BURTONS OF STAFFORD

1680 to 1930

A Partial Chronology of Documented References to
Burtons of Stafford County, Virginia

in Four Volumes, with Source Material from 1587 to 2014

VOLUME I

MARK BURTON

Cover design by Mark Burton.

Front and Back Cover: Composite aerial photograph of Falmouth, Virginia, 1937.
Courtesy of Stafford County Department of Information Technology, Office of
Geographic Information Systems.

Back Cover: Portrait photograph from the author's private collection.

Back of Contents page: A Civil War era map of Stafford County, Virginia, 1864.
Courtesy of the Library of Congress (with labels by the author).

ISBN-13   978-1502398871
ISBN-10   1502398877

CONTENTS

PRINCE WILLIAM CO.

FAUQUIER CO.

MARINE CORPS
BASE QUANTICO
(20TH CENTURY)

STAFFORD
COURTHOUSE
*

HARTWOOD

AQUIA CREEK

THE POTOMAC RIVER

HOLLY
CORNER

BEREA

U.S.
FORD

POTOMAC CREEK

FALMOUTH

BANKS
FORD

WHITE OAK

FREDERICKSBURG

KING GEORGE CO.

MUDDY CREEK

SPOTSYLVANIA CO.

RAPPAHANNOCK R.

Map of Stafford County.
Made under direction of Capt. A. H. Campbell.
Chief of Topogr. Departmt.
SCALE, 1=80000
912 755

Maj. Gen. J. F. Gilmer, Ch. of Eng. Bur.

MAPS FROM THE CONFEDERATE ENGINEER BUREAU
IN RICHMOND, VA. GENERAL J. F. GILMER, CHIEF ENGINEER
PRESENTED TO
THE WEST POINT MILITARY ACADEMY

ACKNOWLEDGMENTS

W HILE RESEARCHING and writing this Chronology, I did not have the luxury of a publisher or editor to guide me, nor did I have any experience as a genealogist. When I first started, I wasn't even planning to write a book, much less a multi-volume collection. I simply wanted to see how far back I could trace my Burton ancestors, not knowing at the time whether they were related to any of the other Stafford Burton families.

But I hit a brick wall about six generations back. At that point, I began collecting as many documented references to Stafford Burtons as I could, hoping to determine which were relatives and which were not. Little did I know that I was embarking on one of the biggest research projects of my life.

And I can ~~blame~~ credit my mother for that. It was her original research into our family history that ~~got me hooked~~ inspired me to take up this historical and genealogical cause. Thanks to her initial research into our branch of the Burton family tree, I was eventually able to determine that I come from a line of Burtons who have lived in southern Stafford County since at least 1680.

I also gratefully acknowledge the help I received from a variety of others while conducting my research. At the top of the list is a wonderful lady who used to work in the Clerk of the Circuit Court's Land Records Office at the Stafford County Courthouse. She gave me a free crash course in title and deed searches, with admirable patience and grace. I got the impression that she didn't want me to mention her by name, but I give her an "A" for effort. I thank her and, to a lesser extent, some of her colleagues. I also thank the helpful personnel at the Culpeper, Fredericksburg, King George, Orange and Spotsylvania courthouses, too.

It is my understanding that some of those court record books would not be available to researchers like me were it not for the preservation efforts supported by the Daughters of the American Revolution (DAR). So I tip my hat to DAR for all the good work they do.

In addition, the reference desk and Virginiana Room staff at the headquarters branch of the Central Rappahannock Regional Library (CRRL) were very helpful to me on far more than one occasion. I would be remiss if I did not also mention those at the Library of Virginia who are responsible for the microfilms of county records, as well as the genealogical and historical records on the library's Web site.

I hope State and local politicians will recognize the immense value of these and other libraries' holdings and fund them appropriately. This work (and many others, I suspect) would not be possible without public libraries.

I am, of course, grateful for the help of various relatives, friends and acquaintances, too, including Janet Cox and Joyce Hall. Even people whom I had never before met, such as Robert Burton, Garry Cooper, Donnie Shelton and Debbie Williams, provided me with invaluable information and research suggestions.

I also thank the authors and compilers of the various reference works and other sources that I found at the library or elsewhere. (As of this writing, I do not know which, if any, require a posthumous acknowledgment.) They include the remarkable Robert Hodge and his wife, Lois, for indexing all of the Fredericksburg newspapers, and certain other materials, from Colonial days to the early 20th century. The folks at the Center for Historic Preservation at the University of Mary Washington also deserve credit for putting many of the Hodges' indexes on the Internet so that they can be searched electronically.

Like the Hodges, Ruth and Sam Sparacio have given local researchers an extraordinary gift. In the 1980s and 1990s, they published volume after volume of indexed abstracts of deeds and other court documents from most of the counties in the Fredericksburg area, covering the 17th, 18th and early 19th centuries. I also thank Therese Fisher, who published at least three or four volumes of marriage records in the 1990s that remain a convenient starting point for anyone researching families who lived in the Fredericksburg area.

In addition, I thank Stafford author Jerrilyn Eby MacGregor for kindly giving me various research tips and suggestions. Her books have been a great help, too. For example, Eby's 2006 book, *Men of Mark: Officials of Stafford County, Virginia, 1664-1991*, is a good source for historical information about business license holders in Stafford.

I also found references to Stafford Burtons in Eby's *Laying the Hoe: A Century of Iron Manufacturing in Stafford County, Virginia*, and her *45th Regiment of Virginia*

Militia, Stafford County, Virginia, 1781-1856, with Biographical Notes on Over 1,600 Militiamen. Stafford Burtons are also mentioned in her latest book (as of this writing), *Land of Hogs and Wildcats: Peoples and Places of Lower Stafford County, Virginia.* (Whether I can get this Chronology published before the prolific Eby gets her next one out remains to be seen....)

I came across *Laying the Hoe* at the Central Rappahannock Heritage Center (CRHC). At the time, CRHC only had relatively sparse holdings about Stafford, but I am nevertheless grateful for their help.

In addition, I was fortunate to have access to some of Mildred Hampton Musselman's genealogical research. Her genealogy of Stafford Boutchyards, for example, is the only one that I know of for that family, although I do not know if it was ever formally published. She and her husband, Carl, published a massive genealogical compendium in 1993, however, titled *Musselman-Powell & Bowling Families of Spotsylvania and Stafford Counties.* I found it very helpful.

I also extend my thanks to King George genealogists and authors William L. Deyo and Elizabeth Nuckols Lee for their help with 17th, 18th and early 19th century Stafford and King George Burtons. Deyo's expertise and publications on the Burton, Porch, and other early Stafford families were invaluable to me. I give credit, too, to the Virginia Genealogical Society for publishing articles by Deyo and others. I am equally grateful to Lee for sharing with me her knowledge of the Burtons of Culpeper County (from whom cousin Elizabeth herself is descended) and their Stafford origins.

I am grateful, too, for the assistance I received from staff members at Sunset Memorial Gardens and Oak Hill cemeteries, and from the Stafford County Cemetery Committee (SCCC). I especially thank the SCCC's Anita Dodd, who was kind enough to provide me with information on a Stafford Burton family cemetery that had been relocated to Prince William County.

I also thank Anita and her co-author M. Amanda Lee for including a photograph of Fielding Burton's store and house (in Old Falmouth) in their 2007 book, *Then & Now: Stafford County.* I don't think they knew it was Fielding's property because he had died decades before the photo was taken in the 1930s. It wasn't too long after the photo was taken that the structures were demolished to make way for a filling station. Were it not for their book, I would not have known the photo existed.

Nor would I know as much about Burtons in Stafford were it not for various church records. I am grateful, for example, to the pastor and secretary of Berea Baptist

Church for loaning me a microfilm copy of their historical records. And I thank D. P. Newton, at the White Oak Museum, for allowing me to peruse a photocopy of the hard-to-find minutes of the Baptist Church of Christ at White Oak (now White Oak Primitive Baptist Church).

I was also able to borrow a microfilm copy of some of the historical records of Hartwood Presbyterian Church from the William Smith Morton Library at Union Presbyterian Seminary. I thank them, as well as the staff of the Presbyterian Historical Society, for their assistance.

Furthermore, I would not have discovered that Burtons played a much greater role in the formation of Falmouth Baptist Church than I had previously known, had various church clerks and other members not kept records dating back to the church's formation in 1891.

I also found important information in the older and more extensive records at the Fredericksburg Baptist Church, which would not have been possible without the gracious assistance of church administrator and Baptist historian Dennis Sacrey. So I thank the good folks at Falmouth Baptist and Fredericksburg Baptist, both past and present, not only for giving me access to their historical membership rolls and other documents, but for having the wisdom and foresight to keep such records in the first place.

I hope that this Chronology, too, will be a useful resource for future researchers, professional and amateur alike. And if I have seen farther into the past of Stafford Burtons than others, it is only because I was able, for almost six years, to spend much of my spare time gazing at history from atop (or buried beneath…) the mounds of records and research of those who came before me.

PREFACE

WHAT DO you call a multi-volume history of Stafford County Burtons that contains more than a quarter of a million words, more than 21,850 indexed names and subjects, more than 1,600 chronological entries, more than 120 surnames of affiliated families, and more than 2,000 source citations culled from more than 940 bibliographic source documents spanning six centuries?

A labor of love? Or the Term Paper from Hell?

Well, I call it a good start. Yet it is only a start, for the historical record contains significant gaps that preclude the compilation of a truly complete history and genealogy of Stafford Burtons. In addition, knowing that a project like this can never really be brought to completion, there came a point when I had to abandon the endless research, lest *Encyclopædia Burtonica* become more than just a highbrow working title.

I would like to point out, however, that in addition to its primary purpose, this lengthy but incomplete Chronology helps to demonstrate just how much work genealogists do behind the scenes when researching even a single family tree. (And this is worth pointing out because most genealogists have the good sense *not* to attempt to summarize every documented reference they use....)

Of course, I would be remiss not to acknowledge the shortcomings of my own research efforts, especially my having relied so heavily on secondary sources for abstracts of early court records, as well as my focus on written sources rather than pictures and photographs. In my own defense, however, many of those 17th- and early 18th-century court records are so difficult to read I doubt that my untrained eye would have been able to discern much of value, even if I had spent the countless man-hours that would have been necessary to read through them line-by-line.

Also, in later court records, indexes are not always reliable, or even available, as I discovered when I actually *did* read through several court record books line-by-line. It is likely, then, that I have missed more than a few non-indexed references to

Burtons among hundreds of years of deed books and other court records, but I was not about to spend the rest of my life reading every line of every page of every record book at every local court house.

Nevertheless, as the subtitle suggests, my main goal in writing this was to compile *documented* references. As a result, I spent little time or effort trying to find pictures and photographs of Burtons. Even when I did come across a photograph, there was often no way to verify the identity of the person or people in it. Still, I must admit that it is a bit disappointing to have gathered so much information on so many people yet not even know what most of them looked like.

I also regret that I was not able to use footnotes when citing sources for all of this information. I usually prefer footnotes rather than endnotes for the convenience of both the reader (no flipping back and forth) and the researcher (being able to photocopy both the desired information and the source on one page).

In this case, however, I ended up with so many citations per page that footnotes became unacceptable for formatting and aesthetic reasons. I admit that endnotes would have looked more professional, but I decided instead to use parenthetical notes which, though unconventional by academic standards, offer conveniences similar to footnotes. Fortunately, the discrete nature of the chronological entries breaks the flow of the text anyway, so the insertion of the notes is only a minor distraction.

I have also used an unconventional format for the index. For multiple reasons, which I will not go into here, I created an index using spreadsheet software, resulting in a separate line item each time a name or subject was indexed. It makes the index longer than it would be otherwise because some names and subjects are repeated many times.

I also chose to index items not by page number but by chronological entry number. This allows me to publish this work as a single printed volume, in multiple volumes or as an ebook without having to create a new index each time. But it also means that names and subjects which appear outside of the two Chronologies, such as those in the Introduction, are not indexed. Still, as with unconventional source citations, an unconventional index is far better than none at all. It was, nevertheless, disappointing to have to make such compromises.

Most disappointing of all, however, is that even after such extensive research, the origin of the Stafford Burtons remains a mystery. Did one or more Burtons come to Stafford directly from England? Or from elsewhere in the colony of Virginia? Or from Maryland or some other colony? Regrettably, I could not trace the Stafford Burtons back to the Old World, or even outside of early Stafford County.

I should point out, by the way, that I often refer to localities within Virginia without actually specifying that they are in Virginia, especially for Stafford's neighboring districts, such as the city of Fredericksburg and the counties of King George, Prince William, Fauquier, Culpeper and Spotsylvania. So, in those cases where I mention a city, town or county without mentioning a state, readers should assume that it is located in Virginia.

Also, while the references in these volumes really do span six centuries—from the list of members of Sir Walter Raleigh's "Lost Colony" in the year 1587 to modern obituaries published in the early 21st century—the bulk of the material covers a period of about 250 years, from the first indisputable reference to a Stafford Burton in 1680 to my 1930 cut-off date. I chose a 1930 cut-off date in part because the 1930 census was the latest one available to the public when I first started researching this subject, and in part because those invaluable indexes for Fredericksburg area newspapers, which begin with Colonial-era papers, end with papers in the late 1920s.

I have, however, included land and property tax records only up to 1900, in part because of constraints on research time, with apologies for the inconsistency. (I think some of the later tax records were still being microfilmed when I was doing my research, so I couldn't have included them up to 1930 even if I had tried.)

In addition, the overall 1930 cut-off date reflects a concern for the privacy of people still living, ensuring that the focus of this work would be on those no longer with us. Members of post-1930 generations are often mentioned as survivors in obituaries, of course, but I have made a deliberate effort to limit the exposure of personal details of people who are still alive.

Finally, the 1930 cut-off date was a practical necessity because of the tremendous population growth in Stafford that began in the mid-20th century. To bring a history of Stafford Burtons up to the present day, or merely to the end of the 20th century, would require many more years of work.

I will leave *that*, however, to someone else, confident that I have provided, with this Chronology, a sufficient foundation for further research.

MB
2014

INTRODUCTION

THIS CHRONOLOGY is not just about *Burtons* in Stafford County, for where would the Burtons be without their spouses? Those spouses came from families with names such as Ballard, (Bartsville?), Beach, Berry, Bettis, Blaisdell, (Bloxton?), Bouchard, Bourne, Boutyard, Boutchyard, Bowler, Bradshaw, Brandenburg, Brooks, Brown, Brummett, Bryant, Buckner, Bullock, Burgess, Burns, Carmine, Carneal, Chatham, Chilton, Coakley, Coghill, Coleman, Cooper, Craig, Curtis, Dallman, DeBruyn, Dickinson, Dillard, (Dodd?), Dorsey, Downs, Dunnington, Dye, Edwards, Ellington, Embrey, Ennis, Fitzhugh, (Fleming?), Foley/Folio, Franklin, Gallahan, Garner, Green, Grinnan, Guy, Hammond, Harding, Harris, (Hearn?), Hewitt, Hove, (Hudson?), Hummer, Humphries, Jacobs, Jefferies, Jefferson, Jett, Johnson, Jones, Kelly/Kelley, Knight, Kurz, Leake, Lee, Limbrick, Littrell, Lowry, Lunsford, Mankey, Marlow, Marquess, McFadden, (McKenney?), (Meade?), Meadows, Mills, Miniclier, Mitchell, Monroe, Moxley, Murphy, Newton, O'Conner/O'Connor, Parker, (Partsville?), Pates, Patton, Payne, (Petit?), Plaskett, Pollard, Porch, Portch, Powell, (Pullen/Puller?), Reed, Rehlander, Rice, Roberts, (Rodgers?), Samuel, Schofield, Sealy, Seay, Shepherd, Sisk, Skidmore, Southard, Spicer, Stephens/Stevens, Sullivan, (Taylor?), Templeman, Truslow, Turner, Tyson, Umphrey, Walker, Way, Webb, Welch, West, Whited, Williams, Wright and Yeatman.

There were a few Burtons from Stafford who married other Burtons, too, but nothing worse than kissing cousins, as far as I know. Of course, if this Chronology had been researched up to the present day, the list of affiliated family surnames would no doubt be much longer.

As one of the oldest families in Stafford County, dating back to at least 1680, the Burtons have had a significant, though largely unheralded, historical impact on the area—especially in Berea, Falmouth, Hartwood and antebellum White Oak. They and their neighbors were the farmers, coopers, laborers, housekeepers, public servants and business owners who built and sustained the Stafford communities through which so many other, more famous, historical figures passed.

It might surprise some people, though, to learn that most, if not all, of the Burtons who resided in Stafford County in the 17th, 18th and 19th centuries were probably part of the same family. Indeed, if my theory is correct that the White Oak, Falmouth, Berea and Hartwood Burtons are branches of the same family tree, then it was not until the 20th century that Burtons from outside of this family began to appear in Stafford in significant numbers.

Although a chronological format seemed to me the easiest and most logical way to organize such a vast amount of information, I can hardly expect people to read through more than 1,600 chronological entries and piece together the story of the Stafford Burtons on their own. The chronological entries are designed primarily for those interested in using this work as a reference document, looking up specific people or focusing on a particular time frame.

I want to use this Introduction, however, to give readers a more concise overview that they can read through from beginning to end, with a few selected highlights but without the cumbersome source citations and other obligatory minutia that bog down the chronological entries. In most cases, the overly suspicious can look up the source information for particular highlights in corresponding chronological entries. Everyone else can simply trust that I've done my homework—and be thankful that I overcame my natural indolence and made at least some effort to provide a more readable overview of Stafford Burton history, which begins in 1608....

America's First Burton

Before I delve into the history of the Burton family of Stafford, I want to point out that the first Burton in North America, the first Burton in Virginia and the first Burton to visit the area that would become Stafford County, were very likely one and the same man. That man was George Burton, a charter member of the Virginia Company, who left England in July 1608, sailing on the ship *Mary and Margaret* under Captain Newport. George arrived in Jamestown in October 1608 as part of the "Second Supply" (which was actually the third company of settlers to arrive in Virginia).

BURTON'S MOUNT. A 1624 edition (above) of Captain John Smith's 1612 map of Virginia is oriented with the west on top and north on the right. It clearly show's "Burton's Mount" north of "Quiyough" (Aquia) creek (below).

In 1608 and 1609, George was among those who accompanied Captain John Smith on his expeditions in Virginia. Interestingly, a hill or ridge containing an antimony mine, called "Burton's Mount," was apparently named after Burton during one of Smith's expeditions and was included on Smith's 1612 map of Virginia. Experts disagree on the exact location of Burton's Mount, but indicate that it was probably near Aquia Creek in today's northern Stafford County, or possibly in Prince William County (which, at one time, was part of the original Stafford County).

To my knowledge, Burton's Mount was the first landmark named after a Burton not only in Virginia but in all of North America. Smith's map was also, presumably, the first map of Virginia, or of North America, or possibly even of the New World, to include a reference to a Burton.

Regrettably, I don't know what became of George. I also don't know if he was related in any way to that family of Burtons who, by 1680, had settled in an area known today as White Oak....

White Oak Origins

Perhaps it is a fitting pun that the main trunk of the Stafford Burton family tree is rooted in the area now known as White Oak, in southeastern Stafford County, in the 17th century. One of the earliest members of this family was probably William Burton. He was born circa 1650, although I don't know where. By 1680, he was in Stafford, according to a court deposition of Richard Bryant, who saw "Will Burton" crossing Potomac Creek in a boat with John Waugh and others. Burton lived in the White Oak area and died sometime after 1703.

A Samuel Burton also lived in the same area during the late 17th and early 18th centuries. Circumstantial evidence indicates that Samuel was related to William. Samuel might have been William's brother or, perhaps, a son.

I do not know for sure if either man had any children, but I strongly suspect that one of them was the father of the second William Burton known to live in Stafford. This "second William," as I refer to him, married Sarah Spicer in 1725 and their descendants grew into the Burton family of Stafford.

In the following 200 years, there would be well over a dozen William Burtons in Stafford, but only one other Samuel Burton. That makes me suspect that the first William Burton, rather than the first Samuel, was the patriarch of the Stafford Burtons, even when I take into account that "William" was one of the most popular male names in the English language at the time.

An Interesting Verdict

I found it interesting that, in 1691, the first William Burton served on a jury which ordered William Harris to free Benjamin Lewis, "a Negroe," on evidence that Lewis had been free in England and had only been a temporary indentured servant, not a slave. Perhaps surprisingly, the jury members decided in favor of the poor and powerless Lewis, despite the potential negative consequences of ruling against a powerful landowner.

Harris appealed the decision, but I regret that I never learned the final verdict. Still, this Harris connection turned up references to two other Burtons.

Harris and Thomas Baxter had received a patent for 3,000 acres in Stafford in 1670. On the same day in 1670 that he received his Stafford patent, Harris was authorized to bring a James Burton and eleven others into the Virginia colony, perhaps to settle his newly acquired land in Stafford. I could find nothing more, however, about this particular James Burton. I don't know if he ever settled in Stafford or even came to Virginia.

Ten years later, in 1680, Harris signed a five-year deed with a John Burton to have Burton farm one of his Stafford plantations near "Neapscoe." I assume this means that John Burton became a tenant farmer for Harris, but I don't know for sure.

I also don't know if James and John were related. Perhaps it is sheer coincidence that Harris was to import a James Burton in 1670 and accepted a John Burton as a tenant farmer in 1680. But both involved Stafford, so I wonder if there might have been a connection. I wonder, too, if the first William Burton and the first Samuel Burton in Stafford might have been sons of this John Burton.

Stafford's First Pre-Nup?

Although I never found out who his parents were, I did learn that the first William Burton married Martha Folio (or Foley) circa 1690, when he was about 40 years old. I don't know if William had been previously married or not, but Martha was the widow of Thomas Folio (or Foley) and had had at least five children by Thomas.

Martha, it appears, was not stupid. She must have known that the laws at the time would give her second husband great control over her property, and she wanted to ensure that her children by Folio received some of their natural father's property before Burton got control of it.

Thus, in what might be the first prenuptial agreement in Stafford County history, Martha Folio had William Burton agree, in writing, to provide specified items to each of Martha's children by Folio as they came of age.

The agreement was signed 5 November 1690 and recorded 8 November 1690. It stated that "...the said William Burton doth grant & promise with ye said Martha before Matrimony to pay her Children as they come of age as followeth."

The children named in the deed were Brian Folio, John, Thomas, Richard and Anne. They were each to receive one mare, one cow and one calf. In addition, Brian and John were each to receive a gun.

On a related note, a few months after they were married, circa 11 March 1690 (1691), William and Martha asked the court to order an appraisement of the estate of Martha's deceased first husband. Such appraisements were routine in those days. In this case, however, I suspect Martha had a special interest in getting an official inventory of her first husband's property.

The Pocahontas Connection

Genealogist William Deyo, who knows more than a little about White Oak history, has theorized that Martha might have been Martha Bryant, the daughter of a Potomac / Patawomeck Indian princess named Keziah Aroyah and an Englishman with the surname Bryant. Keziah Aroyah, in turn, was purportedly a daughter of Wahanganoche, king of Patawomeck. If I understand it correctly, Wahanganoche was a cousin of Pocahontas and a nephew of Powhatan.

According to Deyo's theory, Keziah Aroyah's children included Martha Bryant; Dr. Richard Bryant, Sr.; Thomas Bryant; Silent Bryant; and another son who was the father of Elinor (Bryant?) Gallop Owens. If true, this theory would explain the apparent close relationship between the Bryant and Burton families in the late 17th and early 18th centuries.

For example, in the 1703 Will of Richard Bryant, Sr., William Burton was one of two men listed as "security" for Richard's wife, Ann, who had been named executrix. In that same Will, it is revealed that Richard Bryant, Sr. had allowed Samuel Burton to live rent-free for the previous four years on a plantation owned by Bryant.

This is the only instance I found in which the first William Burton and the first Samuel Burton are both mentioned in the same document. It also seems to imply that

Samuel was living alone at that time, which might reduce the likelihood that he fathered the second William Burton, who was probably born in the 1690s or early 1700s.

In addition, in 1726, the second William Burton was living on a plantation owned by Richard Bryant's grandson. (The grandson, who apparently inherited the plantation from Bryant, sold it to John Fitzhugh that same year.)

These sources make me wonder if the first Samuel Burton and the second William Burton lived on the same plantation originally owned by Dr. Richard Bryant. It would make sense if (1) Martha and Richard Bryant were siblings; and (2) Samuel Burton was related to both Martha's husband and the second William Burton.

By the way, if the Bryants really were the grandchildren of Pocahontas' cousin, it might mean that hundreds or even thousands of Stafford Burton descendants could claim Potomac / Patawomeck Indian ancestry. Before I claim to be related to Pocahontas, however, I will need more substantive evidence that Martha and the first William were the parents of the second William Burton, rather than Samuel and some unknown consort.

POCAHONTAS. A 1616 portrait reportedly depicts Pocahontas after she married John Rolfe, converted to Christianity and took the name Rebecca. (Another version of this portrait exists that is more flattering to its subject.)

The Tie That Binds

Regardless of his parentage, the second William Burton is the tie that binds together the various Stafford Burtons of later generations. Regrettably, historical records of Stafford Burtons during the 18th century are very sketchy. My research and analysis indicate that the second William had at least two sons, both of whom had male children of their own, causing an early split in the main trunk of the Stafford Burton family tree.

The second William Burton married Sarah Spicer on 14 December 1725. Their daughter Lettice was born about eight months later, on 19 August 1726. Almost twenty years after that, on 17 January 1746, a Priscilla Burton was born to a William Burton, but the mother was not mentioned.

To my knowledge, these are the only documented births for Stafford Burtons during that time period. Later records imply, however, that during that same period, two Stafford Burton brothers were born: the elder Nathaniel Burton (who died in 1809) and, as I call him, the "third" William Burton (who reportedly died in 1778). (The "third William" was probably only in his forties when he died, which makes me wonder if he might have died fighting in the Revolutionary War. Regrettably, I was unable to find any evidence about the cause of death.)

In addition, there is evidence that a Charles Burton and a John Burton were married adults living in or near King George County in the 1770s, but I don't know if they were related to the Stafford Burtons. I suppose it's possible that they might have been younger brothers of the elder Nathaniel and the third William, but I have no evidence of that.

If they were all brothers, then it's possible that one or more of the children I assume were the elder Nathaniel's might, instead, have been children of Charles or John. Without clear evidence, though, I have chosen not to include either Charles or John as Stafford Burtons, but I do provide the information I have on them in the Pre-Stafford Chronology.

I know of no other Burton families in Stafford at the time, so the original family tree would look something like this:

1st Generation: (1) William Burton (circa 1650-after 1706)
                                  married Martha (Bryant?) Foley/Folio

                          (2) Samuel Burton (16??-17??) ("first" William's brother or son?)

2nd Generation: William Burton (?-17??)
                                  (Probably the son of William or Samuel, above)
                                  married Sarah Spicer in 1725
                                  Children:

3rd Generation: Lettice Burton (19 Aug 1726-?)
                                  William Burton (17??-1778?) (implied son)
                                  Nathaniel Burton (17??-1809) (implied son)
                                  Priscilla Burton (1746-?) (unknown mother)

Lettice Burton married Alexander Jefferies on 30 September 1741 at the age of 15. I do not know if they had any children. Also, I do not know if Priscilla Burton married or had children.

I know that both a Nathaniel Burton and a William Burton lived in Stafford during the mid-1700s and that they knew each other, because they inventoried and appraised at least two estates together during the 1760s. I found no records specifying their exact relationship, but there is documented evidence that William had a brother who had children.

This "third" William Burton married Rachel Porch (born in 1736) on 7 October 1753. Other records reveal that their children included Mary (born in 1754), Samuel (born in 1756), William (born between 1760 and 1770), Nancy (Ann) (born circa 1770), George (born between 1770 and 1780?), Gerard and Susanna.

Nancy's Will and a related codicil reveal that Nancy was the sister of Samuel Burton and the cousin of James B. Burton. This Burton cousin confirms that Nancy's father must have had a brother.

By this and by process of elimination, I can speculate that James and any other Stafford Burtons born between the 1750s and the early 1770s, who are not included in the list of William and Rachel's children, would probably be children of Nathaniel. These would include James Burton (born circa 1756), John Burton, the younger Nathaniel Burton (born between 1760 and 1770), Isaac Burton (born in 1771) and Lucy Burton (born circa 1779).

So a continuation of the Burton side of the family tree (i.e., for the two brothers) would look something like this:

3rd Generation: (1) William Burton (17??-1778?)
                        married Rachel Porch (circa 1736-1780?) in 1753

                  (2) Nathaniel Burton (17??-1809)
                        unknown consort(s)

4th Generation: (1) Children of William Burton & Rachel Porch:

                        Mary Burton (30 May 1754-?)
                        Samuel Burton (20 April 1756-Oct 1831)
                        William Burton (176?-died by Sep 1833)
                        Nancy (Ann) Burton (circa 1770-1861)

George Burton (177?-after 1830)
Gerard/Gerrard Burton (17??-?)
Susanna Burton (17??-?)

(2) Suspected children of the elder Nathaniel Burton:

James Burton (circa 1756-1850 or 1851)
John Burton (17??-?)
Nathaniel Burton (176?-after 1840) (the younger)
Isaac Burton (Dec 1771-15 Apr 1843)
Lucy Burton (circa 1779-1 Jun 1859)

Spreading Out

In the late 18th and early 19th centuries, these 4th generation Burtons spread out from White Oak to Falmouth, Berea, Holly Corner and Hartwood in Stafford County, and to King George and Culpeper Counties as well. I assume that those who left White Oak moved their families up the Rappahannock primarily because land was cheaper up river. (Some ended up living in an area known at the time for its gold mines, but I have no evidence that any Burtons were miners. One 5th generation Burton, though, ran a store that apparently catered to his gold-mining neighbors.)

White Oak/Falmouth. I should point out, however, that not all of the Burtons moved up river. The "fourth" William Burton remained in White Oak and eventually acquired about half a dozen slaves and just over 290 acres of land "at the head of Muddy Creek," on the border with King George County. He had at least two children by his first wife, Susannah Jett, who was also his first cousin.

Susannah died by about 1820 and William appears to have fathered a second family late in life with a much younger woman, Catharine "Kate" McKenney. It is not known if William married Kate, but a court record reveals that Kate accepted William Burton as her guardian in 1826. They had the first of at least three children that same year or possibly the following year.

William died in 1833. Tax records indicate that he left most of his White Oak land to Barsheba Burton, his surviving daughter by his first wife. Barsheba's brother, Thomas S. Burton, was already dead by then. Barsheba's nephew, William J. Burton (presumably Thomas' son), inherited about 50 acres.

Unfortunately, I could not find a surviving copy of the fourth William's Will, so I don't know if he left anything to Kate. In any case, over the next six generations, his descendants grew into one of two Falmouth branches of the Burton family tree.

Falmouth. The other Falmouth branch were descendants of the younger Nathaniel Burton, although I'm not sure if Nathaniel himself lived in Falmouth. He married a woman named Jane. They are the "missing link" that for many years prevented members of one of the Falmouth Burton families from tracing their Burton roots beyond the early 1800s. Based on analysis of census, marriage and other records, I suspect that Nathaniel and Jane were the parents of William E. Burton, Sr., some of whose descendants lived for decades across the street from the fourth William's Falmouth descendants, apparently without either family knowing that they were related to the other.

King George County. Little is know about the fourth William's brother, George Burton, except that he married a woman named Mary and moved to King George. Census records indicate that George moved back to Stafford late in life.

Culpeper County. Another 4th generation brother, Samuel Burton, also married a woman named Mary and they apparently lived briefly in King George before moving back to Stafford. This "second" Samuel became the patriarch of the Culpeper County Burtons when he moved his family from Stafford to Culpeper circa 1798.

Berea/Holly Corner/Hartwood. Like their cousin Samuel, many if not all of the elder Nathaniel Burton's sons moved up the Rappahannock in the late 18th or early 19th centuries. Unlike Samuel, however, they apparently remained in Stafford. James Burton appears to have lived the longest, surviving well into his 90s. He probably fathered at least two sons and a daughter. His probable grandson, Marshall Burton, became the patriarch of a large branch of the Stafford Burton family tree in the Holly Corner area, northwest of Falmouth near the Rappahannock.

James's suspected son or brother, John Burton, might have become the father of the Hartwood branch of the Stafford Burtons late in his life. This is assuming that he was the same John Burton who married a woman named Susan and fathered brothers James A. Burton and Richard Burton, both of whom lived near U.S. Ford on the Stafford side of the Rappahannock. (Richard, by the way, was the one who ran the store near the gold mines.)

(It is possible that Marshall Burton might also have been a son of John and Susan, even though Marshall's parents are listed as William and Susan on his death certificate. I suspect that Marshall's father might have been John William Burton or William John Burton, son of the elder James Burton, in part because both John and

Marshall's father apparently died in the 1820s and both had wives named Susan. I was unable to confirm this theory, but readers might want to keep the possibility in mind.)

Isaac Burton, another probable son of the elder Nathaniel, married Mary Marquess and fathered a very large family with her. From 1800 to the early 1820s, Mary gave birth to at least eleven children, averaging about one birth every two years for more than 20 years. Many of their descendants lived in the Berea area.

Like his White Oak cousin, the fourth William, Isaac was one of the more successful Burtons of his generation. It would not be surprising if he and fourth William viewed each other as rivals.

Like fourth William, Isaac owned two tracts of land. Indeed, he and fourth William are the first Burtons listed as landowners in Stafford County in land tax records. And, like fourth William, Isaac's land totaled about 290 acres. In addition, Isaac's land, located about four miles northwest of Falmouth near the Rappahannock River, Horsepen Run and Rocky Run, was about the same distance west of Falmouth as fourth William's land was east of Falmouth. Isaac also owned several slaves, about the same number as fourth William.

Well, rivals or not, Isaac and fourth William were, perhaps, the two most prominent Burtons in Stafford at the time. I hesitate to say so definitively, however, because gaps in the historical record, as well as the limits of my own research efforts, preclude a comprehensive analysis of all of the Stafford Burtons of that generation, especially female Burtons who might have "married well."

Mystery Men

I do not know if there were any other 4th generation Stafford Burton children besides those listed above. There are, however, documented references to a few mysterious male Burtons in Stafford during the late 18th and early 19th centuries whose parents are unknown.

Some of these are one-time references which I have been unable to corroborate. For example, a Richard Burton was listed in a 1785 personal property tax record for Stafford County, but I have no other information about him. Also, militia records indicate that a Jonathan Burton from Stafford served in the Virginia Militia during the War of 1812 and that a Joshua Burton from Stafford served in the Virginia Militia in 1822, but I have no further information on either man.

In addition to these one-time references, I have two Stafford Court references to a possible Walker Burton, one in 1826 and another in 1832. In both cases, however, the source documents are barely legible and I cannot be sure if "Walker" is the actual name. In any case, I have no other evidence of a Walker Burton in Stafford at that time.

I also have multiple sources indicating that an Ira Burton from Stafford served in the Virginia Militia during the War of 1812 and in 1817, and paid taxes in Stafford from 1816 to 1818. Census records indicate that he might have moved to Culpeper County by 1820. Still, I do not know who his parents were or if he was related to any of the other Stafford Burtons.

Jesse Burton. I do not know who Jesse Burton's parents were, either, but his name suggests that he was probably related to the original White Oak Burtons. Jesse Burton (a.k.a. Burden) was born circa 1784, presumably in Stafford (because he got married in Stafford and lived in Stafford). He married, circa 1809, Elizabeth Musselman Brummett (circa 1788-after 1870), the widow of John Brummett and mother of William E. Brummett. Jesse apparently died between 1834 and 1840.

If the third William Burton died in 1778, as some sources suggest, then Jesse could not have been his son. So was Jesse a late son of the elder Nathaniel? Or was he an early grandson (i.e., 5th generation) of either the third William or the elder Nathaniel? I should point out that the name "Jesse" shows up more than once in later generations, as in William Jesse Burton (a descendant of the third William) and Parker F. "Jesse" Burton (a descendant of the elder Nathaniel).

Except for his wife and stepson, I found no records of any of Jesse's relatives, but it's important to note that he lived and died during the "dark ages" of Stafford, from the late 1700s to the early 1800s. Many of the Stafford court records from that period are missing, and it was a time when census records only included the names of heads of households, not spouses or children. Furthermore, government birth, death and marriage records were not kept until the 1850s.

The Unknown Husbands. In general, pre-1850 census, tax and other historical records are more likely to provide the names of males than females. Sometimes, however, the reverse is true, as in the cases of Sarah Limbrick Burton and Sarah Coakley Burton, who were probably born in the late 1700s or very early 1800s. Both women were from Stafford and both married unknown Burtons. Of course, I cannot say with certainty that their husbands were Stafford Burtons, but it seems likely.

For example, the 1810 Census for Stafford indicates that Sarah Limbrick's father, John Limbrick, was a neighbor of James Burton and that both were the heads of large households. It is possible, then, that Sarah Limbrick married one of James Burton's sons. (By the way, John Limbrick's 1826 Will specifically mentions that he had a daughter named Sarah Burton, which also suggests that she was still alive at the time.)

Sarah Coakley's father, Benjamin Coakley, lived in southern Stafford, which was home to many Burtons. She and her unknown husband had apparently died by 1839, because by then her two children had become wards of her brother, Daniel Coakley.

An 1815 court case indicates that a William and Sarah Burton lived in the Fredericksburg area at the time, but I do not know if they were from Stafford, or if the wife was Sarah Limbrick or Sarah Coakley. In any case, I find it frustrating that I cannot identify these unknown husbands, because they were probably fourth or fifth generation Stafford Burtons, and it would be nice to know who they were and what happened to them.

Mystery Women

In addition to these mystery men, I came across a few mysterious female Burtons in Stafford. The 1850 census for Stafford County, for example, lists an 86-year-old Rachel J. Burton. Her name and age suggest that she might have been a daughter of the third William Burton and Rachel Porch, but I do not know for sure.

The 1850 census also lists a Susan Burton, 38, and a Delphia Burton, 55, living in the same household. I have no further information on either woman, except that this Susan might be the 45-year-old Susan Burton listed in the 1860 census living with a Sarah B. Littrell, 56.

In addition, a 68-year-old Levenia Burton is listed in the 1900 census, in a household with Martha E. Jeffries, 68, and Harriot S. Lowry (*sic*), 67. I have no further information on Levenia, but her two housemates had connections to other Burtons.

The 1870 census indicates that Martha and two other Jeffryes (*sic*) were living with Rachel Burton, probably a daughter of Harris W. Burton. (I do not know, however, if these Jeffries/Jeffryes were related to the Alexander Jefferies who married Lettice Burton in 1741.) Another daughter of Harris W. Burton, Elizabeth Burton Harding, might have named one of her daughters Levenia (Levenia Harding Wine?), so perhaps the elder Levenia Burton was a niece or other relative of Harris W. Burton.

Harriot might have been Harriet, the mother of Margaret "Maggie" Lowry Burton, wife of John Broaddus Burton, Sr. I assume that Levenia, Martha and

Harriot/Harriet lived together in part for financial reasons, because they were elderly and single (either unmarried or widowed).

I should also point out that many female Stafford Burtons are never named in this Chronology because they were born and married prior to 1850, and I have no way to discover their names. If I had some way to determine who they were and whom they married, the list of affiliated family surnames would be significantly longer. Given these gaps in the historical record, readers should bear in mind that many more families in Stafford and the surrounding area probably have Stafford Burton ancestors than I have documented in here.

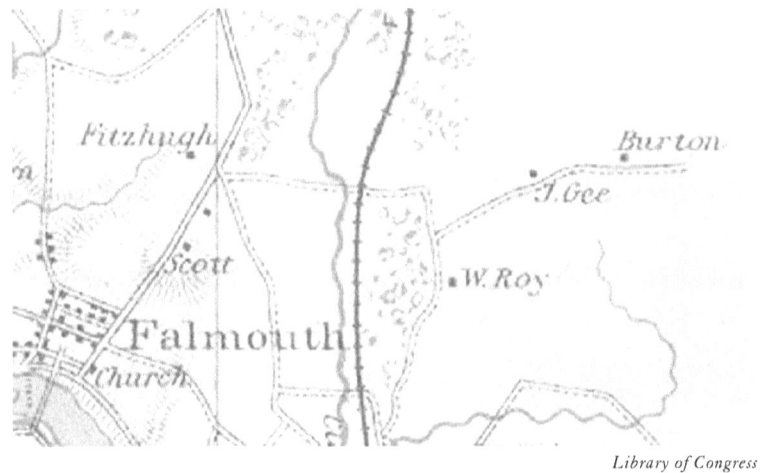

Library of Congress

ANOTHER MYSTERY. Some Civil War maps, like this one from 1864, show a Burton property or residence located, very roughly, in the vicinity of today's Grafton Village Elementary School. The Burton or Burtons referred to remain unidentified.

The 5th & 6th Generations

Despite these numerous information gaps, I have been able nevertheless to determine many of the grandchildren and great-grandchildren of the third William and the elder Nathaniel. Along with a few anecdotes about selected individuals, I devote the next 16 or so pages to providing an at-a-glance summary of pre-Civil War Stafford Burton families. I begin with third William's descendants, including those for whom I have little information.

I do not know what happened to "third" William and Rachel's daughter, Mary, and I don't know if Mary had any children of her own. Another daughter, Ann (also known as Nancy) apparently never married and ended up living with her cousin James in her old age.

Tax records indicate that William and Rachel's son, Gerard, grew to adulthood in Stafford, but I do not know if he remained here or moved away. Some genealogists speculate that he might have married Jane Porter in Bourbon County, Kentucky on 21 August 1792, but I have my doubts about that.

I also don't know if William and Rachel's son, George Burton, and his wife, Mary, had any children. Census records indicate that he had moved from King George back to Stafford by 1830, where he was a 50- to 60-year-old head of a household that included himself, a a 30- to 40-year-old woman, a 5- to 10-year-old boy and a girl under the age of 5.

Had he remarried and started a new family? Or did he move in with relatives after his wife died? I don't know. Fortunately, considerably more information is available on some of George's brothers and their children.

Samuel Burton's Family. Like his brother George, Samuel Burton married a woman named Mary and apparently lived in King George briefly before moving back to Stafford. Samuel and Mary's son, William, was reportedly born in King George County in 1787, and Samuel is listed in King George tax records for that year. But Samuel is listed in Stafford tax records in following years, and his son, Cary, was born in Stafford in 1790.

As noted above, Samuel and his family moved to Culpeper County circa 1798. I regret that I could not research the Culpeper Burtons in depth, and what information I do have is sketchy and not necessarily confirmed. Still, Samuel's family looked something like this:

4th Generation:	Samuel Burton (20 Apr 1756-Oct 1831)
(Stafford)	married Mary (unknown last name)
	Children:
5th Generation:	Lettice "Lettie" Burton (circa 1784-15 Oct 1871 ?)
(Stafford/Culpeper)	William (L. or S.) Burton (1787-18 Sep 1859)
	Jane Burton
	Cary Burton (circa 1790-circa 1860)

Catherine Burton Southard
Mary Burton Rodgers

Samuel's son William was probably William L. Burton, although one source indicates that he might have been William Spicer Burton. (In those days, handwritten capital L's and S's were very similar in appearance.) William married Margaret Pollard.

5th Generation:	William (L. or S.) Burton (1787-18 Sep 1859)
(Stafford/Culpeper)	married Margaret Pollard
	Children:

6th Generation:	Mary Ann Burton (circa 1818-30 Mar 1894)
(Culpeper)	Catherine (or Lucy Catherine) Burton Jones (circa 1824-?)
	George W. Burton (circa 1826-?)
	James/John W. (Wesley?) Burton (circa 1827-?)
	Virginia F. Burton Ellington (circa 1829-12 Feb 1915)

Samuel's son Cary married twice. His first wife was Susanna Walker. His second wife was Nancy Burns.

5th Generation:	Cary Burton (circa 1790-circa 1860)
Stafford/Culpeper:	married (1) Susanna Walker (7 Sep 1799-before 1832)
	married (2) Nancy Burns (circa 1794-1870)
	(possibly Nancy Pollard)
	Children:

6th Generation:	Absalom Spicer Burton (circa 1812-18??) (s/o Susanna)
(Culpeper)	Amanda Burton (circa 1814-1894 ?) (d/o Susanna)
	Thomas (S. or C.) Burton (circa 1833-?) (s/o Nancy)
	Lucy M. Burton Elley (circa 1835-?) (d/o Nancy)
	William Peter Burton (30 Mar 1839-1 Mar 1914) (s/o Nancy)

The Fourth William Burton's Families. As noted above, the fourth-generation William Burton, brother of George, Gerrard and Samuel, had children with his wife, Susannah Jett, but also appears to have fathered children with Catharine "Kate" McKenney after Susannah's death. It is not clear if William formally married Kate.

One source indicates that he was William J. Burton, Sr., and that seems likely, given that he had one son and two grandsons also named William J. Burton. William remained in the White Oak area of Stafford and prospered, but his children by Susannah had both died by 1845 and the White Oak property fell out of Burton hands. William apparently left no land to Kate or her children. His sons by Kate eventually established themselves and their families in Falmouth.

4th Generation: William Burton (176?-died by 9 Sep 1833)
                     (William J. Burton, Sr.?)
                     married Susannah Jett (17??-before 1821)
                     married/consorted with Catharine "Kate" McKenney
                     (circa 1805-after 1870)
                     Children:

5th Generation: Thomas S. Burton (died before 20 Jun 1845) (s/o Susannah)
                     Barsheba Burton (died before 20 Jun 1845) (d/o Susannah)
                     Lucinda/Lucindy "Lucy" Burton Turner (circa 1826-after
                          1860) (d/o Kate)
                     Fielding Burton (circa 1826-November 1903) (s/o Kate)
                     William J. Burton (13 Mar 1834-20 Mar 1896) (s/o Kate)
                     Sarah "Sally" (Burton or Tyson) Southard (183?-15 Mar 1919)
                          (d/o Kate; father unclear)

Thomas S. Burton apparently died fairly young, but he lived long enough to father at least one child with an unknown consort.

5th Generation: Thomas S. Burton
                     Unknown consort
                     Child:

6th Generation: William J. Burton (circa 1820-186?)
                     (possibly died in Civil War)

This particular William J. Burton (the son of Thomas S. Burton) has a terrible reputation, so much so that I have dubbed him "the notorious William J." As of this writing, there are *still* people in White Oak who speak of him with derision, even though he died a century and a half ago!

I, personally, did not find much evidence of wrongdoing, though I did see some indications of possible fiscal irresponsibility. For example, William inherited about 50 acres in White Oak when his grandfather died, but he quickly lost it. (One distant relative of his wife thinks that he lost her house, too, but I found no evidence to confirm or deny it.)

Also, a court record indicates that William provided security for a man accused of forgery. The accused was probably a relative of William's wife and was apparently acquitted. So William and the accused were not *necessarily* cronies engaged in crime.

In addition, there has been some confusion because there were at least three, if not four, William J. Burtons living in southern Stafford in the 19th century. Some people, having heard the tales about this particular William J. Burton, have mistakenly confused him with some of the other William J. Burtons. For example, some people might believe, mistakenly, that it was this William J. Burton who fathered children with Kate McKenney (thus adding the charge of adultery to his misdeeds), but it's not true. The "notorious" William J. was only 6 or 7 years old when Kate started having children.

Well, I hope this Chronology helps to clear up who's who. There is, however, one incident that raises doubts even in my mind about the notorious William J.'s character. His aunt, Barsheba Burton, apparently left him nothing when she died, even though he might have been her only surviving "legitimate" relative. For example, she left specific instructions that the roughly 240 acres she inherited from her father (and his grandfather) be sold.

She also wrote in her Will that "my object particularly in making my will is for the ultimate emancipation of my slaves." Her slaves included Betty, Henry and Henry's wife, Nancy.

(By the way, Barsheba noted in her Will that her slaves should only be freed on condition that they agree to leave Virginia. This condition was apparently a requirement of State law at the time. According to June Purcell Guild, in her 1996 book *Black Laws of Virginia*, an 1806 law stated "if any slave hereafter emancipated shall remain within this Commonwealth more than twelve months after his freedom, he shall forfeit such right, and may be sold by the overseers for the benefit of the poor."

Exceptions were possible, though, as noted by Guild: "courts on proof of the extraordinary merit of an applicant could permit a slave emancipated for extraordinary merit since May 1, 1806, to remain, and also his emancipated wife, husband or children on proof of their good character and conduct.")

So why didn't Barsheba leave her land or her slaves to her closest surviving relative, William J. Burton? Did she simply dislike him? Or did she consider him too irresponsible? Even if she was an abolitionist, or merely a compassionate slave owner who wanted to reward her slaves after her death, she still could have left the *land* to her nephew.

It is equally interesting that Barsheba apparently left nothing to her father's second consort, Kate McKenney, or to Kate's children. Does this imply that Kate was not a second wife but merely a mistress, and her children "illegitimate"? I don't know. Perhaps Barsheba just didn't like her relatives. In any case, Barsheba had two half-brothers, Fielding Burton and William J. Burton, who would carry on the Burton name along with her allegedly notorious nephew.

Fielding Burton was one of the most interesting of all the Stafford Burtons, as I explain in more detail under "Manslaughter in Falmouth," in the highlights section (below). Fielding's descendants would live in Falmouth for generations.

5th Generation: Fielding Burton (circa 1826-November 1903)
                       married Virginia Webb (18??-28 Jan 1887)

                       Children:

6th Generation: William Jesse Burton (3 Jul 1850-28 Jan 1922)
                       Warren Burton (21 May 1853-5 Jul 1854)
                       Thompson Burton (circa 1854-5 Aug 1902)
                       Mary Burton (born circa 1857?) (suspected child)
                       Ida R. Burton Hewitt (3 Aug 1863-17 Jul 1926)

Like his brother Fielding, William J. Burton (the "fifth" William) lived and worked in Falmouth from at least 1866 up to the time of his death, or close to it. There has been some confusion about him, however, because a newspaper death notice indicates that he died "at his home" in Lance, Virginia (in what is today Hartwood). I suspect, however, that William either died at the home of a friend or relative in Lance while being cared for at the very end of his life, or that the newspaper mistakenly printed "Lance" instead of Falmouth because there were so many other Burtons who lived near Lance.

Deed records reveal that William owned a residence in Falmouth beside the Union Church and that he owned a shop or other property in Falmouth that fronted the west side of Cambridge Street and backed up to Falls Run. Unfortunately, deed records refer to both his residence and his other property with the same confusing lot number designator, perhaps because some clerk didn't realize that the same man owned two different properties in Falmouth. To make matters worse, William's properties aren't listed in tax records until the 1890s, because he apparently did not record the deeds when he purchased them (or, perhaps, because he bought them during 1866 and the records were lost during the post-Civil War Union occupation).

Mark Burton © 2014

FORMER SITE OF BURTON RESIDENCE. Deed records confirm that the Master Hobby School is located on the former William J. Burton residential lot, but the exact site of Burton's house is not known.

In any case, his was yet another Falmouth Burton family. Unlike his brother Fielding's children, though, it appears that all of William's sons either moved away or died before having children, leaving no further Burton descendants of his in Falmouth. Sadly, he was preceded in death by two wives, two daughters and at least one son.

WILLIAM BURTON HOUSE, FALMOUTH. The photo above, labeled "William Burton House, Falmouth," was taken between 1927 and 1929, but no street is specified. I suspect that this was William J. Burton's house, located roughly where the Master Hobby School is now (below). I don't know if the house's foundation stones were used for the school.

5th Generation: William J. Burton (13 Mar 1834-20 Mar 1896)
married (1) Mary A. Franklin (circa 1837-20 May 1864)
married (2) Drucilla B. Knight (circa 1846-15 Jun 1888)

Children:

6th Generation: Milton H. Burton (circa 1858-after 1893) (s/o Mary)
Alma Burton (circa 1859-8 or 9 November 1889) (d/o Mary)
William Franklin Burton (30 May 1861-after 1893) ("sixth" William, s/o Mary)
Olga Belle Burton Franklin (20 Dec 1868-after 1893) (d/o Drucilla)
Fielding (F. or T.) Burton (28 Feb 1872-1 April 1893) (s/o Drucilla)
Gilbert Cecil Burton (circa 1884?-after 1905) (s/o Drucilla)
Lizzie May Burton (8 May 1888-10 Jun 1888) (d/o Drucilla)

James Burton's Family. As I mention above, circumstantial evidence suggests that James Burton (possibly James B. Burton, Sr.) was one of at least four sons of the elder Nathaniel Burton. I'm not exactly sure where he lived, although an 1810 census tally sheet suggests that he was, at the time, a neighbor of John Limbrick (whose daughter, Sarah Limbrick, had married an unknown Burton).

James appears to have married a sister of Richard Taylor, but I don't know her first name. Circumstantial evidence indicates that they had at least one daughter. Census records reveal that a Dully Burton, who was 20 to 25 years younger than James, lived in his household in Stafford in 1850, when James was about 94 years old. She was a niece of Richard Taylor and spent nearly the entire decade of the 1820s in court with her relatives.

First, Dully teamed up with another niece of Taylor's, Lucy Carter Green, and her husband, Timothy Green, to sue their deceased uncle's heirs for possession of two of his slaves. (I do not know, by the way, if this Timothy Green was related in any way to the founder of Fredericksburg's *Virginia Herald* newspaper, who shared the same name.)

In his Will, Richard Taylor left his slaves first to his wife, Hannah, then to his two nieces, Dully and Lucy, upon Hannah's death. Taylor's wife, however, must have died either before he did or shortly after. Her heirs presumably tried to keep the slaves for themselves.

After several years in court, Dully and the Greens won their case and were awarded at least two slaves. So how did Dully celebrate?

She sued the Greens!

So *Green, et al v. Taylor* was followed by *Burton v. Green*. In May 1828, more than eight years after it all started, Dully emerged from court victorious, having won possession of both slaves.

The slaves, however, had little reason to celebrate—unless, of course, Dully's motive was to inherit them in order to free them, as her second cousin Barsheba would do in the 1840s for the slaves that she (Barsheba) had apparently inherited from her father. In Dully's case, I have no evidence for such a happy ending. Census records of Stafford slave inhabitants indicate that Dully Burton owned three slaves in 1850 and that a Dolly Burton (probably Dully) owned eight slaves in 1860 (presumably having inherited more slaves after her father died).

Dully probably had at least two brothers or half-brothers, James B. Burton (possibly James B. Burton, Jr.) and William Burton (possibly John William Burton or William John Burton). I don't know if they had the same mother or if they had any other siblings.

4th Generation:	James Burton (circa 1756-1850 or 1851)
	married FNU Taylor (suspected)
	Children:
5th Generation:	Dully Burton (circa early 1780s-after 1860) (suspected daughter)
	William Burton (circa 1780s-circa 1826/1827) (known son)
	James B. Burton (circa 1793-after 1870) (suspected son)

I do not know if Dully ever married. She, her father, her Aunt Lucy and a man named Hiram Burton lived in the same household in 1850. Dully and Hiram were still living together in 1860. So who was this Hiram, who was more than 20 years younger than Dully? Did James father a son late in life, perhaps with a second wife? Or was Dully (or Lucy) a widow with a son? Or did Dully (or Lucy) have a son out of wedlock? He only shows up once in tax records, in 1854, and only twice in census records.

Dully's likely brother, James B. Burton, married a woman named Elizabeth (born circa 1797 and died between 1860 and 1870), but I don't know if they had any children. (This James B. Burton, by the way, should not be confused with at least two younger James B. Burtons who also lived in Stafford in the 19th century.)

Dully's other likely brother, William Burton, had the greatest procreative impact of the three siblings. With so many William Burtons in Stafford at the time, however, and so little information available, I am hesitant to make any declarations without some reservations. Still, I know that (1) a James Burton had a son name William because an 1807 Stafford tax record lists one of three William Burtons as "the son of James"; (2) according to a death record, Marshall Burton's parents were William and Susan Burton; and (3) a William Burton's estate was listed in an 1827 Stafford tax record and, by process of elimination based on numerous other records, the deceased was probably the son of James Burton.

5th Generation:	William Burton (circa late 1780s/early 1790s; died circa 1826/1827)
	probably married Susan LNU
	Suspected Child:
6th Generation:	Marshall Burton (circa 1818-8 July 1882)
	married Jane F. Bettis (or Dunnington?) (18??-7 Feb 1887)

My research indicates that Marshall and Jane had at least 9 children, at least 27 grandchildren and at least 21 great-grandchildren. And I've probably missed many of the great-grandchildren who were descended from Marshall's daughters and had Burton grandparents but not Burton parents. This section, however, is limited to the 5th and 6th generations, so I will forego naming Marshall's children and move on to the family of John Burton, who might have been a son of the elder Nathaniel Burton who had children late in life, but who also might have been Marshall Burton's father (that is, John William Burton or William John Burton).

John Burton's Family. There is clear evidence that brothers James A. Burton and Richard Burton lived near U.S. Ford on the Stafford side of the Rappahannock River during the 19th century and that their father was named John Burton. Had this John Burton lived near U.S. Ford when that area was part of King George? Had the two brothers simply divided their father's property between them after his death? Was Marshall Burton their brother?

If Marshall Burton was not their brother, was their father the same John Burton who, in 1779, signed a petition to have the Stafford Courthouse moved following Stafford's 1777 land-swap with King George County? Did that land-swap, which gave Stafford its current frontage along the Rappahannock, suddenly make John a resident on Stafford's extreme southwest border rather than a resident of King George, spurring him to sign the petition to move the Courthouse to a more central location in Stafford?

More importantly, was this John Burton a son of the elder Nathaniel Burton? Only two other Stafford Burtons had signed that petition to move the Courthouse: Nathaniel Burton and James Burton. They were probably the elder Nathaniel (because the younger Nathaniel might not have been old enough to sign) and his son.

But if John was old enough to sign the petition in 1779, then he would have been in his fifties when he had his son James and in his early sixties when he had Richard. That's not impossible, of course, but it raises doubts.

It's also possible that James and Richard were the sons of a John Burton who is not related to the Stafford Burtons at all. That would mean that the huge Hartwood branch of the Stafford Burton family tree (for James and Richard had many descendants) would have to be pruned off entirely from the original White Oak trunk.

If I had to guess, I would say that Marshall, Richard and James A. Burton were brothers, and that their father was John William Burton or William John Burton, who was the son of James B. Burton, Sr., the husband of Susan Burton and who died circa 1826. He might have used the name John to avoid being confused with other William Burtons. I cannot prove this theory, though, so I will treat Marshall as a cousin of Richard and James, not as their brother.

I had hoped to solve the mystery of this particular John Burton when I learned that Robert G. Burton, owner of Burton's Automotive on Route 17 and a descendant of the said Richard Burton, had a Burton Family Bible that included handwritten names of his ancestors inside the cover, dating back to the early 1800s. Alas, by the time I contacted Robert, the Burton Family Bible had been lost!

Given such a devastating loss, I will proceed under the assumption that John Burton was the son of the elder Nathaniel, rather than a grandson, and that he fathered James and Richard late in life, with a caveat to the reader that this has yet to be documented. There is evidence that John, whoever he was, had a wife named Susan, so his family looked something like this:

4th Generaton: John Burton (17??-after 1820)

married Susan LNU (?-after 1820)

Children:

5th Generation: James A. Burton (circa 1809-20 Nov 1885)

Richard Burton (circa 1821-Apr 1860)

Both James and Richard were prolific, so much so that I suspect 19th-century Hartwood would have been a much lonelier place had these two men decided against having children. James' family looked something like this:

5th Generation: James A. Burton (circa 1809-20 Nov 1885)

married Ellen Dunnington (b. circa 1811-20 Apr 1906)

Children:

6th Generation: Richard Burton (1845-7 Feb 1919)

Elijah J. Burton (circa 1850-Nov 1895)

James B. Burton (circa 1854-died after 1905)

John Broaddus Burton, Sr. (12 May 1857-5 or 7 May 1925)

Of these four sons, I'm not sure if James B. Burton had any children. All of his brothers, however, had large families and numerous descendants. So did their uncle, Richard, whose family looked something like this:

5th Generation: Richard Burton (circa 1821-Apr 1860)

married (1) (Mary LNU?) (suspected marriage)

married (2) Willie Ann Monroe (circa 1821-23 September 1895)

6th Generation: Wesley Burton (circa 1840-18 May 1884) (s/o Mary ?)

Children by Willie Ann:

Pemiley G. Burton Kelley/Kelly (circa 1851-1 Jul 1927)

Isabella Burton Monroe (27 May 1852-25 Jan 1919)

Haswell Burton (20 Jan 1854-4 Aug 1940)

Wellington Burton (16 Apr 1855-8 Apr 1930)

Mary F. Burton Littrell (28 July 1856?-after 1899)
Willie Ann Burton Burgess (4 Dec 1857-after 1 Jul 1927)
Alvena "Allie" Burton Mills (20 Nov 1858-21 Oct 1942)

Richard died about a year before the start of the Civil War. His home, however, would play an important role as a temporary Union hospital during the famous Civil War battle of Chancellorsville, in which the outnumbered Confederates under General Robert E. Lee defeated the Union forces under General Joseph Hooker, albeit with the devastating loss of famed Confederate General Thomas "Stonewall" Jackson to friendly fire.

As I explain in more detail in the "Widow Burton" highlight (below), Richard's wife filed a detailed claim with the Southern Claims Commission after the war to be reimbursed for losses incurred. The claim is the only source I know of which reveals that her husband, Richard, was the brother of James Burton and the uncle of James' son, who was also named Richard. (The name of the nephew is important because there was more than one James Burton in Stafford at the time, but only one with a son named Richard.)

The Younger Nathaniel Burton's Family. Unfortunately, I have no documented confirmation that the elder Nathaniel Burton was the father of the younger Nathaniel Burton. Still, there is evidence of a younger Nathaniel Burton living in Stafford after the elder Nathaniel died in 1809. Census and tax records, for example, indicate that a Nathaniel Burton was the head of a household in Stafford until at least 1840.

There is also an 1866 marriage record of crucial importance which indicates that a Nathaniel and Jane were the parents of a William Burton, who was born in the very early 1800s. Analysis of the details of this marriage record and other related records indicates that the son was probably William E. Burton, Sr., who was an elderly widower when he remarried in 1866, just after the Civil War. (His own son, William E. Burton, Jr., had died in the war.)

William E. Burton, Sr.'s second wife, Sarah Williams, was a young widow (presumably a war widow). She was probably the daughter of John Burton and Missouri Simpson Burton, who had lived in Spotsylvania before the war.

(I suspect that John and Missouri might have been the Burtons who had rented a farm in Spotsylvania that included the hill from which Stonewall Jackson observed Union forces before launching his famous flank attack in the Battle of Chancellorsville, but I did not have time to research this intriguing tangent thoroughly. In 2013, Park Rangers at the Chancellorsville Battlefield Visitors' Center told me that, while the Burton Farm property was important enough to be acquired by the Park Service, historians to date have been unable to identify which Burtons had lived there. Perhaps someday someone will be able to confirm or deny my suspicions.)

Anyway, assuming that the younger Nathaniel was the son of the elder Nathaniel, the marriage record of William Burton to Sarah Williams is the only source I know of that connects one of the Falmouth Burton families to the rest of the Stafford Burtons. Regrettably, little else is known about the younger Nathaniel, his wife or his other children.

4th Generation: Nathaniel Burton (the younger) (176?-after 1840)
                     married Jane LNU
                     Children:

5th Generation: William Burton (circa 1805-after 1880)
                     (William E. Burton, Sr.?)
                     married (1) Elizabeth Bowler (circa 1807-18??)
                     married (2) Sarah Williams (circa 1840-after 1880)
                     Children:

6th Generation: William E. Burton, Jr. (circa 1835-1862) (s/o Elizabeth)
                     Margaret Burton (circa 1837-?) (d/o Elizabeth)

Census records indicate that Nathaniel and Jane might have had six or more children, but William is the only one for whom I have a name. I think I have all the names, however, for the children of Nathaniel's suspected brother, Isaac Burton, who was probably the youngest son of the elder Nathaniel.

Isaac Burton's Family. I don't know exactly when Isaac Burton married Mary Marquess, but they had their first child in 1800. In 1802, Isaac bought 114.5 acres from the estate of James Hunter (1721-1784), who had owned the ironworks just up river from Falmouth during the Revolutionary War. About 20 years later, Isaac acquired an additional 175 acres from either Mary's father, Anthony Marquess, or one of her brothers. This was probably part or all of the land that Anthony Marquess had purchased in 1803 from Hunter's estate.

Isaac was a slave owner and did not sit idly by when one of his slaves ran away. For example, he published a notice in the 24 June 1820 edition of the *Virginia Herald* newspaper offering a $20 reward for the return of a 12-year-old runaway slave named

Dennis. Dennis' grandmother was named Pallas and she lived at William Beale's in Fauquier County. Dennis's uncle was named Gerard and he lived in Stafford County with a man named Wood Cutting Peter. Isaac thought the child might be hiding with one of these relatives or with a woman named Flora who lived in Fredericksburg.

The following year, Isaac was granted a search warrant to look for his slave Mary in the house of Flora, a free black woman residing in Fredericksburg. A 17 May 1821 entry indicates that the search was executed but "the property" was not found.

I don't want to jump to false conclusions about the implications of these run-away incidents. Do they indicate that Isaac was a harsh slave owner, whose cruelty spurred his slaves to run away? Or do they indicate that he was an easy-going slave owner, whose laxity allowed for frequent escapes? Or is it more reasonable to assume that anyone kept as a slave would be apt to run away whenever possible, regardless of conditions?

I don't know much else about Isaac, but a mysterious source of information about his family provides many names and dates. Much of the information is corroborated by other sources.

4th Generation: Isaac Burton (circa Dec 1771-15 Apr 1843)
                     married Mary Marquess (12 May 1779-13 Apr 1843)
                     Children:

5th Generation: Harris W. Burton (17 Mar 1800-21 Sep 1883)
                     Strother M. Burton (5 Apr 1802-5 Jun 1851)
                     Terrissa M. Burton Guy (23 Aug 1804-23 Feb 1889)
                     Emily M. Burton Brown (29 Jan 1806-19 Dec 1856?)
                     Joseph S. Burton (31 May 1808-29 May 1890)
                     Eliza A. Burton (Petit?) (15 Aug 1810-28 Jul 1841)
                     Robert I. Burton (29 Dec 1812-21 Jul 1840)
                     Elijah M. Burton (1 Jun 1815-20 Aug 1890)
                     Arthur A. Burton (29 Oct 1817-Dec 1905?)
                     John Edwin Burton (11 Mar 1820-12 Feb 1901)
                     Mary E. Burton (Bloxton?) [7 Jun 1822/1825? -17 May 1906?]

Isaac's eldest son, Harris W. Burton, reportedly disagreed with his father about slavery. That might be why Isaac apparently excluded Harris from his Will, leaving land to his other surviving children and even to Harris' children, but not to Harris himself. Isaac also specifically stated in his Will that his slaves were to be divided among his children after his wife's death, but that Harris was not to receive any part of the slaves.

Harris did, however, end up getting some of his father's land. When Harris' son, Arastus (or Erastus?), died a minor in 1845, Harris inherited Arastus' portion of the 50 acres that Isaac had left to Harris' children.

In addition, late in his life, Harris clearly demonstrated his opposition to slavery. In 1863, during the Union occupation of Stafford during the Civil War, Harris signed the following oath: "State of Virginia, County of Stafford. I, Harris W. Burton, do solemnly swear that I will bear true faith and allegiance to the Government of the United States of America and will support the constitution ther of (*sic*) and that I will not give aid or comfort to its enemies so help me God."

It was a risky move. At the time, it wasn't clear if the Confederates might one day re-occupy Stafford and arrest or execute anyone deemed a traitor to their cause. Nevertheless, Harris helped the Union troops in various ways. For example, he once accompanied a "bearer of dispatches" to show him the way to Banks Ford (on the Rappahannock River), and on another occasion he kept a sick Union lieutenant at his home.

After the war, in 1879, Harris filed a claim for damages, revealing in his deposition that he "was a 78-year-old wheelwright. He lived on a 30-acre farm about four miles from Falmouth in Stafford County, Virginia, and owned a wheelwright shop about one mile from his farm. He had lived there since 1840 and stated that he never went more than two miles from his home during the war, except on one occasion in August 1863 when he went to see the Provost Marshall to take the oath of allegiance to the United States. He further stated that his sympathies were on the side of the Union and that he never wanted it [the union] broken up."

Despite his loyalty and cooperation, the Union troops did not treat him very well. They took property from Harris' farm, including 25 bushels of potatoes, 10 bushels of corn, and apparently corn from a field that was fed to the army's horses. Union picket guards also burned 200 (parcels?) of Harris' fences.

Even worse, they confiscated most, if not all, of the tools and other valuables from his wheelwright shop, and then burned the shop building itself to the ground. I suppose one could argue that the Union troops were following a "scorched earth" policy and couldn't leave behind anything of use that might fall into the hands of the enemy. Still, it was a poor way to treat a loyal citizen.

Interestingly, witnesses who testified on behalf of Harris' claim included Robert Lawson, a colored blacksmith, and Peyton Washington, a former slave from Culpeper who later lived near Harris. Both claimed to have known Harris for about 50 years, confirmed that he was pro-Union and corroborated his claims about the wheelwright shop being burned. In the end, however, only $269 of Harris' $669.50 claim was approved, and by then Harris only had a few more years left to live.

5th Generation:	Harris W. Burton (17 Mar 1800-21 Sep 1883) married Elizabeth (Betsy/Bettie/Betty) LNU (born by 1819-died after 1880)
	Children:
6th Generation:	Arastus (or Erastus?) Burton (born by 14 Feb 1840; died a minor in 1845)
	Rachel D. Burton (circa 1832-Nov 1903]
	Seldon Wellington Burton (8 Dec 1833-25 Jul 1913)
	Parker F. "Jesse" Burton (circa 1838-10 Mar 1901)
	Ann Eliza "Annie" Burton Brooks (14 Feb 1840-27 Nov 1923)
	Mary H. Burton Brown (before 1843-19??)
	Elizabeth H. "Bettie" Burton Harding (14 Aug 1843-22 Aug 1916)

Despite his father's opposition to slavery and pro-Union beliefs, Seldon Wellington Burton fought for the Confederacy during the Civil War, although one source indicates that he only volunteered to avoid conscription. According to his obituary, by the time he died in 1913, he was the oldest Confederate veteran in Stafford County. His tombstone, and that of his sister, Elizabeth, are reportedly the only ones still visible in the old Burton cemetery off Fleet Road, just west of Berea Baptist Church.

Of Isaac Burton's other sons, Strother, Robert, Arthur and John Edwin apparently did not have any children. I'm not sure if Elijah had children; if so, I do not know their names. (I was unable to confirm claims that he was Elijah Marquess Burton, who married Margaret Hearn in 1841 in Tuscaloosa, Alabama.)

Joseph S. Burton married and had children, and eventually moved his family out of Stafford. I know very little about him or his family.

5th Generation: Joseph S. Burton (31 May 1808-29 May 1890)
                             married Maria A. LNU (circa 1821-?)
                             Children:

6th Generation: Arthur A. Burton (circa 1843-?)
                             Cornelia T. Burton (circa 1845-?)
                             Laura F. Burton (circa 1847-?)
                             Sarah Burton (circa 1849-?)

This ends my summary of 5th and 6th generation Stafford Burtons who were, for the most part, pre-Civil War Stafford Burton families. (To avoid confusion, I point out that I have included the families of 5th generation Stafford Burton men who started families prior to the war but also had children who were born during or after the war.)

Highlights From Later Generations

The Stafford Burtons of later generations were primarily working-class or middle-class farmers or laborers who led relatively ordinary lives. By the mid-19th century, though, there were so many Stafford Burtons that I have decided to refrain from listing all of the known families here. There are, however, a few additional highlights from the Civil War era and later that I think are worth mentioning.

The Widow Burton. As I mention above, during the Civil War battle of Chancellorsville, Confederate General Thomas "Stonewall" Jackson reportedly decided to launch his famous flank attack after spying the positions of Union forces from a hill located on the Burton Farm in Spotsylvania County. (I leave it to others to confirm or refute the possibility that the farm was rented by John Burton and his wife, Missiouri Simpson.) The farm, or at least the hill in question, is now part of the battlefield park.

I was surprised to discover, however, that that was not the only Burton farm to play a significant role in the battle. Before the battle, not surprisingly, military cartographers made maps of the Rappahannock River valley. These maps typically noted important homes in the area, usually marked by the names of the owners or residents, as well as major roads, waterways, river fords and other features of military significance.

On the Stafford side of the river, one of the homes marked on both Union and Confederate maps was that of the mysterious "Mrs. Burton." On at least one map, she is listed as the "Widow Burton."

But who was this Widow Burton? And why was her humble home deemed important enough to be highlighted on military maps?

Her name, it turns out, was Willie Ann Monroe Burton. Her husband, Richard Burton, had died in 1860. In the spring of 1863, she was a 45-year-old widow with seven children who lived on a 200-acre Stafford farm on the Rappahannock River. She had ten acres in cultivation and the rest in timber.

And hers was the closest house to U.S. Ford....

CROSSING U.S. FORD. In this Edwin Forbes sketch of Union troops crossing the Rappahannock River at U.S. Ford, from Stafford into Spotsylvania, the house on the hill in the background might be that of the Widow Burton.

Imagine her surprise when Union General Joseph Hooker and a large portion of his army stopped at her house before crossing the Rappahannock on their way to the Battle of Chancellorsville. The biggest shock, however, must surely have come after the battle, when the bulk of Hooker's bloodied and defeated army retreated back across the river and commandeered the Burton house and farm for use as a hospital.

While there, the Union troops confiscated vast quantities of Mrs. Burton's property, including: 6 or 7 hogs; 3 cattle; 1 cow; 1 calf; 50 bushels of corn; 1,500 pounds of hay; 48-50 fowls (which Mrs. Burton used to make soup for the wounded, the surgeons and the officers); knives and forks; a one-horse wagon and harness; and an estimated 8,000 (!) fence rails. According to Mrs. Burton, Col. Sharp and Col. Skinker promised to pay for all that had been taken, but they never did.

When the troops finally pulled out a few weeks later, they took all of Mrs. Burton's quilts, comforts, pillows and other items (which she had made herself), "to make the soldiers easy in their ambulances." They promised to pay her for them, but Mrs. Burton conceded that she gave those particular items freely, stating "I could not object, the suffering was so great."

And the suffering really was terrible. For example, according to Willie Ann's neighbor, Robert E. Patton, "the badly wounded" were taken to her house and "many amputations performed." At one point, according to Patton, Mrs. Burton had to flee her own home when it came under bombardment from Confederate artillery located on the southern side of the river.

Many of these details are known because, years later, Willie Ann filed claim number 16818, dated 26 November 1872, with the Southern Claims Commission, for $680.00 for losses incurred during the war. Fortunately for her, the claim was approved, indicating that the Commission believed she had been pro-Union during the war. And fortunately for historians and genealogists, the story of her wartime ordeal was preserved in the process, surviving more than 150 years to give future generations a better understanding of the Civil War's impact on Stafford Burtons and their neighbors.

On the Waterfront. For about 100 years, from the early 19th to the early 20th centuries, Stafford Burtons like Willie Ann owned much of the waterfront property along the Stafford side of the Rappahannock River, from about Horsepen Run (a few miles northwest of Falmouth) to the Fauquier County line. By the early 20th century, however, most of these Burton properties had been divided among heirs, many of whom apparently viewed such inheritances as potential financial windfalls. Many of those waterfront properties were sold off, in whole or in part, to a local electric power company in 1907.

According to a 16 February 2014 *Free Lance-Star* newspaper article and other sources, the Fredericksburg Water Power Company built the Embrey Dam in 1910 on the Rappahannock River just above Fredericksburg. The Virginia Electric and Power Company bought the dam in 1926 and also ended up owning thousands of acres on both banks of the Rappahannock and Rapidan rivers. Decades later, in 1968, the City of Fredericksburg acquired the dam and most or all of that waterfront land. And that is why much of the waterfront land remains undeveloped to this day.

Someone Did the Math. Were she here today, Annie Laura Downs Burton could testify that churches in the 19th century were much stricter then than they are now. Even though Annie and her beau, Wellington Burton, did the right thing by getting married (back in 1877), it wasn't good enough for the folks at Annie's church, Hartwood Presbyterian.

Mark Burton © 2014

HARTWOOD PRESBYTERIAN CHURCH. Many Stafford Burtons are buried in the cemetery at Hartwood Presbyterian Church. Wellington and Annie Laura ended up with one of the more prominent grave sites, suggesting that the fornication charge was eventually followed by forgiveness and reconciliation.

Annie, it turns out, gave birth to her first child only *five* months after getting married, rather than the ususal and customary nine. And—surprise, surprise—someone at church cared enough to do the math. According to the church's 8 July 1877 minutes, the pastor of the church charged Annie with fornication and suspended her from "communion with the church" for four months.

Wellington was not mentioned, suggesting that he might not have been a member of the church. Or perhaps Wellington was not the father but married the pregnant Annie in a chivalrous attempt to save her from impending dishonor. I have no evidence, however, that Wellington was not the father, and I would not be surprised if certain church members considered Wellington an unindicted co-conspirator.

I *was* surprised by the number of cases of fornication, both explicit and implied, that I came across in my research. I would not want to suggest, however, that Stafford Burtons thought *impatience* a virtue....

The Burton School House. At least some Stafford Burtons must have believed in the virtue of education because there is evidence that a Burton School House existed in southern Stafford at some point prior to 1882. I, however, had never heard of a Burton School House in Stafford until I inadvertently came across a reference to it in an 1882 tax record. Apparently, the school house was no longer in use by then, but it was mentioned in descriptions of land parcels that were in the same vicinity as the school house. I don't know exactly where the school house was located, but I suspect that it was in or near Berea.

The tax records are the only sources I know of that mention a Burton School House in Stafford. (I saw no reference to the school in Dr. Helen Stewart Jones' 1970 dissertation on the history of public education in Stafford County, which suggests that the Burton School House was privately owned.)

I don't know if modern historians are aware that a Burton School House existed in Stafford in the 19th century. If not, I hope this highlight brings it to their attention.

Burtons, Hewitts and Berry's Store. Unlike the Burton School House, Berry's Store in Old Falmouth (which still stands today on the northwest corner of Washington and West Cambridge streets) has received lots of attention ever since it was painted in the 1920s by artist Gari Melchers, who had moved into the Belmont mansion just up Washington Street. By then, the store was owned by N. N. Berry, whose name is clearly visible in the painting, which explains why most people today think of it as Berry's Store.

But that's not the whole story.

The store's original owner was probably Thomas H. Hewitt, a 19th-century Falmouth businessman. Tax records indicate that Hewitt purchased the corner lot in question circa 1848 from Thomas C. Scott (then owner of Clearview mansion), after moving to Stafford from Connecticut. It's not clear, however, when the building itself was built, so perhaps Scott was the original owner.

Hewitt died in 1872 at the age of 53. The store remained in his family for years, but a dispute apparently developed among his heirs after his wife died in 1885. As a result of the court case of *Hewitt v. Honey*, the Hewitt store was put up for sale at public auction.

Another Falmouth businessman, Fielding Burton, who owned his own store on the southwest corner of the same intersection, bought the Hewitt store at the public auction for $775 on 14 November 1885. At the time, the purchase price was a lot of money, but Fielding had his reasons.

Stafford County Historical Society

BERRY'S STORE. N. N. Berry purchased the Hewitt-Burton store in Falmouth from Ida R. Burton Hewitt and her children in 1920. A few years later, Berry's name was immortalized in a painting by Gari Melchers (above), and the store's Hewitt and Burton history was soon forgotten.

Fielding's daughter, Ida Burton, had married Thomas Hewitt's son, Peter Hewitt, in 1878. Fielding gave the former Hewitt store to Ida and her children, jointly, on 5 May 1888. By then, Peter was a business partner of Ida's brother, William

Jesse Burton. The company was listed as *Hewitt and Burton* in Chaitaigne's 1888-1889 business directory for Fredericksburg.

Had someone else bought the store, Fielding would have had a new rival to contend with just across the street, and his relatives would have had to find a new location for their business. So it's not surprising that Fielding spent so much to buy it.

Also, Fielding's wife had died suddenly in 1887. Perhaps her death made Fielding worry about what would happen to Ida and her children if Peter should suddenly die, so he gave the store to them to provide for their future financial security.

As it turns out, Peter did die young, in 1907. Shortly after her husband's death, Ida moved her family to Fredericksburg. In her later years, she apparently lived with one or more of her children in Richmond and in Washington, D.C. In 1920, she and her children sold the Falmouth store to N. N. Berry. (It is not clear who, if anyone, ran the store between 1908 and 1920, but I would not be surprised if it was Ida's brother, William, who remained in Falmouth until his death in 1922.)

So the store in Melchers' painting was actually a Hewitt store for up to 37 years, then it was a Burton store for two and a half years, then it was a Hewitt-Burton store for another 32 years. Only then did it become Berry's Store.

The Founding of Falmouth Baptist Church. In addition to owning the store, Ida R. Burton Hewitt played a key role in the founding of the current Falmouth Baptist Church in Falmouth, Virginia, in August 1891. She and her sister-in-law, Mary E. Boutyard Burton, were two of ten charter members of the church.

I have learned, however, that the current Falmouth Baptist Church was not the first, which complicates matters. Now, I know this is supposed to be a mere highlight, but please indulge me while I go off on a tangent and provide some rather tedious details regarding the church's history that I wish to document but could not justify including in the chronological entries.

Elmer Hedrick, a former clerk at Falmouth Baptist, wrote a history of the church back in the 1960s, titled *Church History, 1891-1966*. He notes that Baptists in Falmouth broke off from Fredericksburg Baptist Church several times throughout the 19th century and quotes "Dr. Darter's" book for details.

(Darter's book was probably *The History of Fredericksburg Baptist Church, Fredericksburg, Virginia*, by Oscar H. Darter. Darter mentions Falmouth Baptist Church on pages 124, 149, 162 and 174. Note that Darter himself listed years of reunification as if they were years of separation in a summary of the two churches' relationship on page 124. This might have been a mistake because it seems to contradict what he wrote on pages 149, 162 and 174.)

In any case, according to Darter's book and Hedrick's excerpts, some members of Fredericksburg Baptist withdrew in 1818 to form a separate Baptist church in Falmouth.

Mark Burton © 2014

BEREA BAPTIST CHURCH. Some members of the antebellum Falmouth Baptist Church left in 1852 to form Berea Baptist, about four miles northwest of Falmouth. In 1866, the then-defunct Falmouth Baptist Church sold some property in Falmouth to William J. Burton and donated the proceeds to their Berea counterparts to help them repair Civil War damage to the Berea church's building. The original building is still in use (shown here in 2014 with additions and upgrades).

In 1861, the Falmouth Baptist Church "dissolved" and was reunited with Fredericksburg. (I am not sure if this was the same church that had been formed in 1818.) I suspect that the onset of the Civil War and the impending Union occupation of Falmouth might have spurred this reunification, but that is just speculation on my part. I should point out that an unknown number of members had withdrawn from Falmouth Baptist in the early 1850s to form Berea Baptist Church, so perhaps the diminished membership at Falmouth also played a role in the Falmouth Baptists' decision to re-join with Fredericksburg in 1861.

In 1868, the Falmouth Baptists again withdrew from Fredericksburg to form their own church. It lasted until about 1888 or 1889. Mary E. Boutyard Burton, of

Falmouth, was a member of this church. For reasons unknown to me, she and the others reunited with Fredericksburg Baptist in 1888 or 1889.

The Darter excerpts indicate that the decision to reunite was made on 3 May 1888. The readmission of Falmouth members does not appear in Fredericksburg Baptist records, however, until the spring of 1889. The membership roster from that time indicates that some Falmouth members were readmitted in April 1889, and a 2 May 1889 entry in the minutes section of the same record book formally recognizes the readmissions.

The statement in the minutes reads: "Brethren and sisters of former Falmouth Baptist Church, now disbanded, received by experience into Fredericksburg Baptist." A list of 25 readmitted members included the name of Mary E. Burton, and this is how I learned that she had been a member of the 1868-1888/9 Falmouth church.

Just two or three years later, on 2 August 1891, the Falmouth Baptists would withdraw from Fredericksburg for the last time and found the current Falmouth Baptist Church.

According to Hedrick, Mrs. Hewit (*sic*) (Ida R. Burton Hewitt) and Mary E. Burton were two of ten charter members of today's Falmouth Baptist Church. These ten were part of a group of 34 members who left Fredericksburg Baptist Church to form Falmouth Baptist. I do not know why all 34 were not considered charter members. Perhaps charter members played a special role.

Mrs. Almeta J. Burton (Ida's other sister-in-law) was also one of the original 34 members, as was Ida's husband, Peter Hewitt. In addition, Almeta's daughter, Rosa Burton, was among the first group of people to be baptized at the new church. (Her name is on a list of 28 people who were baptized at the Falmouth church on its first day, 2 August 1891.)

As noted in the Berry Store highlight, Ida R. Burton Hewitt was the daughter of Falmouth businessman Fielding Burton. Mary E. Burton and Almeta Jane "Virginia" Burton were Fielding's daughters-in-law. Rosa was Fielding's granddaughter. So it was the Burton women who played crucial roles in the founding of Falmouth Baptist. I do not know, however, if Fielding himself attended any church.

On the Falmouth church's membership roster, Mrs. Ida R. (Burton) Hewitt was listed as member number 3 and the wife of member number 2, Peter Hewitt. They had both been members of Fredericksburg Baptist since 1888.

Mark Burton © 2014

THE 1892 FALMOUTH BAPTIST CHURCH. The Falmouth Baptist Church completed this building (above), at the corner of Cambridge and Forbes Streets, about a year after their final separation from Fredericksburg Baptist in 1891. (The Falmouth Baptists moved to new facilities in the mid-20th century and this building is now used by Golgotha Church.)

The view from Route 17 (below) became possible in 2014 when trees were removed during construction to improve the intersection of Routes 1 and 17 in Falmouth.

Mark Burton © 2014

Peter was baptized at Fredericksburg Baptist Church on 29 April 1888. Ida became a member of Fredericksburg Baptist Church on 3 June 1888 by a letter of transfer. (She transferred from Berea Baptist Church, where she had been a member since at least 1883.)

As noted above, Peter was the son of prominent Falmouth businessman Thomas H. Hewitt, whose store was on the corner across the street from Fielding Burton's store. Not only did Peter marry Fielding's daughter, but he was a business partner with Fielding's son, William Jesse Burton.

Peter's mother, Jane, was listed as a member of Fredericksburg Baptist in April 1861. (I wonder if Jane was one of those from the Falmouth church that reunited with Fredericksburg that year.) I saw no indication that Peter's father, Thomas, was ever a member of Fredericksburg Baptist. Thomas is buried near Berea Baptist in the same acre of land that he had donated to the Berea community for use as a cemetery, but I don't know if he was ever a member of the church.

Mark Burton © 2014

BEREA CEMETERY. Ida R. Burton Hewitt's father-in-law, Thomas H. Hewitt, donated one acre of land for the Berea Cemetery (above), which is adjacent to, but not part of, Berea Baptist Church. He acquired the acre from Piney Latham and Nancy Burton just after the Civil War, when Nancy bought the surrounding land from Piney. Hewitt and his wife, and various Burtons, are among those buried there.

(A private Burton family cemetery is reportedly located just to the west/northwest, but only the markers of Seldon Wellington Burton and his sister, Elizabeth Burton Harding, are said to be discernable.)

Mrs. Almeta J. Burton was listed as member number 8 on the original Falmouth Baptist membership roster. Mary E. Burton was listed as member number 9. Rosa Burton was listed as member number 44.

Fredericksburg Baptist records also indicate that these Burtons were among the original 34 members of Falmouth Baptist. A 6 September 1891 entry in an untitled Fredericksburg Baptist Church record book confirms that 34 members left to form Falmouth Baptist Church in 1891: "the large number of dismissals by letter is accounted for in the fact that 34 of our members withdrew to form a church in Falmouth, where most of them reside."

In addition, Fredericksburg Baptist membership records mention 2 August 1891 as the date that the Falmouth members transferred their memberships by letter. The entry for Mary E. Burton, "no. 63.," included a remark that she left "to organize the church at Falmouth." Miss Almeta Jane Burton, "no. 65," also went "to Falmouth ch" on that date, as did Peter Hewitt, "no. 200," and his wife, Mrs. Ida R. Hewitt, "no. 239."

I could not find a complete list of the 34 original members of Falmouth Baptist Church, but I found two nearly identical lists containing 32 and 33 names, respectively. One list comes from 3 September 1891 meeting minutes on page 287 of an untitled and undated Fredericksburg Baptist record book. (The book begins with 4 October 1883 meeting minutes.) The other list comes from a loose sheet of paper attached to the inside front cover of that same record book.

I present the names from the two lists side-by-side for comparison. Names of charter members are followed by a (C). I use parentheses and question marks for names that are illegible in the original.

3 September 1891 Minutes:	Inside Front Cover:
Mrs. Mary E. Green	Mrs. Mary E. Green
Mrs. Nannie Sullivan	" Nannie Sullivan
Miss Nettie Sullivan (C)	Mifs Nettie Sullivan (C)
Mrs. (Zilla?) Casey	Mrs. Zilla Casey
Mrs. Almeta Burton	" Jinnie Burton (Almeta Jane)
Mrs. Susan Heflin	" Fannie Roberson
Mrs. Sallie (Leitch?) (C)	" Susan Heflin
Mrs. James Heflin	" Sallie Leich (C)

Mr. James Heflin	Mr. James He(flin?)
Robt. Tyson	Mrs. Nannie Heflin
Mrs. Marguret (?) Payne	Mr. Robert Tyson
Mrs. (Thos.?) Sullivan (*sic*)	Mrs. Margaret Payne
Thos. Sullivan (*sic*)	" Thomas Snellings (*sic*)
Chas. Wine (C)	Mr. Thomas Snellings (*sic*)
Mary Wine (C)	" Chas Wine (C)
Sarah Young (C?)	Mrs. Mary Wine (C)
Douglas Young (C)	" Anna Young (C?)
J. W. Mills	Mr. Dug (*sic*) Young (C)
M. A. Mills (C?)	" Joseph Mills
Ida Hewitt (C)	Mrs. Alice Mills (C)
Peter Hewett (*sic*)	" Ida Hewitt (C)
Jennie (?) Edwards	Peter Hewitt
Maria (?) Edwards	Mrs. Jinnie (sp?) Edwards
Alice O'Bryhim	" Maria Edwards
Mary Littrell	" Alic O'bryant (*sic*)
John Jett	Mifs Mary Littrel
Mrs. John Jett	Mrs. John Jett
Ann Garner	Mr. John Jett
Thos. Musselman	Mifs An (*sic*) Garner
Mary E. Burton (C)	Thomas Musselman
Frank K. Tyler (C)	Mrs. Mary E. Burton (C)
James Wooddy	Frank K. Tyler (C)
	Jas. P. Wooddy

Fannie Roberson appears on the second list but not the first. I assume that Mr. and Mrs. Thos. Sullivan, on the first list, and Mr. and Mrs. Thomas Snellings, on the second list, were the same couple, but I don't know which surname is correct.

I also do not know with certainty the name of the unlisted 34th member, but it might have been Mary A. Tyson, Robert Tyson's sister. In her obituary, Mary was referred to as a "charter" member of the Falmouth Baptist Church.

Another source, however, lists "Miss May Tyson" as one of the first 28 people to be baptized into the church on 2 August 1891. If this was actually Mary A. Tyson, then Mary was not the 34th member to transfer from Fredericksburg. Georgia Tyson,

Robert's second wife, was also a possible candidate for the missing 34th member, but she, too, is listed among the first 28 to be baptized.

These Tysons, by the way, were probably related to Stafford Burtons. Robert Tyson was probably Fielding Burton's half-brother and Mary A. Tyson was probably his half-sister.

As noted in the Chronology, many more Stafford Burtons would join Falmouth Baptist in subsequent years, which is another reason I wanted to include this as a highlight. Today, only a few Burtons attend the church, but several of the non-Burton members are related to Burtons in one way or another.

140,000 Burtons. The involvement of Burtons in southern Stafford businesses and churches during the late 19th century, such as Hewitt's Store and Falmouth Baptist, is not surprising simply because there were so many Burtons in Stafford at the time. I very roughly estimate that, in the early 1890s, this single, though very extended, Burton family comprised more than one percent of the entire population of Stafford, which was about 7,500. This is even more remarkable when one considers that almost all of those Burtons lived in the southern half of the county.

Furthermore, the estimated percentage of Burtons in Stafford's population far exceeded the estimated percentage of Burtons in the U.S. population. For example, according to a 30 November 1892 Fredericksburg *Star* newspaper article, Arthur Anthony Burton of Stafford attended an 1892 national gathering of American Burtons in Mitchell, Indiana.

The article included an estimate of 140,000 Burtons in the United States at the time. If accurate, this would have been about two-tenths of one percent of the U.S. population, which was, roughly, a mere 65 million back then. Of course, with so many Burtons in southern Stafford, one of them was bound to make the news sooner or later....

Manslaughter in Falmouth. In July 1894, just a few years after his daughter and daughters-in-law helped to found Falmouth Baptist Church, Fielding Burton was arrested for killing Burrell "Burley" Payne. He was tried that September. Like the founding of Falmouth Baptist, the story of Fielding Burton's murder trial is really too long to be a highlight, but I want summarize it here because it is one of the most interesting events in Stafford Burton history.

At the time, it was the biggest murder trial in Stafford County's history. The crowd of people who showed up to watch, estimated at 600 people, was so large that three candidates for Congress stopped by to campaign. Even the mayor of Fredericksburg, A. P. Rowe, attended.

But was Fielding Burton really a murderer? What had spurred a 68-year-old grandfather and store owner to kill? What kind of man had he been? What kind of life had he led?

By the time of the killing, Fielding had become a prominent Falmouth businessman despite the fact that he, according to his own testimony, "never went a day to school and had no education." He further revealed that he had been born in Stafford, had worked as a cooper for about 20 years before going into the grocery business and had lived in Falmouth since about the 1850s.

If he was really 68 in 1894, then Fielding was probably born in 1826 or 1827. Also, it's not surprising that Fielding started out as a cooper, or barrel-maker, which must have been a popular profession in what were then the bustling port towns of Falmouth and Fredericksburg. Although Fielding's father had been a successful farmer with hundreds of acres in land, he died when Fielding was only six or seven years old. Fielding's stepfather, William Tyson, was a cooper who, in 1841, had to mortgage his land, his hogs and his cooper's tools to Walker P. Conway in order to pay a debt.

By 1850, Fielding was apparently living in Fredericksburg with his sister Lucy and her husband, Newton A. Turner, where both men worked as coopers. Fielding married Virginia Webb, presumably while living in Fredericksburg, and they had their first three children there. Sadly, their second child, Warren, died at the age of 11 months.

Tax records indicate that Fielding and his family had moved back to Stafford by 1856. The 1860 census indicates that he had at least three children by then: Willie, 10; Thompson, 4; and Mary, 3. (It appears that Mary did not survive childhood.) Fielding and his family probably remained in or near Falmouth during the Civil War, but I found no records to prove it. He does not appear to have served in the military. His daughter, Ida, was born during the war.

After the war, in 1865, Fielding obtained a license to sell liquor, which he might have held jointly with George J. Lightner, a Falmouth businessman, that year and the next. It must have worked out well, because Fielding would continue to get liquor licenses until at least 1896, although perhaps not every year.

By 1867, Fielding had a store in Falmouth. The exact location of the store is not known, and it is unclear if Fielding owned the real estate or merely rented. Fielding's store was hit by burglars that year in a heist so big it caught the attention of the local newspaper.

According to a 19 November 1867 article in the Fredericksburg *Ledger*, burglars broke into Fielding's store in Falmouth on a Saturday night and stole approximately $800 worth of goods, along with $10-12 in cash. (In those days, $800 could buy an entire house.) The burglars first stole tools from a nearby blacksmith shop, which they then used to cut the lock from Burton's store. Among the goods taken were sugar, coffee, beef, bacon, whiskey, tobacco and twenty-five pairs of boots.

I don't know if the burglars were ever caught or if any of the stolen goods were recovered. If nothing else, this indicates that Fielding was a legitimate grocer and not just a liquor store manager.

In 1869, Fielding purchased 131 acres of land in or near Falmouth for $1,200 from two New York men, George and Kirtland Arnold. The land had previously been part of John Newton's estate. That was a lot of money back then, and it seems odd that the owners were from New York. Were they carpetbaggers? Or did they have a local connection of some sort?

In any case, in the 1870 census, Fielding was listed as a farmer, not a cooper or grocer, perhaps because he owned so much land. But things would soon change.

In the mid-1870s, when Falmouth businessman George J. Lightner decided to purchase the old Basil Gordon warehouse and convert it into a store, he sold his old combination house and store to Fielding, presumably to raise money to buy the warehouse. Fielding jumped at the opportunity, for Lightner's old store was ideally situated at the corner of Carter (now West Cambridge) and Washington streets, which was the main intersection in Falmouth at the time.

But Fielding had to raise money himself, so he and his wife sold their 131-acre farm, that they had purchased just a few years earlier, to Thomas J. Moncure for only $900 (a $300 loss). Fielding apparently used most of the money from the sale of the farm to make a down payment of about one-third of the $2100 purchase price for Lightner's old store.

Fielding and his wife had to borrow the rest, taking out a mortgage in 1876, but it paid off handsomely. Fielding not only paid off his mortgage in the next four years, but he was able to purchase the house next door and the shop next to it during that same time frame. These purchases gave Fielding significant frontage along Cambridge Street in Falmouth, from what is today Washington Street south to the brick building that now houses Amy's Café.

(These three properties survived into the 1930s, but had been replaced by an Esso filling station by the early 1940s. The location later became an auto body shop.)

In 1883, Fielding purchased Lot 28 along River Road in Falmouth from Henry O'Connor (probably William Henry O'Conner/O'Connor, Sr.). This 1.5-acre property, on the corner of River Road and the road that used to run up the hill to Union Church, might have included the building now known as Shelton's Cottage (which was moved to a different location in the 20th century). I cannot say with certainty that Fielding owned Shelton's Cottage, though, because the records do not clearly indicate if Fielding bought the western corner lot or the eastern corner lot.

In 1885, Fielding purchased Thomas H. Hewitt's store at public auction. This purchase gave Fielding control of both corners of Warrenton Road (now Washington Street) in the heart of old Falmouth. At the time, it was prime commercial real estate, because Routes 1 and 17 did not exist, and all traffic passing through Falmouth had to go past his stores.

In 1887, Fielding purchased the northern half of Lot 61, one of the lots in the original town plan of Falmouth. It was located on the east side of what is now Route 1 in Falmouth, and the lot's northern border was part of Falmouth's original northern boundary.

Thus, in little more than a decade, Fielding Burton had acquired at least six properties in Falmouth. He appears to have purchased at least some of these properties via public auction and county "tax sales." In other words, long before the invention of late-night television "infomercials," Fielding had learned one of real estate investors' biggest secrets.

Sadly, in 1887, near the height of his financial success, Fielding's wife, Virginia, died. Her early death might have spurred Fielding to think about his own mortality and about providing for his children and grandchildren.

The following year, Fielding deeded the former Hewitt store and house to his daughter Ida and her children (Peter Hewitt's family). He deeded the Lot 28 property on River Road to one of his daughters-in-law, Mary E. Burton, and her children (i.e., his son William Jesse Burton's family). He deeded the Lot 61 property to his other daughter-in-law, Virginia (a.k.a. Almeta Jane) Burton, and her children (i.e., his son Thompson Burton's family).

I don't know why he excluded his sons' names from the deeds. Perhaps there was a tax advantage in doing so. Or perhaps Fielding was unusually prescient in entrusting the properties to the women. His son Thompson, his son-in-law Peter, and five of his six grandsons would all be dead by 1912.

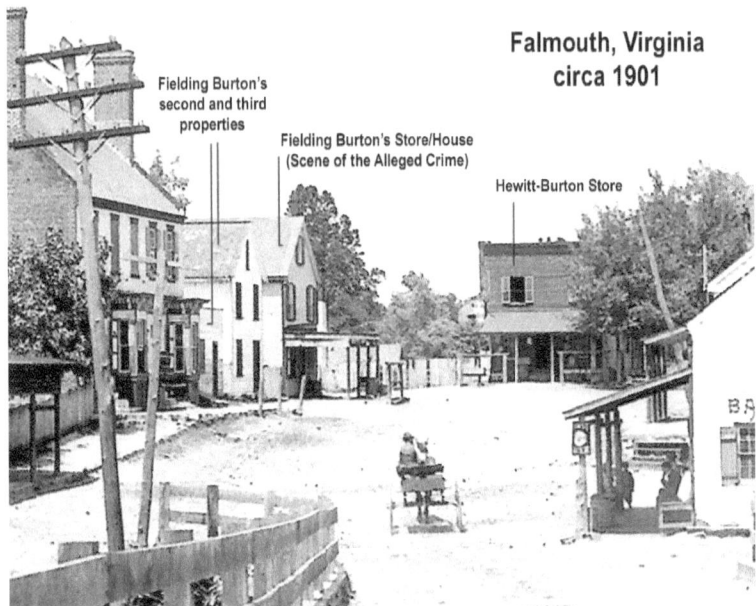

Fielding Burton's
second and third
properties

Fielding Burton's Store/House
(Scene of the Alleged Crime)

Hewitt-Burton Store

**Falmouth, Virginia
circa 1901**

Stafford County Historical Society (cropped and labeled by author)

SCENE OF THE CRIME. Fielding Burton was probably still alive when this photo of Falmouth (above) was taken circa 1901, about seven years after Burley Payne's death. The same street in 2014 is shown below. The building that housed the Hewitt-Burton store still stands (on the right in photo below), although its facade has been modified.

Mark Burton © 2014

In the summer of 1894, however, Fielding was a successful family patriarch with three children and at least 12 grandchildren. He had gone from cooper to farmer to store owner to real estate entrepreneur. That's not bad for a man who was apparently illiterate and, by his own admission under oath, never went to school a day in his life.

This certainly does not seem to be the kind of life a murderer would lead. So what happened that fateful summer evening in 1894 that would ruin the final years of an otherwise successful life?

The facts seem simple enough. Fielding Burton, 68, while working at his store in Falmouth, struck Burrell "Burley" Payne, about 22, in the head with a stick at about 8:30 or 9 p.m. on Saturday evening, 21 July 1894.

Payne was examined by Docter H. B. Hales at about 9:30 p.m. and was then taken home, where he died early the next day, Sunday, 22 July 1894, at about 4:30 or 5 a.m. The same doctor did a postmortem a few hour later, just before noon.

A funeral for Payne was held in Falmouth at Union Church on Monday, 23 July, and he was buried in the cemetery there. Fielding was indicted by a special grand jury a few weeks later, in August 1894, and released on $6,000 bail, with his son-in-law Peter Hewitt as his surety.

The trial was held the following month and covered in detail in Fredericksburg's *Free Lance* newspaper, whose staff included Mayor A. P. Rowe's son, A. P. Rowe, Jr. The *Free Lance* called the trial "one of Stafford's most celebrated cases" and noted that "the trial of Burton consumed more time than any other trial that ever took place in the history of Stafford." The trial lasted four days, from 19 to 22 September 1894.

(Thanks in large part to the extensive coverage provided by the *Free Lance*, I was able to include many details regarding the trial in the 1894 section of the Chronology, which is far longer than any of the other years. Readers who wish to know more details, such as the names of the jurors or those of nearly three-dozen witnesses, should see the related entries under 1894.

Regrettably, I do not have the news coverage of the incident by the other local paper, the Fredericksburg *Daily Star*. Although most of the *Daily Star* issues are preserved on microfilm, the second of half of 1894 is missing.)

According to the *Free Lance*, at one point during his testimony in court, the 230-pound Fielding wept as he expressed remorse over the incident, stating that he had had no ill will toward Payne and wished that he had been the one killed instead of Payne.

According to the newspaper summary, Fielding's lawyers, St. George R. Fitzhugh and William A. Little, Jr., argued that "Burrell Payne was seeking in an angry and menacing manner to enter Burton's home for the purpose of assaulting him or his son, and that in an effort to keep him out he was accidentally killed, and that therefore the homicide was justifiable...."

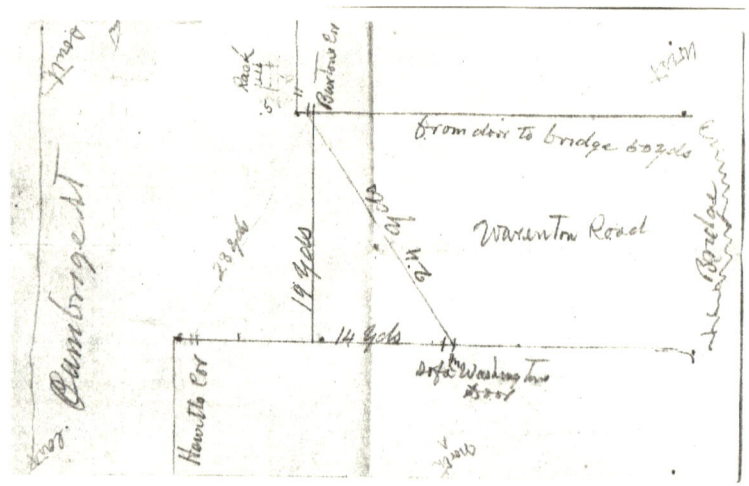

Records Office, Clerk of the Circuit Court, Stafford County, Virginia

HEWITT'S DIAGRAM. Fielding Burton's son-in-law, Peter Hewitt, drew this diagram of the crime scene, apparently to demonstrate that some alleged witnesses had committed perjury, because they were not in a position to have seen what happened.

The jury had a choice of five possible verdicts: first degree murder, second degree murder, voluntary manslaughter, involuntary manslaughter or acquittal. According to the newspaper account, nine members of the jury were originally in favor of acquittal, but the other three were in favor of involuntary manslaughter and apparently would not give in.

The jury ended up convicting Fielding of involuntary manslaughter and fining him $200, plus about $700 for court costs. Fielding's total costs, however, including attorneys' fees, were estimated at $2,000, which was a small fortune in those days.

So, was Fielding guilty or not? After reading the summaries of witnesses' testimonies in the newspaper, as well as handwritten affidavits and jury instructions formerly on file at the Stafford Courthouse, I get the impression that Burrell Payne was drunk and belligerent, and tried to force his way into Fielding's store (which was also Fielding's home).

The incident reportedly began when Payne saw Fielding's adult son, William Burton, drag an unconscious drunkard, Ben Snellings, out of the doorway of Fielding's store. Was Payne sincerely concerned for Snellings when he complained that it was inappropriate for William to drag the drunken man, or was Payne just looking for an excuse to take offense?

The latter appears to be the case. Payne's own words suggest that he was looking for a fight and trying to provoke others. Multiple witnesses testified that Payne was drunk and boasting that he was "the best G-d d–n man in Falmouth," and that Payne called Fielding's son, William, a "damn fool."

When Payne tried to follow William into Fielding's store, Fielding blocked him at the doorway and told him repeatedly to go away. After Payne literally put his foot in the doorway, Fielding struck him with a some sort of stick or cane.

According to the newspaper account, several witnesses testified that they had known Fielding for decades and that he had always been a peaceful man. My own research into Fielding's life suggests the same.

For example, both before *and after* his trial, Stafford County officially recognized Fielding as a person of "good moral character" when granting his annual liquor license applications. If Fielding had had a violent or criminal history, other than the manslaughter case, I doubt his applications would have been approved.

Even the prosecutor in Fielding's trial, W. Seymour White, referred to Fielding as "a respectable citizen of the Commonwealth," and said that prosecuting him for murder was a "disagreeable duty of the Commonwealth's Attorney." I don't think White meant to imply Fielding's innocence, but White apparently could find nothing in Fielding's past with which he could impugn Fielding's character. (White, by the way, would later become mayor of Fredericksburg.)

I cannot say, of course, whether or not the verdict was appropriate. I have no way to know how aggressive Payne was and whether Fielding truly felt threatened enough to justify the use of force. It does seem unlikely, though, that a responsible, 68-year-old businessman and devoted grandfather, with no history of violence or criminal behavior, would attack a 22-year-old, in public, in front of witnesses, if it were not in self-defense.

Furthermore, Payne did not die at the scene. It is therefore possible that Payne died of some other cause at his home. For example, if he was drunk, he might have died of alcohol poisoning, or fallen during the night and exacerbated his wound.

Stafford County Historical Society

TOBACCO WEIGHT. This 1930s photo of a tobacco weight (foreground) reveals that Fielding Burton's three Falmouth properties (center right background) were still standing decades after his death in 1903. By the early 1940s, all three buildings had been razed to make way for an Esso gasoline station. The view in 2014 is shown below.

Mark Burton © 2014

The doctor even testified that he "had seen many other wounds of similar character, which had not produced death." Even without the benefit of modern forensics, this raises doubts about whether Fielding's blow was the sole cause of death, regardless of Fielding's motives.

Although he avoided prison, Fielding paid a heavy financial price for defending himself, his son and his property from an angry drunkard. Tax assessments indicate that back then, $2,000 was enough to buy two or more houses. The combined value of Fielding's store / house and two adjacent buildings, for example, was assessed at $1,000 in 1894.

So the purchasing power of that $2,000 would be roughly equivalent to hundreds of thousands of dollars today. Other records indicate that, after the trial, Fielding had to mortgage all of his properties (the store / house, plus the two adjacent properties he had purchased), presumably to pay the fine, court costs and lawyers' fees. Still, he must have been thankful that he did not have to spend his remaining nine years in prison.

According to his obituary, Fielding Burton died suddenly of heart trouble at 11 o'clock on a Tuesday night (probably 24 November) in 1903. He was reportedly one of the oldest citizens in Stafford County at the time. (He was probably about 76 or 77 years old when he died.)

His funeral and interment were to take place at Union Church in Falmouth. The location of his grave is not known.

Deed records indicate that the sheriff who arrested Fielding, Charles Lewis Kennedy, ended up buying Fielding's store and adjacent properties. A few years after Fielding's death, Kennedy, or possibly Kennedy's son, would sell the properties to the wealthy W. E. Brooks, who had served on the coroner's inquest that led to Fielding's indictment.

Fielding's death and Kennedy's purchase of his store marked the end of an era in old Falmouth. From the end of the Civil War to the beginning of the 20th century, Fielding Burton had been a Falmouth storekeeper, and had owned and operated his store on the corner for at least 25 of those years. His son, William Jesse Burton, would carry on as a Falmouth businessman, but never again would a Burton be so prominent a figure in Falmouth.

Saturday Night's All Right for Fighting. In his opening statement for the Defense in Fielding Burton's 1894 murder trial, St. George R. Fitzhugh reportedly waxed eloquent about his boyhood days in Falmouth, providing some insight into one particular aspect of Falmouth social life from the 1850s to the 1890s (albeit with an ulterior motive). According to a newspaper account, Fitzhugh said that the people of Falmouth were peculiar, but generous and brave.

Back then, "'her streets were busy marts of business, and also frequently the scene of a knock-down fight. You were welcome to a drink, or they would divide their last mouthful with you, and then, at the first insult, knock you down.' He had frequently seen as many as a dozen fights on a Saturday night, and though business had disappeared, the custom of Saturday evening brawling had not." Fighting, and even killing, were not confined to the southern end of the county, however, as another Burton would find out in the 1920s.

Following in Plessy's Footsteps. Frank Burton was born in Madison County, Virginia, but he eventually moved to Widewater in northeastern Stafford. He might have been the first black Burton to live in Stafford. Even if he wasn't, he's the main subject of the earliest documented reference to black Burtons in Stafford that I found.

That reference, an 18 August 1902 special dispatch to the Richmond *Times* newspaper, states that "Frank Burton, a negro, of Stafford County, was to-day fined $3 and costs by Mayor Willis for refusing to go in the car provided for colored people and insisting on riding in the car for white people when he boarded a train on the Richmond, Fredericksburg and Potomac Railroad here" [in Fredericksburg].

I do not know why Frank insisted on boarding the white passenger carriage that day, but I wonder if his actions were somehow related to the tenth anniversary of the famous case of *Plessy vs. Ferguson*. According to an encyclopedia article, the Supreme Court did not rule on the case until 1896, but it had originated in Louisiana in June 1892 when Homer A. Plessy was arrested for the same offense as Frank.

Unfortunately for Frank, a far more tragic event would put his family in the news again just over 20 years later. According to newspaper accounts, one of Frank's sons was murdered by Willie Bowen in Widewater on Saturday night, 3 March 1923, near the store of Wilson Decatur. The younger Burton died quickly after Bowen allegedly severed Burton's throat with a butcher knife following an altercation.

Bowen then allegedly telephoned Commonwealth's Attorney F. P. Moncure and requested that an officer be sent to Widewater to take him (Bowen) into custody. (Bowen, by the way, was also black and was reportedly the first prisoner to be incarcerated in the jail at what was then the new brick courthouse in Stafford.)

The journalists, however, might have gotten a crucial part of this story wrong. The 1920 Census indicates that the elder Frank Burton had at least four sons. One was named Frank and another was named Eugene. The newspapers listed Frank as the murdered son, but a death record indicates that it was actually Eugene who died that day of a stab wound to the throat.

I don't know which source is correct, but I do know that not all news accounts of Stafford Burtons are so sorrowful. For example, less than a year after the elder black Frank Burton was fined in the railroad car incident, one droll reporter put tongue firmly in cheek….

Quilting Party Animals. In a 21 March 1903 dispatch from Fredericksburg, a newspaper reporter lamented that "this has been the dullest week socially in this city since the Lenten season set in." The reporter then resorted to describing a recent Burton birthday party.

"Mr. and Mrs. R. L. Burton, of Stafford county, gave a birthday party in honor of their son, Bennie L. Burton, which was largely attended by the young people of the neighborhood. There was music and dancing. The feature of the occasion was a quilting party, in which many of the young ladies took part, and an entire quilt was finished during the evening."

Who says Burtons don't know how to party?

Carved in Stone. Sometimes "carved in stone" isn't all that it's cracked up to be—even if it's a tombstone. The year of death on William Jesse Burton's tombstone, for example, is 1921, but he actually died in 1922. The 27 February 1919 date of death on Stella Burton's tombstone is also wrong. Other sources indicate that she died on 25 February 1918.

In addition, the dates on the tombstone of Rosa Burton Sullivan's husband, Hunter Sullivan, do not match the dates given in his obituary. The date of death on Gilmer Burton's tombstone is also wrong, but it's only off by one day.

How could such errors go unnoticed regarding information that is, literally, of monumental importance to the loved ones of the deceased? Perhaps in some cases, when a funeral occurred at the beginning of the year, the carver mistakenly chiseled the previous year out of habit, and then hoped no one would notice. In other cases, it is possible that a tombstone might not be placed on a grave until long after the burial, by which time the customer ordering the stone might have forgotten the exact date, or might have faulty information from a third party.

Any of those are preferable to the possibility that someone was trying to save money by opting for a discounted leftover: "It's Discount Tombstone's January Clearance Event! All previous model year tombstones up to 50% off! Sale ends soon, so die now and save big!"

I guess the moral of the story is that tombstone carvers are not always reliable, so those who wish to be remembered should make names for themselves *before* they die. And some Burtons did exactly that.

A Million Miles Without an Accident. Major Burton was born in Stafford circa 1895. (Although he served in World War I, "Major" was his first name, not a rank.)

He became the safest truck driver in the history of the Esso Oil Company (one of ExxonMobil's predecessors). In his 40-year career, it was estimated that he drove more than a million miles and delivered more than 300 million (!) gallons of gasoline and other petroleum products *without a single accident*. (And that was back when neither the trucks nor the roads had the safety features that they have today....)

I wonder if his record still stands, whether in terms of (1) distance driven without an accident; (2) number of years without an accident; or (3) amount of fuel delivered without an accident. In any case, he made a name for himself, even if it's now just a minor highlight in an obscure chronology about Stafford Burtons.

Getting the Name Drop on Hollywood. When it comes to names, Stafford Burtons were often way ahead of Hollywood. For example, long before *Happy Days* ever aired, there was a Fonzie Burton in Stafford. And long before there was a *Streetcar Named Desire*, Stafford had Stella Burton. There was even a Gilmore Burton in Stafford long before there was a *Happy Gilmore*.

There was also more than one Richard Burton, but I don't think any of them pursued (over-) acting. In most cases, of course, the stories of working-class Stafford Burton farmers and laborers would hardly be of interest to a Hollywood producer, but the next and final highlight really could be made into a movie.

An Unsung Hero. Private First Class Everett E. Burton, son of Ollie and Lillie Burton of Berea, was one of the unsung heroes of World War II. (Even though World War II is technically beyond the scope of this Chronology, which stops at 1930, Everett was born in 1919, so I include him and the sacrifice he made.)

Everett was wounded in the North Africa campaign and spent three months in the hospital. But that didn't stop him. When he recovered, he went on to fight in Sicily. Then he and his unit returned to England, but he wasn't there for very long.

His unit was among the first to land at Normandy on D-Day. Regrettably, he died on 8 June 1944 of wounds he received in action in France while serving with the First Infantry Division.

Well, Everett's heroic story brings me to the conclusion of this Introduction, which I hope provides enough information on early Stafford Burton families to whet the appetites of genealogists while also providing sufficiently interesting highlights to keep other readers from falling asleep. In the next section, I provide summarized genealogical information, listing selected Stafford Burtons alphabetically and chronologically, and also listing known, implied and suspected marriages.

Those lists are followed by a special, "Pre-Stafford" Chronology of documented references to Burtons who might have lived in or near Stafford County's predecessor districts. I begin that Pre-Stafford Chronology with some cursory information on early Virginia Burtons, for anyone who might be interested.

Then, finally, comes the Main Chronology of documented references to Stafford Burtons, which makes up the bulk of this work and is divided into three parts. Only Part I, which includes entries from the 17th and 18th centuries, is included in this volume.

Volume II contains Part II of the Main Chronology, which includes entries for the 19th century. Volume III contains Part III, which includes entries for the early 20th century. Volume III also includes a bibliography for the entire four-volume collection. Volume IV contains an index for the Pre-Stafford and Main chronologies.

GENEALOGICAL SUMMARIES

I N LIEU of a formal genealogy of Stafford Burtons, which would not only be incomplete and speculative, but would require another volume or two, I have instead compiled several lists of summary information. These include:

- Selected Stafford Burtons, listed alphabetically
- Selected Stafford Burtons, listed chronologically by birth
- Selected Marriages, listed chronologically
- Selected Marriages, listed alphabetically by Burton
- Selected Marriages, listed alphabetically by Consort

If nothing else, these listings should help readers quickly find names of parents; names of consorts; and dates of birth, death and marriage. Such information, in turn, can be used to locate additional related details and source citations in the Main Chronology.

I do not provide an alphabetical listing of parents. Still, it should not be too difficult for readers who wish to find children of known parents to look up the parents in the chronological listing of Burtons, given that most children in a family are born within a span of twenty years or so.

Regrettably, the automatic sort software that I used to create these lists had trouble with punctuation marks and did not offer a way to ignore titles and suffixes, like "Mrs." or "Jr." (which it treated like first names). I tried my best to manually correct such errors in these lists, but I cannot guarantee perfect order.

In the marriage lists, I chose to list Burtons and their consorts, rather than grooms and brides. In cases where a Burton married another Burton, the marriage is listed twice.

I have also included some marriages that took place after the 1930 cut-off date. These should be thought of as "bonus material" and might not be as well-researched as earlier marriages.

Finally, in some cases, I had to have numbers appear prior to any letters to facilitate automated numerical sorting. As a result, phrases such as "after 1850" sometimes appear in reverse, such as "1850 after."

Selected Stafford Burtons

Alphabetical Listing

NAME	DOB	DOD	FATHER	MOTHER
Burton, Abner	circa 1885 or circa 1886	1950.09	Burton, James B. "J. B."	West, Mary W. "Mollie /Molly"
Burton, Addie T. [Addie T. Burton Harding]	1881.01.13	between 1921 and 1926.10.18 ?	Burton, Wellington W.	Downs, Annie Laura
Burton, Agnes Elizabeth Miniclier	1921.11.13	1991.04.27		
Burton, Agnes Margaret	1908.03.24	2003.12.07	Burton, Joseph Lee	Humphries, Nora V. Burton
Burton, Alfred E. (?) [NFI]	1880.12.23		Burton, Jr., William J. (*sic*)	Burton, Mary V. (*sic*)
Burton, Alfred Eugene	1881.12.08	1903.08.23	Burton, William Jesse	Boutyard, Mary E. (Ellen?)
Burton, Alfred Wilson	1923	1976.06.30	Burton, Ernest William	Boutyard / Boutchyard, Florence Mary
Burton, Alice L. Dickerson / Dickinson	1863	1952.04.01	Dickinson, William	LNU, Ellen
Burton, Aline McGill Payne	circa 1934	2011.08.28	Payne, Oliver	LNU, Pearl
Burton, Alma	circa 1859	1889.11.08 or 1889.11.09	Burton, William J. (William J. Burton, Jr. ?) ["fifth"]	Franklin, Mary A.

NAME	DOB	DOD	FATHER	MOTHER
Burton, Alma May [Alma May Burton Johnson] [F'burg?]	1927.04.09	after 1980	Burton, Renald / Reynold Vinson	Yeatman, Bertha M.
Burton, Almeta Jane "Virginia / Jennie / Jenny"	circa 1857	1910.01.02 or 1910.01.03	Burton, William J.	Chilton, Elizabeth
Burton, Alphonso "Fonsie/Fonzie"	1882	1940.10.25	Burton, Elijah J.	Bettis, Letha / Lethe Anne
Burton, Alvena "Allie" [Alvena "Allie" Burton Mills]	1858.11.20	1942.10.21	Burton, Richard	Monroe, Willie Ann
Burton, Ann "Nancy"	circa 1770	by 1861.09.18	Burton, William ["third"]	Porch, Rachel
Burton, Ann "Nancy" [the younger]	circa 1793	by 1885.12.16		
Burton, Ann Eliza "Annie" [Ann Eliza "Annie" Burton Brooks]	1840.02.14	1923.11.27	Burton, Harris W.	LNU, Elizabeth
Burton, Ann Eliza [Ann Eliza Burton Conner/Connor/O'Conner/O'Connor]	circa 1842		Burton, Marshall	Bettis, Jane F.? [Jane F. Dunnington?]
Burton, Anne E. "Annie" [Anne E. "Annie" Burton Way Berry]	circa 1882	after 1942	Burton, Elijah J.	Bettis, Letha / Lethe Anne
Burton, Anne "Annie" Lee [black] [Anne "Annie" Lee Burton (Dawson or Dorsey)] [F'burg?]	before 1888.06.28			
Burton, Annette J. "Nettie" [Annette J. "Nettie" Burton Cooper]	1881.12.04	after 1933	Burton, James B. "J. B."	West, Mary W. "Mollie / Molly"
Burton, Annie Laura Downs	1858.12.16	1926.10.18	Downs, Thomas	Smith, Amanda

NAME	DOB	DOD	FATHER	MOTHER
Burton, Annie Virginia [Annie Virginia Burton Way]	circa 1910	after 1998	Burton, Joseph Lee	Humphries, Nora V. Burton
Burton, Arastus (or Erastus?)	between 1821 and 1840.02.14	1845 (died a minor)	Burton, Harris W.	LNU, Elizabeth
Burton, Archibald B. "Archie"	1878.03.03 or 1879.08.09	1962.12.06	Burton, Elijah J.	Bettis, Letha / Lethe Anne
Burton, Archibald Lee "Archie" "Buck"	1908	1985	Burton, Archibald B. "Archie"	Payne, Susan (B.?) "Susie"
Burton, Archie [black]	circa 1908		Burton, Frank [black]	Pullen / Puller, Lucy Kate [black]
Burton, Arnita Ellen [Arnita Ellen Burton Beach]	circa 1929	2006.04.12	Burton, Sr., Benjamin Lewis / Louis "Bennie / Benny"	Monroe, Iva Davis
Burton, Arthur A.	1817.10.29	1905.12.17	Burton, Isaac	Marquess, Mary
Burton, Arthur A.	circa 1843		Burton, Joseph S.	LNU, Maria A.
Burton, Sr., Arthur James	1891	1985.05.19	Burton, Sr., John Broaddus	Lowry, Margaret "Maggie"
Burton, Jr., Arthur James "Junior"	1922.09.06	1977.10.10	Burton, Sr., Arthur James	Craig, Blanche May
Burton, Arthur M.	circa 1882 or circa 1883	1970.10.08	Burton, James B. "J. B."	West, Mary W. "Mollie / Molly"
Burton, Barsheba	by 1794	between 1843.02.01 and 1843.11.27	Burton, William (William J. Burton, Sr.?) ["fourth"]	Jett, Susannah "Sukey"
Burton, Sr., Benjamin Lewis / Louis "Bennie / Benny"	1883.08.08	1977.03.01	Burton, Robert L.	Patton, Georgeanna / Georgianna "Anna / Annie"
Burton, Jr., Benjamin Lewis / Louis	1913.08.17	1984.10.30	Burton, Sr., Benjamin Lewis / Louis "Bennie / Benny"	Monroe, Iva Davis
Burton, Bertha M. Yeatman [Fredericksburg / Stafford]	1897	1980.07.21	Yeatman, Fitzhugh	LNU, Dolly

NAME	DOB	DOD	FATHER	MOTHER
Burton, Bessie Larkin Jones	circa 1909	1973.09.21		
Burton, Beverly [Beverly C. Burton?]	circa 1849	after 1882 (circa 1912.01.03)	Burton, Marshall	Bettis, Jane F.? [Jane F. Dunnington ?]
Burton, Blanche May Craig	1898	1962	Craig, Henry D.	unknown first wife
Burton, Carrie [Carrie Burton Hoover]	between 1903.10.04 and 1927.08.26	after 1969.12	Burton, Clarence	Jones, Carrie L.
Burton, Carrie Irene [Carrie Irene Burton Knight]	1880.11.15	1953.07	Burton, Robert L.	Patton, Georgeanna / Georgianna "Anna / Annie"
Burton, Carrie L. Jones [Spotsy/Stafford]	1882.04.03	1927.08.26	Jones, E. F.	Burton, Lucy P.
Burton, Sr., Carroll Eugene [Fredericksburg]	1923.11.27	1979.01.07	Burton, Sr., Arthur James	Craig, Blanche May
Burton, Cary	circa 1790	circa 1860	Burton, Samuel ["second"]	LNU, Mary
Burton, Catharine	circa 1857		Burton, Marshall	Bettis, Jane F.? [Jane F. Dunnington ?]
Burton, Catharine [Catharine Burton Southard]	before 1831.10		Burton, Samuel ["second"]	LNU, Mary
Burton, Catherine [black]	circa 1930	2003.01.14	Burton, Edward James [black]	Buckner, Mildred Virginia [black]
Burton (?), Catharine "Kate" McKenney [Catharine "Kate" McKenney (Burton?) Tyson]	circa 1805	after 1870		
Burton, Cecil Melvin	1925	2001.03.17	Burton, Elwood Winston [the elder]	Harding, Myrtle V.
Burton, Cecil Preston	1921	2005.07.28	Burton, Oliver R. "Ollie"	Monroe, Lillian Bell "Lillie / Lilly"
Burton, Charles	circa 1868	1892.08.(16?)	Burton, Richard	LNU, Dulcibella "Dulcie"

NAME	DOB	DOD	FATHER	MOTHER
Burton, Charles "Charlie"	1894.06.04	1964.08.03	Burton, William F.	Burton, Mary "Mollie"
Burton, Charles Ford	1917.08.15 or circa 1918	1986.11.13	Burton, Archibald B. "Archie"	Payne, Susan (B.?) "Susie"
Burton, Charlotte Bourne	circa 1926		Bourne, Henry S.	Newton, Gladys H.
Burton, Christine [Flossie ? Christine Burton Sealy]	circa 1929	after 2008.11.09	Burton, Oliver R. "Ollie"	Monroe, Lillian Bell "Lillie / Lilly"
Burton, Clarence	1877.05.11	after 1930	Burton, Wellington W.	Downs, Annie Laura
Burton, Clementine [Clementina / Clementine Burton Walker]	1855.04.15	1916.12.17	Burton, William J.	Chilton, Elizabeth
Burton, Clemma (*sic*)	circa 1850		Burton, William J.	Chilton, Elizabeth
Burton, Clifford Emory	1910.01.15	1961.02.21	Burton, John [son of Elijah J. Burton]	Portch, Nettie M.
Burton, Clifton [NFI]	before 1909.09.17			
Burton, Columbus Ashby	1884.10.23 ?	after 1955.02.08	Burton, Haswell	Moxley, Leatha Ann
Burton, Cornelia T.	circa 1845		Burton, Joseph S.	LNU, Maria A.
Burton, Daniel	before 1835	after 1881	Burton, FNU	Coakley, Sarah
Burton, David E.	circa 1906 or circa 1908	1955.02.08	Burton, Columbus Ashby	Curtis, Marietta "Flossie"
Burton, Delia [1860 slave owner; NFI]	1860 before			
Burton, Delphia	circa 1795			
Burton, Dollie / Dolly M. Garner [King George / Stafford ?]	1913.02.03 or 1914.02.03	1938.12.19	Garner, Lucien ?	Montieth, Dollie ?
Burton, Dora Lee [Dora Lee Burton Edwards]	1882.08.08 ?		Burton, Haswell	Moxley, Leatha Ann

NAME	DOB	DOD	FATHER	MOTHER
Burton, Doris	before 1933.08.11		Burton, Judson Marshall	
Burton, Dorothy Virginia Sisk [Dorothy Virginia Sisk Burton Seay]	1922.06.16	2010.11.22	Sisk, James A. (Ashby?)	Leake, Bertha
Burton, Dorothy Virginia [Dorothy Virginia Burton Ellington] [Fredericksburg / Stafford]	1922.12.14	2009.05.07	Burton, Renald / Reynold Vinson	Yeatman, Bertha M.
Burton, Drucilla B. Knight	circa 1846	1888.06.15	Knight, Austin	Cloe, Elizabeth
Burton, Dulcibella "Dulcie"	circa 1842	1907.08.27		
Burton, Dully	circa 1780s ?	after 1860	Burton, Sr., James B.?	Taylor, FNU ?
Burton, Eddie	circa 1898		Burton, Thomas R.	Limbrick / Limerick, Hester A.
Burton, Edith [Stafford ?]	before 1930.01.25	after 1930.01.25	Burton, Edward M. "Eddie"	Williams, Elizabeth
Burton, Edith [Edith Burton Umphrey]	circa 1893	1920.04.15 ?	Burton, Thomas R.	Limbrick / Limerick, Hester A.
Burton, Edna C. Way [Edna C. Way Burton Dallman]	1928.10.09	2007.01.31	Way, Ashton Cleveland	Burton, Annie Virginia
Burton, Edna E. [Edna E. Burton Leake]	1932.06.02		Burton, William M.	Burton, Winnie Davis
Burton, Edward James [black]	circa 1907 or circa 1910	1984.03.30 ?	Burton, Frank [black]	Pullen / Puller, Lucy Kate [black]
Burton, Edward Henry	circa 1920	1989.08.27	Burton, Archibald B. "Archie"	Payne, Susan (B.?) "Susie"
Burton, Edward M. "Eddie"	1890.09.20	1930.01.25	Burton, Sr., John Broaddus	Lowry, Margaret "Maggie"
Burton, Edwin Emory "Ed"	1933.07.28	2011.11.21	Burton, Frank Edwin	Burton, Agnes Margaret

NAME	DOB	DOD	FATHER	MOTHER
Burton, Elijah J.	circa 1850	1895.11.25	Burton, James A.	Dunnington, Ellen
Burton, Elijah M. [Elijah Marquess Burton ?]	1815.06.01	1890.08.20	Burton, Isaac	Marquess, Mary
Burton, Eliza A. [Eliza A. Burton Petit?]	1810.08.15	1841.07.28	Burton, Isaac	Marquess, Mary
Burton, Eliza V. Ballard	circa 1838	after 1907.02.18	Ballard, Flavius Josephus	LNU, Eliza
Burton, Elizabeth [wife of James B. Burton, Jr.]	circa 1797	between 1860 and 1870		
Burton, Elizabeth	before 1812			
Burton, Elizabeth [wife of Harris W. Burton]	by 1819	after 1880		
Burton, Elizabeth "Betsy" Bowler	circa 1807	before 1866	Bowler, Charles	Donahoe, Elizabeth
Burton, Elizabeth Chilton	circa 1820	after 1870	Chilton, Thomas	Limbrick, Charlotte
Burton, Elizabeth H. "Bettie / Betty" [Elizabeth H. "Bettie / Betty" Burton Harding]	1843.08.14	1916.08.22	Burton, Harris W.	LNU, Elizabeth
Burton, Elizabeth Musselman Brummett [Elizabeth Musselman Brummett Burton Reed]	circa 1788	after 1870	Musselman, Henry	LNU, Elizabeth
Burton, Elizabeth Williams	before 1917 ?			
Burton, Ella [Ella Burton Payne]	circa 1876, 1881 or 1886	1933	Burton, Elijah J.	Bettis, Letha / Lethe Anne
Burton, Ellen Dunnington	circa 1811	1906.04.13 or 1906.04.20		
Burton, Ellen Jane	before 1835		Burton, FNU	Coakley, Sarah

NAME	DOB	DOD	FATHER	MOTHER
Burton, Elsie Mae / May [Elsie Mae / May Burton Hove] [Fredericksburg]	1921.05.21	after 1981.03.07	Burton, Major	Curtis, Fleda C.
Burton, Elwood Winston [the elder]	1904.06.06	1948.08.05 or 1948.08.08	Burton, Sr., Benjamin Lewis / Louis "Bennie / Benny"	Monroe, Iva Davis
Burton, Emily M. [Emily M. Burton Brown]	1806.01.29	1856.12.19 ?	Burton, Isaac	Marquess, Mary
Burton, Ernest William	1894.07.09	1970.09.28	Burton, Wilson	Dickerson / Dickinson, Alice L.
Burton, Erva V. "Billie" "Sis" [Erva V. "Billie" "Sis" Burton Murphy]	1925.12.16	2008.11.09	Burton, Oliver R. "Ollie"	Monroe, Lillian Bell "Lillie / Lilly"
Burton, Estelle [Stafford?]	by 1925	after 1929.11.16	Burton, James Grover	LNU, Grace
Burton, Esther [Esther Burton Grinnan]	circa 1920	2010.01.24	Burton, Sr., Benjamin Lewis / Louis "Bennie / Benny"	Monroe, Iva Davis
Burton, Eugene [black]	1902.10.20	1923.03.04 ?	Burton, Frank [black]	Pullen / Puller, Lucy Kate [black]
Burton, Eula Meadows	1922	1988		
Burton, Everett E.	1919.09.19	1944.06.08	Burton, Oliver R. "Ollie"	Monroe, Lillian Bell "Lillie / Lilly"
Burton, Fannie D. Guy	circa 1889		Guy, Robert ?	
Burton, Fielding B.	circa 1826 or 1827	1903.11.24	Burton, William (William J. Burton, Sr.?) ["fourth"]	McKenney, Catharine "Kate" [Catharine "Kate" McKenney (Burton?) Tyson]
Burton, Fielding B.	1882.12.26	1896.08.20	Burton, Thompson	Burton, Almeta Jane "Virginia / Jennie / Jenny"

NAME	DOB	DOD	FATHER	MOTHER
Burton, Fielding (F. or T.?)	1872.02.28	1893.04.01	Burton, William J. (William J. Burton, Jr. ?) ["fifth"]	Knight, Drucilla B.
Burton, Fielding W.	circa 1906	after 1969.12	Burton, Clarence	Jones, Carrie L.
Burton, Fleda C. Curtis	1899	1981.03.07	Curtis, E. L. [Edwin L. Curtis ?]	Downs, Maggie ?
Burton, Ernestine Florence / Florence Ernestine [Ernestine Florence / Florence Ernestine Burton Payne]	1918	1993	Burton, Ernest William	Boutyard / Boutchyard, Florence Mary
Burton, Florence Mary Boutyard / Boutchyard	1899.02.05	1994.05.29	Boutyard, Ashton Sanford	Bryant, Elizabeth G. "Lizzie"
Burton, Flossie Almeda [Flossie Almeda Burton Plaskett]	circa 1896	after 1970.10.08	Burton, James B. "J. B."	West, Mary W. "Mollie / Molly"
Burton, FNU [infant son of James B. "J. B." Burton]	1888.06.09 or 1889.06.09	1888.07.01 or 1889.07.01	Burton, James B. "J. B."	West, Mary W. "Mollie / Molly"
Burton, FNU [son of Wilson Burton]	1892.04.12		Burton, Wilson	Dickerson / Dickinson, Alice L.
Burton, FNU [Mrs. George Burton]	before 1919.02.07	after 1919.02.07		
Burton, Frances Eunice "Fannie / Fanny" Cooper [Frances Eunice "Fannie / Fanny" Cooper Burton Berry]	1885.10.05	1960.11.26	Cooper, Henry L.	Fritter, Emma Ideler / Idella "Della / Dellie"
Burton, Frank [black] [the elder black Frank Burton]	1879	1949.04.19	Burton, Wm. [black?]	LNU, Susan [black?]
Burton, Frank [black]	circa 1905	1923.03.03 ?	Burton, Frank [black]	Pullen / Puller, Lucy Kate [black]
Burton, Frank Edwin	1903.04.10	1980.03.06	Burton, John [son of Elijah J. Burton]	Portch, Nettie M.

NAME	DOB	DOD	FATHER	MOTHER
Burton, George	circa 1770s ?	after 1830	Burton, William ["third"]	Porch, Rachel
Burton, George ?	1885.05.08 ?		Burton, James (*sic*) [James B. "J. B." Burton ?]	LNU, Mary (*sic*) [Mary W. "Mollie / Molly" West ?]
Burton, George B.	circa 1865 or 1868.04.15 ?	1944.04.04 ?	Burton, Richard	LNU, Dulcibella "Dulcie"
Burton, George Farrar [Albemarle? / Stafford]	1921.04.15	2008.12.13		
Burton, Georgeanna / Georgianna "Anna / Annie" Patton	1854.02.09	1934.02.06	Patton, Elliot / Elliott	LNU, Delia
Burton, Gerrard	after 1753		Burton, William ["third"]	Porch, Rachel
Burton, Gilbert Cecil	circa 1884 ?	after 1905	Burton, William J. (William J. Burton, Jr. ?) ["fifth"]	Knight, Drucilla B.
Burton, Gilmer / Gilmore W.	1892.04.12 ? or 1894.05.19 ?	1939.09.26 or 1939.09.27	Burton, Wilson	Dickerson / Dickinson, Alice L.
Burton, Glendie S. [Glendie S. Burton Johnson]	circa 1905	after 1964.02.24	Burton, John [son of Elijah J. Burton]	Portch, Nettie M.
Burton, Grace [wife of James Grover Burton] [Stafford?]	before 1915.12	after 1929.11.16		
Burton, Harold L.	1912.01.04	after 1979.03.12	Burton, Leonard	Burton, Minnie C.
Burton, Harris W.	1800.03.17	1883.09.21	Burton, Isaac	Marquess, Mary
Burton, Haswell	1854.01.20	1940.08.04	Burton, Richard	Monroe, Willie Ann
Burton, Helen Elizabeth Newton [Elizabeth Helen Newton Burton ?]	1923	2007.06.22	Newton, Richard	LNU, Effie
Burton, Helen [granddaughter of Haswell Burton ?]	before 1929.06.07			
Burton, Henry Bernard	1890.03.28	1918.07.28	Burton, William Henry	Portch, Sarah E.

NAME	DOB	DOD	FATHER	MOTHER
Burton, Hester A. Limbrick / Limerick	circa 1869	after 1919	Limbrick, Lanius (?)	LNU, Margaret
Burton, Hiram	circa 1808 or circa 1815	after 1860		
Burton, Hugh M.	circa 1895	after 1933	Burton, William Henry	Portch, Sarah E.
Burton, Ida V. [Ida V. Burton Skidmore]	1870.08.03 ?	after 1910	Burton, Parker F. "Jesse"	Brown, Mahala
Burton, Ida R. [Ida R. Burton Hewitt]	1863.08.03	1926.07.17	Burton, Fielding B.	Webb, Virginia "Jennie"
Burton, Ida Bell / Belle Humphries [Ida Bell / Belle Humphries Burton McGhee]	1869.01.26	1943.07.28	Humphries, William H.	LNU, Charlotte
Burton, Inez Marguerite [Inez Marguerite Burton Payne]	1905 or 1906	1963.03.20	Burton, Maurice Walter	Cooper, Frances Eunice "Fannie / Fanny"
Burton, Ira	before 1814	after 1830 ?		
Burton, Ira Richard	1889.03.08	1965.05.05	Burton, Haswell	Moxley, Leatha Ann
Burton, Irene Lee Grinnan	1916.01.06	1973.01.22	Grinnan, Edward	Monroe, Katherine
Burton, Isaac	1771.12	1843.04.15	Burton, Nathaniel [the elder] ?	
Burton, Isabella [Isabella Burton Monroe]	1852.05.27	1919.01.25	Burton, Richard	Monroe, Willie Ann
Burton, Iva Davis Monroe	1882.12.02	1964.11.30	Monroe, George E.	LNU, Mary
Burton, J. Alvin	1909.09.25	1979.03.12	Burton, Leonard	Burton, Minnie C.
Burton, James [James B. Burton, Sr.?]	circa 1756	1850 or 1851	Burton, Nathaniel [the elder] ?	
Burton, Jr., James [James B. Burton, Jr.?]	circa 1793	after 1870	Burton, Sr., James B.?	Taylor, FNU ?

NAME	DOB	DOD	FATHER	MOTHER
Burton, James A.	circa 1809	1885.11.20	Burton, John	LNU, Susan
Burton, James Alexander "Sandy"	circa 1832	1896.11.(08?)	Burton, James ?	Burton, Ann "Nancy"
Burton, James B.	circa 1852	circa 1941 ?	Burton, James A.	Dunnington, Ellen
Burton, James B. "J. B."	1857.12.09	1897.02.23	Burton, Marshall	Bettis, Jane F.? [Jane F. Dunnington ?]
Burton, James Edward	1887.03.25 or 1887.03.31	1959 ?	Burton, Haswell	Moxley, Leatha Ann
Burton, James Grover	circa 1884 or 1885.05.08 ?	1915.12	Burton, James B. "J. B."	West, Mary W. "Mollie / Molly"
Burton, James Lester	between 1925.11.25 and 1954.09.25	after 2006.03.25	Burton, Lester Clifton	Bryant, Mae
Burton, James William	1918.06.16	1945.05.08	Burton, James Edward	Humphries, Minnie Elizabeth
Burton, Jane McKinley "Janie" [Jane McKinley "Janie" Burton Marlow/Marlowe]	1896.11.31	after 1933	Burton, William Henry	Portch, Sarah E.
Burton, Jane	circa 1844	1870.07.16		
Burton, Jane	circa 1770			
Burton, Jane	before 1831.10		Burton, Samuel ["second"]	LNU, Mary
Burton, Jane F. [Jane F. (Bettis or Dunnington?) Burton]	circa 1813 to circa 1819	1887.02.07 or 1887.02.09 or 1887.02.10		
Burton Jarrett	before 1777	after 1833		
Burton, Jesse [Jesse Burden/Burton]	circa 1784	between 1833 and 1840		
Burton, John	before 1680			
Burton, John	before 1779		Burton, Nathaniel [the elder] ?	
Burton, John [son of Elijah J. Burton]	circa 1869	1919.02.26 ?	Burton, Elijah J.	Bettis, Letha / Lethe Anne

NAME	DOB	DOD	FATHER	MOTHER
Burton, John (or Robert?) [son of William J. Burton]	circa 1848		Burton, William J.	Chilton, Elizabeth
Burton, John ?	1890.02.25		Burton, John [John Broaddus Burton, Sr. ?]	LNU, Margaret [Margaret "Maggie" Lowry ?]
Burton, Sr., John Broaddus	1855.07.17 or 1857.05.12	1925.05.07	Burton, James A.	Dunnington, Ellen
Burton, Jr., John Broaddus	1896.03.13	1960.03.12	Burton, Sr., John Broaddus	Lowry, Margaret "Maggie"
Burton, John Edwin "Ned"	1820.03.11	1901.02.12	Burton, Isaac	Marquess, Mary
Burton, John H. [Washington, DC/Stafford]	circa 1883			
Burton, John Pershing "Percy"	circa 1919	1961.01.04	Burton, Joseph Lee	Humphries, Nora V. Burton
Burton, John Wesley [Spotsy/Stafford]	circa 1871	1911.07.15	Burton, George W. [Spotsy]	Johnson, Virginia S. [Spotsy]
Burton, John [John William Burton or William John Burton ?]	before 1779 ? or circa 1780s ?	1826 or 1827 ?	Burton, Nathaniel [the elder] ? or James B. Burton, Sr.?	
Burton, Jonathan	before 1814			
Burton, Joseph Eustace "Josie"	1914.03.23	1958.10.26	Burton, Joseph Lee	Humphries, Nora V. Burton
Burton, Joseph Lee	1886.06.10	1981.05.27	Burton, Sr., John Broaddus	Lowry, Margaret "Maggie"
Burton, Joseph S.	1808.05.31	1890.05.29	Burton, Isaac	Marquess, Mary
Burton, Joshua ? (NFI)	before 1822			
Burton, Joyce Ann Shepherd	1931.09.16	1956.03.24	Shepherd, Charles F.	
Burton, Judson Marshall	1885.10.07	1933.08.11	Burton, Robert L.	Patton, Georgeanna / Georgianna "Anna / Annie"
Burton, Julia A. [Stafford or Louisa?]	before 1881.06.11	after 1881.06.11		

NAME	DOB	DOD	FATHER	MOTHER
Burton, Julian [Julia Burton ?]	1895.09.27		Burton, Thomas R.	Limbrick / Limerick, Hester A.
Burton, Julian	circa 1875	1911.06.17 ?	Burton, Elijah J.	Bettis, Letha / Lethe Anne
Burton, Julian	1924.01.07	1956.12.29 or 1956.12.30	Burton, Archibald B. "Archie"	Payne, Susan (B.?) "Susie"
Burton, Katherine E. "Katie" [Katherine E. "Katie" Burton Hudson]	circa 1897	1948 ? (by 1948.12.28)	Burton, John [son of Elijah J. Burton]	Portch, Nettie M.
Burton, Kimmie (or Kennie?) A. [Kimmie A. Burton (Schofield?) Reed ?]	1881	1925.06.04	Burton, Haswell	Moxley, Leatha Ann
Burton, Lady Mazella Trigger	circa 1907		Trigger, B. J. ?	LNU, Lucy
Burton, Laura F.	circa 1847		Burton, Joseph S.	LNU, Maria A.
Burton, Leatha Ann Moxley	1858.10.09 or 1859.10.09	1939.07.26	Moxley, James	Monroe, Roberta
Burton, Leathea / Leathie Virginia [Leathea / Leathie Virginia Burton Blaisdell]	1909	2003.07.27	Burton, Archibald B. "Archie"	Payne, Susan (B.?) "Susie"
Burton, Leona M. [Leona M. ("Lizzie"?) Burton Mills]	1887.07.27 ?	after 1959	Burton, Robert L.	Patton, Georgeanna / Georgianna "Anna / Annie"
Burton, Leonard	1889.03.03	1955.09.03	Burton, Wellington W.	Downs, Annie Laura
Burton, Leslie Hall	1915.08.18	1972.04.30	Burton, Sr., Benjamin Lewis / Louis "Bennie / Benny"	Monroe, Iva Davis
Burton, Lester Clifton	1925.11.25	1954.09.30	Burton, James Edward	Humphries, Minnie Elizabeth
Burton, Letha / Lethe Anne Bettis	circa 1852 or circa 1854	1889.12.08	Bettis, Thomas	LNU, Sarah

NAME	DOB	DOD	FATHER	MOTHER
Burton, Lettice [Lettice Burton Jefferies]	1726.08.19		Burton, William ["second"]	Spicer, Sarah
Burton, Lettice "Lettie"	circa 1784	1871.10.15 ?	Burton, Samuel ["second"]	LNU, Mary
Burton, Levenia [NFI]	circa 1832	circa 1900		
Burton, Levenia J. ? [Levenia J. Harding Wine?]	circa 1883	after 1900	Harding, E. P. ?	Burton, Elizabeth H. "Bettie / Betty" ?
Burton, Lillian Bell "Lillie / Lilly" Monroe	1897.11.06	1983.09.15	Monroe, James D.	LNU, Sis ? [LNU, Willetta L. ?]
Burton, Lillian Embrey	1897.02.19	1985.09.04	Embrey, James	LNU, Emma
Burton, Sr., Linwood Ashby "Dober"	1928.12.08	1996.06.08	Burton, Frank Edwin	Burton, Agnes Margaret
Burton, Lizzie M.	1880.11.15	1897.02.22 or 1897.02.23	Burton, James B. "J. B."	West, Mary W. "Mollie / Molly"
Burton, Lizzie May [Lucy May Burton ?]	1888.05.08	1888.06.10 or 1888.06.13	Burton, William J. (William J. Burton, Jr. ?) ["fifth"]	Knight, Drucilla B.
Burton, Lucille [Stafford ?]	before 1930.01.25	after 1930.01.25	Burton, Edward M. "Eddie"	Williams, Elizabeth
Burton, Lucinda "Lucy" Truslow	circa 1832	1896.02.18	Truslow, William	LNU, Elizabeth
Burton, Lucinda / Lucindy "Lucy" [Lucinda / Lucindy "Lucy" Burton Turner]	circa 1826	after 1860	Burton, William (William J. Burton, Sr.?) ["fourth"]	McKenney, Catharine "Kate" [Catharine "Kate" McKenney (Burton?) Tyson]
Burton, Lucy	circa 1779	1859.06.01	Burton, Nathaniel [the elder] ?	
Burton, Lucy H.	1927.03.16	1927.06.28	Burton, Fielding W.	Trigger, Lady Mazella
Burton, Lucy Kate Pullen / Puller [black ?]	circa 1886	1937.04.01	Pullen / Puller, Eugene [black ?]	Coleman, Margaret ? [black ?]

NAME	DOB	DOD	FATHER	MOTHER
Burton, Lucy P. [Lucy P. Burton Jones]	circa 1862 or circa 1864	after 1917	Burton, Parker F. "Jesse"	Brown, Mahala
Burton, Lucy Virginia [Lucy Virginia Burton Berry ?]	1890.11.16	after 1942 ?	Burton, Charles	Burton, Ida V.
Burton, Mae Ballard Cooper [Stafford ?]	1885.11.04	1968.03.08	Ballard, James	
Burton, Mae Bryant [Mae Bryant Burton Boutchyard]	1924.01.08	2006.03.25	Bryant, James Murray	Withers, Gloria
Burton, Mae Lawhorne ? [Stafford ?]	circa 1921	1986.04.28		
Burton, Mahala Brown	circa 1837	1915.09.04 or 1915.09.05	Brown, William	LNU, Lucy
Burton, Major	circa 1895	1972.01.09	Burton, Haswell	Moxley, Leatha Ann
Burton, Margaret	1837		Burton, Sr., William E.	Bowler, Elizabeth
Burton, Margaret A.	before 1929.06.07	after 1955.02.08		
Burton, Margaret A. "Margie" ? [Margaret A. "Margie" Burton Fitzhugh ?]	circa 1926 ?	after 1976.04.30 ?	Burton, David E. [son of Columbus Ashby Burton]	LNU, Margaret A.
Burton, Margaret (A.?) Pollard	circa 1780s or 1790s ?		Pollard, FNU ?	
Burton, Margaret Lloyd ?	1911	after 1957.06.14		
Burton, Margaret "Maggie" Lowry	1867	1949.01.06 or 1949.01.07	Lowry, Thomas	LNU, Harriet
Burton, Margaret Mae Carneal	1915	1991.11.11		
Burton, Maria A.	circa 1821			

NAME	DOB	DOD	FATHER	MOTHER
Burton, Marie [Marie Burton Grinnan]	1911	1999	Burton, Sr., Benjamin Lewis / Louis "Bennie / Benny"	Monroe, Iva Davis
Burton, Marie Elizabeth [Marie Elizabeth Burton Mitchell]	1921	2007.08.15	Burton, Ernest William	Boutyard / Boutchyard, Florence Mary
Burton, Marietta "Flossie" Curtis	circa 1885	1976.04.30	Curtis, E. L. [Edwin L. Curtis ?]	Downs, Maggie ?
Burton, Marshall	circa 1817	1882.07.02	Burton, William [son of James B. Burton, Sr.?]	LNU, Susan
Burton, Martha [Martha (Bryant?) Foley/Folio Burton]	before 1690		Bryant, FNU ?	Keziah Aroyah ?
Burton, Martha [Martha A. Burton Bradshaw?]	circa 1823 or circa 1829	circa 1880	Burton, James ?	Burton, Ann "Nancy"
Burton, Mary	1754.05.30		Burton, William ["third"]	Porch, Rachel
Burton, Mary	1750s or 1760s ?			
Burton, Mary	circa 1770s ?			
Burton, Mary [Mary Burton Rodgers]	before 1831.10		Burton, Samuel ["second"]	LNU, Mary
Burton, Mary	circa 1857		Burton, Fielding B.	Webb, Virginia "Jennie"
Burton, Mary	1891.12.27		Burton, Thomas R.	Limbrick / Limerick, Hester A.
Burton, Mary A. (Ann?)	circa 1820s	1897.03.30 ?		
Burton, Mary A. Ballard	circa 1806	1883.12.26	Ballard, James	LNU, Mary
Burton, Mary A. Franklin	circa 1832 or circa 1833	1864.05.20	Franklin, William	LNU, Agnes

NAME	DOB	DOD	FATHER	MOTHER
Burton, Mary Curtis [Mary Dodd Burton ?] [Fredericksburg ?]	1930	1972.12.12		Dodd, Ethel Desrosiers
Burton, Mary E. [Mary Elizabeth Burton Bloxton ?]	1822 or 1825.06.07	1906 ?	Burton, Isaac	Marquess, Mary
Burton, Mary E. (Ellen ?) Boutyard	1854.01.31	1936.06.07	Boutyard, William James	Snellings, Jane Sarah
Burton, Mary F. [Mary F. Burton Littrell]	1856.07.28 ?		Burton, Richard	Monroe, Willie Ann
Burton, Mary I. [Mary I. Burton Jefferson]	before 1929	1983.10.30	Burton, Sr., Benjamin Lewis / Louis "Bennie / Benny"	Monroe, Iva Davis
Burton, Mary G. [Mary G. Burton Bullock]	1892.05.15	1968.02.19	Burton, James B. "J. B."	West, Mary W. "Mollie / Molly"
Burton, Mary H. [Mary H. Burton Brown]	before 1843		Burton, Harris W.	LNU, Elizabeth
Burton, Mary J. [Mary J. Burton Brandenburg]	circa 1862	after 1925	Burton, Marshall	Bettis, Jane F.? [Jane F. Dunnington ?]
Burton, Mary M. [Mary M. Burton Templeman] [Stafford ?]	before 1922.12			
Burton, Mary Marquess	1779.05.12	1843.04.13	Marquess, Anthony	Winlock, Elizabeth ?
Burton, Mary "Mollie"	circa 1869, circa 1870 or 1874.04.18	1922.02.15 or 1922.04.14	Burton, Richard	LNU, Dulcibella "Dulcie"
Burton, Mary Virginia "Virgie" [Mary Virginia "Virgie" Burton Harris]	1877.09.17	1963.03.10	Burton, William Jesse	Boutyard, Mary E. (Ellen?)

NAME	DOB	DOD	FATHER	MOTHER
Burton, Mary W. "Mollie / Molly" West	1858.06.09	1937.11.25	West, James	O'Bryhim, Annette
Burton, Maude Virginia Hummer [Loudoun ?]	before 1912			
Burton, Maurice Walter	1879.08.04	1912.06.30	Burton, William Jesse	Boutyard, Mary E. (Ellen?)
Burton, Maurice V.	circa 1885	1980.12.17	Burton, William Henry	Portch, Sarah E.
Burton, Media V. [Media V. Burton Patton]	1907	1943	Burton, William F.	Burton, Mary "Mollie"
Burton, Melvin Strother	1859	after 1925	Burton, Marshall	Bettis, Jane F.? [Jane F. Dunnington ?]
Burton, Merritt Dickinson "Dippy"	circa 1906	1990.02.06	Burton, Wilson	Dickerson / Dickinson, Alice L.
Burton, Mildred [Mildred Burton Cassiday] [Stafford?]	by 1925	after 1929.11.16	Burton, James Grover	LNU, Grace
Burton, Milton H.	circa 1858	after 1893	Burton, William J. (William J. Burton, Jr. ?) ["fifth"]	Franklin, Mary A.
Burton, Minnie C.	1889.03.01 or 1889.04.07	1979.03.12	Burton, Sr., John Broaddus	Lowry, Margaret "Maggie"
Burton, Minnie Elizabeth Humphries	1892	1970	Humphries, James	Monroe, Elizabeth Gordon
Burton, Minnie V. (Virginia?) Stephens / Stevens	circa 1872 or circa 1875	1956.06.18	Stephens, Wm.	LNU, Jennie
Burton, Myrtle V. Harding [Myrtle V. Harding Burton Dallman]	1907	1989.03.23	Harding, Archie	LNU, Jennie
Burton, Nancy Burns [Nancy Pollard Burton ?]	circa 1794	1870		Burns, Lucy ?

NAME	DOB	DOD	FATHER	MOTHER
Burton, Nancy E. Madison Stevens ? [Fredericksburg ?]	1913	1973.06.20	Madison, Ollie C.	
Burton, Nannie Lee [Nannie Lee Burton Berry]	1887.01.11	1932.08.09	Burton, Thompson	Burton, Almeta Jane "Virginia / Jennie / Jenny"
Burton, Nathaniel [the elder]	between 1726 and 1740 (est.)	1809	Burton, William ["second"] ?	Spicer, Sarah ?
Burton, Nathaniel [the younger]	between 1760 and 1770 ?	after 1840	Burton, Nathaniel [the elder] ?	
Burton, Nettie M. Portch	1871.11.24	1948.12.28	Portch, John	LNU, Susan
Burton, Nina Annabelle	1894.09.22	1975.02.18	Burton, John [son of Elijah J. Burton]	Portch, Nettie M.
Burton, Noel Robert	1894.03.07 or 1896.03.07	1985.03.04	Burton, Sr., John Broaddus	Lowry, Margaret "Maggie"
Burton, Nora V. [Nora V. Burton Humphries Burton ?]	1887.05.03	1919.01.30 or 1919.01.31	Burton, Wellington W.	Downs, Annie Laura
Burton, Norman "Chip"	1912.09.27	1998.12.05	Burton, Joseph Lee	Humphries, Nora V. Burton
Burton, Olga Belle [Olga Belle Burton Franklin]	1868.12.20	after 1893	Burton, William J. (William J. Burton, Jr. ?) ["fifth"]	Knight, Drucilla B.
Burton, Oliver R. "Ollie"	1898.06.01	1980.08.02	Burton, William F.	Burton, Mary "Mollie"
Burton, Sr., Oliver Stansbury "Ollie"	1917.03.22	2010.03.08	Burton, Oliver R. "Ollie"	Monroe, Lillian Bell "Lillie / Lilly"
Burton, Parker F. "Jesse"	circa 1838	1901.03.10	Burton, Harris W.	LNU, Elizabeth
Burton, Pauline Bernice Powell [Pauline Bernice Powell Burton Daniels]	1920.12.09		Powell, Eugene Franklin	
Burton, Pauline Kurz	1909.11.28	1993.05.06	Kurz, Sr., Gustave "Gus"	Berry, Fannie

NAME	DOB	DOD	FATHER	MOTHER
Burton, Pauline M. [Pauline M. Burton Lee]	circa 1898	after 1964	Burton, John [son of Elijah J. Burton]	Portch, Nettie M.
Burton, Pearl Vivian [Pearl Vivian Burton Jett]	circa 1907	after 1980	Burton, John [son of Elijah J. Burton]	Portch, Nettie M.
Burton, Pemiley [Pemiley G. Burton Kelley/Kelly]	circa 1851	1927.07.01	Burton, Richard	Monroe, Willie Ann
Burton, Priscilla	1746.01.17		Burton, William ["second"?]	
Burton, Rachel Porch	circa 1736		Porch, Richard ?	LNU, Mary ?
Burton, Rachel D.	circa 1832 or circa 1838	1903.11	Burton, Harris W.	LNU, Elizabeth
Burton, Rachel J.	circa 1764	after 1850		
Burton, Ralph Monroe	1923.09.08	1957.06.22	Burton, Sr., Benjamin Lewis / Louis "Bennie / Benny"	Monroe, Iva Davis
Burton, Raymond E.	1895.04.16	1986.02.04	Burton, William Henry	Portch, Sarah E.
Burton, Renald / Reynold Vinson	1895	1964.02.22	Burton, John [son of Elijah J. Burton]	Portch, Nettie M.
Burton, Richard [son of John Burton]	circa 1822	1860.04	Burton, John	LNU, Susan
Burton, Richard [NFI]	before 1785			
Burton, Richard	1845	1919.02.07	Burton, James A.	Dunnington, Ellen
Burton, Robert (or John?) [son of William J. Burton]	circa 1849		Burton, William J.	Chilton, Elizabeth
Burton, Dr. Robert Elmore	1890.06.12	1959.01.24	Burton, Robert L.	Patton, Georgeanna / Georgianna "Anna / Annie"
Burton, Robert Franklin "Bobbie"	1910	1969.12	Burton, Clarence	Jones, Carrie L.

NAME	DOB	DOD	FATHER	MOTHER
Burton, Robert Gilbert	1929.10.17		Burton, Ernest William	Boutyard / Boutchyard, Florence Mary
Burton, Robert I.	1812.12.29	1840.07.21	Burton, Isaac	Marquess, Mary
Burton, Robert L.	1846.01.20	1923.04.14	Burton, Marshall	Bettis, Jane F.? [Jane F. Dunnington ?]
Burton, Robert L.	1922.01.22	1994.03.16	Burton, Sr., Benjamin Lewis / Louis "Bennie / Benny"	Monroe, Iva Davis
Burton, Rosa B. [Rosa B. Burton Sullivan]	1875.04.06	1965.06.09	Burton, Thompson	Burton, Almeta Jane "Virginia / Jennie / Jenny"
Burton, Ruby Jane Ellington [Ruby Jane Ellington Burton Allen]	circa 1910		Ellington, James M.	Heflin, Cora L.
Burton, Ruth Gallahan	1920s ?	after 2010.01.24		
Burton, Samuel ["first" Samuel]	before 1699	after 1703		
Burton, Samuel ["second" Samuel]	1756.04.20	1831.1	Burton, William ["third"]	Porch, Rachel
Burton, Sarah	circa 1849		Burton, Joseph S.	LNU, Maria A.
Burton, Sarah [Sarah Burton Way]	1889	1959	Burton, Elijah J.	Bettis, Letha / Lethe Anne
Burton, Sarah Coakley	before 1835.03.28		Coakley, Benjamin	LNU, Margaret
Burton, Sarah E. [Sarah E. "Nannie" Burton Green Dye]	1926.03.07	2009.04.07	Burton, Archibald B. "Archie"	Payne, Susan (B.?) "Susie"
Burton, Sarah E. Portch [Sarah E. Portch Burton Mankey]	1857.01.14	1933.10.25	Portch, John	LNU, Susan
Burton, Sarah Limbrick	before 1826.04.11		Limbrick, John	LNU, Sarah

NAME	DOB	DOD	FATHER	MOTHER
Burton, Sarah "Sallie/Sally" [Sarah "Sallie/Sally" (Burton or Tyson) Southard]	1830s	1919.03.15	William Burton (William J. Burton, Sr.?) ["fourth"] (or possibly William Tyson)	McKenney, Catharine "Kate" [Catharine "Kate" McKenney (Burton?) Tyson]
Burton, Sarah Spicer	before 1725			
Burton, Sarah Williams [Sarah "Sallie" Berton / Burton Williams Burton?]	circa 1840 or circa 1844	after 1880	Burton, John [John or Robert Berton/Burton ?]	Simpson, Missouri
Burton, Seldon Wellington	1833.12.08	1913.07.25	Burton, Harris W.	LNU, Elizabeth
Burton, Jr., Sidney Ellsworth	between 1928 and 1974 ?	after 1988	Burton, Sr., Sidney / Sydney Ellsworth	Way, Edna C.
Burton, Sr., Sidney / Sydney Ellsworth	1926.08.09	1974.05.15	Burton, Elwood Winston [the elder]	Harding, Myrtle V.
Burton, Stella E.	circa 1898 or 1899.09.10	1918.02.25	Burton, Wilson	Dickerson / Dickinson, Alice L.
Burton, Stonewall J.	1891.12 ?	1892.08.04	Burton, Haswell	Moxley, Leatha Ann
Burton, Strother M.	1802.04.05	1851.06.05	Burton, Isaac	Marquess, Mary
Burton, Susan [wife of John ?]	before 1809			
Burton, Susan [wife of William Burton or John Burton ?]	1780 to 1790 ?	after 1840		
Burton, Susan	circa 1812			
Burton, Susan (same as Susan b. 1812?)	circa 1815			
Burton, Susan [NFI]	before 1869.11.18			
Burton, Susan A. [Susan A. Burton Sullivan]	circa 1843 or circa 1847	1909.11.(27?)	Burton, William J.	Chilton, Elizabeth
Burton, Susan (B.?) "Susie" Payne	1884.02.11	1956.01.30	Payne, George Washington	LNU, (Sarah?) "Sallie"
Burton, Susanna Walker [Culpeper ?]	1799.09.07	before 1832	Walker, Solomon	Taylor, Frances

NAME	DOB	DOD	FATHER	MOTHER
Burton, Susannah "Sukey" Jett	circa 1760s	between 1810-1820	Jett, Sr., Francis	Porch, Barsheba
Burton, Terrissa M. [Terrissa M. Burton Guy]	1804.08.23	1889.02.23	Burton, Isaac	Marquess, Mary
Burton, Thelma [Thelma Burton Miller] [Stafford ?]	before 1929.06.07		Burton, Ira Richard	
Burton, Thelma H. [Thelma H. Burton Coghill]	circa 1904	1965.08.17	Burton, Sr., Benjamin Lewis / Louis "Bennie / Benny"	Monroe, Iva Davis
Burton, Thelma Samuel [Caroline / Stafford]	1928.10.15	2000.04.16		
Burton, Theodore R. T.	1908.11.13	1936.01.09 or 1936.01.10	Burton, Sr., Benjamin Lewis / Louis "Bennie / Benny"	Monroe, Iva Davis
Burton, Thomas J.	circa 1888 or circa 1889	1938	Burton, James B. "J. B."	West, Mary W. "Mollie / Molly"
Burton, Thomas (L. or M.)	circa 1851		Burton, Marshall	Bettis, Jane F.? [Jane F. Dunnington ?]
Burton, Thomas R.	1861.11.27	1919.02.26	Burton, Jr., William E.	Truslow, Lucinda "Lucy"
Burton, Thomas S.	by 1794	between 1814 and 1843	Burton, William (William J. Burton, Sr.?) ["fourth"]	Jett, Susannah "Sukey"
Burton, Thompson	circa 1855	1902.08.05	Burton, Fielding B.	Webb, Virginia "Jennie"
Burton, unnamed infant	1871	1871	Burton, Richard	LNU, Fanny
Burton, Virgie	1911.11.20	1915.12.10	Burton, Archibald B. "Archie"	Payne, Susan (B.?) "Susie"
Burton, Virginia B. "Virgie" [Virginia B. "Virgie" Burton Ennis]	circa 1884	between 1906.04.25 and 1921.03.26	Burton, Elijah J.	Bettis, Letha / Lethe Anne

NAME	DOB	DOD	FATHER	MOTHER
Burton, Virginia F. [Virginia F. Burton Ellington]	circa 1829	1915.02.12	Burton, William (L. or S.?) Burton	Pollard, Margaret
Burton, Virginia "Jennie" Webb	by 1844	1887.01.28	Webb, John	LNU, Lucy Ann
Burton, Walker ? [NFI]	before 1826			
Burton, Walter Eugene	1907.10.27	1969.06.09	Burton, Maurice Walter	Cooper, Frances Eunice "Fannie / Fanny"
Burton, Warren	before 1933.08.11	after 1933.08.11	Burton, Judson Marshall	
Burton, Wellington W.	1855.04.16 or 1856.02.28	1930.04.08	Burton, Richard	Monroe, Willie Ann
Burton, Wesley	circa 1840	1884.05.18	Burton, Richard	LNU, Mary ?
Burton, William ["first"]	circa 1650			
Burton, William ["second"]	before 1725			
Burton, William ["third"]	between 1726 and 1736 (est.)	1778 ?	Burton, William ["second"] ?	Spicer, Sarah ?
Burton, William [William J. Burton, Sr.?] ["fourth"]	circa 1760s	by 1833.10	Burton, William ["third"]	Porch, Rachel
Burton, William [William John Burton or John William Burton ?]	circa 1780s ?	1826 or 1827	Burton, Sr., James B.?	Taylor, FNU ?
Burton, William [William Breuton ?]	circa 1832			Gallahan, Alice ?
Burton, William B. [NFI]	before 1826			
Burton, Sr., William E.	circa 1805	after 1880	Burton, Nathaniel [the younger] ?	LNU, Jane
Burton, Jr., William E.	circa 1835	1862	Burton, Sr., William E.	Bowler, Elizabeth
Burton, William F.	1866 or 1868.07.05 or 1868.07.06	1939.04.13	Burton, Parker F. "Jesse"	Brown, Mahala

NAME	DOB	DOD	FATHER	MOTHER
Burton, William Franklin ["sixth"]	1861.05.30	after 1893	Burton, William J. (William J. Burton, Jr. ?) ["fifth"]	Franklin, Mary A.
Burton, William Henry	circa 1844	circa 1896	Burton, Marshall	Bettis, Jane F.? [Jane F. Dunnington ?]
Burton, William J.	circa 1820	1860s ? (poss. died in Civil War)	Burton, Thomas S. ?	
Burton, William J. [William J. Burton, Jr. ?] ["fifth"]	1834.03.13	1896.03.20	Burton, William (William J. Burton, Sr.?) ["fourth"]	McKenney, Catharine "Kate" [Catharine "Kate" McKenney (Burton?) Tyson]
Burton, William Jesse	1850.07.03 or 1851.07.03	1922.01.28	Burton, Fielding B.	Webb, Virginia "Jennie"
Burton, William [William (L. or S.) Burton]	circa 1787 (in King George)	1859.09.18	Burton, Samuel ["second"]	LNU, Mary
Burton, William M.	1873.03.26	1942.04.10	Burton, Elijah J.	Bettis, Letha / Lethe Anne
Burton, William T.	1880.07.09	1910.02.28	Burton, Thompson	Burton, Almeta Jane "Virginia / Jennie / Jenny"
Burton, Willie Ann [Willie Ann Burton Burgess]	1857.09.04 or 1857.12.04	1931.11.06 ?	Burton, Richard	Monroe, Willie Ann
Burton, Willie Ann Monroe	circa 1821	1895.09.23		
Burton, Wilson	1858.10.02 or 1858.10.03	1924.07.27	Burton, Jr., William E.	Truslow, Lucinda "Lucy"
Burton, Winnie	circa 1893	before 1914 ?	Burton, Robert L.	Patton, Georgeanna / Georgianna "Anna / Annie"
Burton, Winnie Davis	1891.06.22	1984.01.14	Burton, William Henry	Portch, Sarah E.

Selected Stafford Burtons

Chronological Listing
(By Date of Birth)

NAME	DOB	DOD	FATHER	MOTHER
Burton, William ["first"]	circa 1650			
Burton, John	before 1680			
Burton, Martha [Martha (Bryant?) Foley/Folio Burton]	before 1690		Bryant, FNU ?	Keziah Aroyah ?
Burton, Samuel ["first" Samuel]	before 1699	after 1703		
Burton, William ["second"]	before 1725			
Burton, Sarah Spicer	before 1725			
Burton, Lettice [Lettice Burton Jefferies]	1726.08.19		Burton, William ["second"]	Spicer, Sarah
Burton, William ["third"]	between 1726 and 1736 (est.)	1778 ?	Burton, William ["second"] ?	Spicer, Sarah ?
Burton, Nathaniel [the elder]	1726 and 1740 between (est.)	1809	Burton, William ["second"] ?	Spicer, Sarah ?
Burton, Rachel Porch	circa 1736		Porch, Richard ?	LNU, Mary ?
Burton, Priscilla	1746.01.17		Burton, William ["second"?]	

NAME	DOB	DOD	FATHER	MOTHER
Burton, Gerrard	after 1753		Burton, William ["third"]	Porch, Rachel
Burton, Mary	1754.05.30		Burton, William ["third"]	Porch, Rachel
Burton, James [James B. Burton, Sr.?]	circa 1756	1850 or 1851	Burton, Nathaniel [the elder] ?	
Burton, Samuel ["second" Samuel]	1756.04.20	1831.1	Burton, William ["third"]	Porch, Rachel
Burton, Mary [wife of "second" Samuel Burton]	1750s or 1760s ?			
Burton, Susannah "Sukey" Jett	circa 1760s	between 1810 and 1820	Jett, Sr., Francis	Porch, Barsheba
Burton, William [William J. Burton, Sr.?] ["fourth"]	circa 1760s	by 1833.10	Burton, William ["third"]	Porch, Rachel
Burton, Nathaniel [the younger]	between 1760 and 1770 ?	after 1840	Burton, Nathaniel [the elder] ?	
Burton, Rachel J.	circa 1764	after 1850		
Burton, George	circa 1770s ?	after 1830	Burton, William ["third"]	Porch, Rachel
Burton, Mary [wife of George Burton]	circa 1770s ?			
Burton, Ann "Nancy"	circa 1770	by 1861.09.18	Burton, William ["third"]	Porch, Rachel
Burton, Jane	circa 1770			
Burton, Isaac	1771.12	1843.04.15	Burton, Nathaniel [the elder] ?	
Burton Jarrett	before 1777	after 1833		
Burton, Mary Marquess	1779.05.12	1843.04.13	Marquess, Anthony	Winlock, Elizabeth ?
Burton, Lucy	circa 1779	1859.06.01	Burton, Nathaniel [the elder] ?	
Burton, John	before 1779		Burton, Nathaniel [the elder] ?	

NAME	DOB	DOD	FATHER	MOTHER
Burton, John [John William Burton or William John Burton ?]	before 1779 ? or circa 1780s ?	1826 or 1827 ?	Burton, Nathaniel [the elder] ? or James B. Burton, Sr.?	
Burton, William [William John Burton or John William Burton ?]	circa 1780s ?	1826 or 1827	Burton, Sr., James B.?	Taylor, FNU ?
Burton, Dully	circa 1780s ?	after 1860	Burton, Sr., James B.?	Taylor, FNU ?
Burton, Jesse [Jesse Burden/Burton]	circa 1784	between 1833 and 1840		
Burton, Lettice "Lettie"	circa 1784	1871.10.15 ?	Burton, Samuel ["second"]	LNU, Mary
Burton, Richard [NFI]	before 1785			
Burton, William [William (L. or S.) Burton]	circa 1787 (in King George)	1859.09.18	Burton, Samuel ["second"]	LNU, Mary
Burton, Margaret (A.?) Pollard	circa 1780s or 1790s ?		Pollard, FNU ?	
Burton, Elizabeth Musselman Brummett [Elizabeth Musselman Brummett Burton Reed]	circa 1788	after 1870	Musselman, Henry	LNU, Elizabeth
Burton, Susan [wife of William Burton or John Burton ?]	1780 to 1790 ?	after 1840		
Burton, Cary	circa 1790	circa 1860	Burton, Samuel ["second"]	LNU, Mary
Burton, Ann "Nancy" [the younger]	circa 1793	by 1885.12.16		
Burton, Jr., James [James B. Burton, Jr.?]	circa 1793	after 1870	Burton, Sr., James B.?	Taylor, FNU ?

NAME	DOB	DOD	FATHER	MOTHER
Burton, Thomas S.	by 1794	between 1814 and 1843	Burton, William (William J. Burton, Sr.?) ["fourth"]	Jett, Susannah "Sukey"
Burton, Barsheba	by 1794	between 1843.02.01 and 1843.11.27	Burton, William (William J. Burton, Sr.?) ["fourth"]	Jett, Susannah "Sukey"
Burton, Nancy Burns [Nancy Pollard Burton ?]	circa 1794	1870		Burns, Lucy ?
Burton, Delphia	circa 1795			
Burton, Elizabeth	circa 1797	between 1860 and 1870		
Burton, Susanna Walker [Culpeper ?]	1799.09.07	before 1832	Walker, Solomon	Taylor, Frances
Burton, Harris W.	1800.03.17	1883.09.21	Burton, Isaac	Marquess, Mary
Burton, Strother M.	1802.04.05	1851.06.05	Burton, Isaac	Marquess, Mary
Burton, Terrissa M. [Terrissa M. Burton Guy]	1804.08.23	1889.02.23	Burton, Isaac	Marquess, Mary
Burton (?), Catharine "Kate" McKenney [Catharine "Kate" McKenney (Burton?) Tyson]	circa 1805	after 1870		
Burton, Sr., William E.	circa 1805	after 1880	Burton, Nathaniel [the younger] ?	LNU, Jane
Burton, Emily M. [Emily M. Burton Brown]	1806.01.29	1856.12.19 ?	Burton, Isaac	Marquess, Mary
Burton, Mary A. Ballard	circa 1806	1883.12.26	Ballard, James	LNU, Mary
Burton, Elizabeth "Betsy" Bowler	circa 1807	before 1866	Bowler, Charles	Donahoe, Elizabeth
Burton, Joseph S.	1808.05.31	1890.05.29	Burton, Isaac	Marquess, Mary
Burton, Hiram	circa 1808 or circa 1815	after 1860		

NAME	DOB	DOD	FATHER	MOTHER
Burton, Susan [wife of John ?]	before 1809			
Burton, James A.	circa 1809	1885.11.20	Burton, John	LNU, Susan
Burton, Eliza A. [Eliza A. Burton Petit?]	1810.08.15	1841.07.28	Burton, Isaac	Marquess, Mary
Burton, Ellen Dunnington	circa 1811	1906.04.13 or 1906.04.20		
Burton, Elizabeth	before 1812			
Burton, Robert I.	1812.12.29	1840.07.21	Burton, Isaac	Marquess, Mary
Burton, Susan	circa 1812			
Burton, Jane F. [Jane F. (Bettis or Dunnington?) Burton]	circa 1813 to circa 1819	1887.02.07 or 1887.02.09 or 1887.02.10		
Burton, Jonathan	before 1814			
Burton, Ira	before 1814	after 1830 ?		
Burton, Susan (same as Susan b. 1812?)	circa 1815			
Burton, Elijah M. [Elijah Marquess Burton ?]	1815.06.01	1890.08.20	Burton, Isaac	Marquess, Mary
Burton, Marshall	circa 1817	1882.07.02	Burton, William [son of James B. Burton, Sr.?]	LNU, Susan
Burton, Arthur A.	1817.10.29	1905.12.17	Burton, Isaac	Marquess, Mary
Burton, Elizabeth	by 1819	after 1880		
Burton, William J.	circa 1820	1860s ? (poss. died in Civil War)	Burton, Thomas S. ?	
Burton, Elizabeth Chilton	circa 1820	after 1870	Chilton, Thomas	Limbrick, Charlotte
Burton, John Edwin "Ned"	1820.03.11	1901.02.12	Burton, Isaac	Marquess, Mary
Burton, Arastus (or Erastus?)	between 1821 and 1840.02.14	1845 (died a minor)	Burton, Harris W.	LNU, Elizabeth
Burton, Maria A.	circa 1821			

NAME	DOB	DOD	FATHER	MOTHER
Burton, Willie Ann Monroe	circa 1821	1895.09.23		
Burton, Richard	circa 1822	1860.04	Burton, John	LNU, Susan
Burton, Joshua ? (NFI)	before 1822			
Burton, Mary E. [Mary Elizabeth Burton Bloxton ?]	1822 or 1825.06.07	1906 ?	Burton, Isaac	Marquess, Mary
Burton, Martha [Martha A. Burton Bradshaw?]	circa 1823 or circa 1829	circa 1880	Burton, James ?	Burton, Ann "Nancy"
Burton, Mary A. (Ann?)	circa 1820s	1897.03.30 ?		
Burton, William B. [NFI]	before 1826			
Burton, Sarah Limbrick	before 1826.04.11		Limbrick, John	LNU, Sarah
Burton, Lucinda / Lucindy "Lucy" [Lucinda / Lucindy "Lucy" Burton Turner]	circa 1826	after 1860	Burton, William (William J. Burton, Sr.?) ["fourth"]	McKenney, Catharine "Kate" [Catharine "Kate" McKenney (Burton?) Tyson]
Burton, Fielding B.	circa 1826 or 1827	1903.11.24	Burton, William (William J. Burton, Sr.?) ["fourth"]	McKenney, Catharine "Kate" [Catharine "Kate" McKenney (Burton?) Tyson]
Burton, Walker ? [NFI]	before 1826			
Burton, Virginia F. [Virginia F. Burton Ellington]	circa 1829	1915.02.12	Burton, William (L. or S.?) Burton	Pollard, Margaret
Burton, Sarah "Sallie / Sally" [Sarah "Sallie / Sally" (Burton or Tyson) Southard]	1830s	1919.03.15	William Burton (William J. Burton, Sr.?) ["fourth"] (or possibly William Tyson)	McKenney, Catharine "Kate" [Catharine "Kate" McKenney (Burton?) Tyson]
Burton, Jane	before 1831.10		Burton, Samuel ["second"]	LNU, Mary

NAME	DOB	DOD	FATHER	MOTHER
Burton, Catharine [Catharine Burton Southard]	before 1831.10		Burton, Samuel ["second"]	LNU, Mary
Burton, Mary [Mary Burton Rodgers]	before 1831.10		Burton, Samuel ["second"]	LNU, Mary
Burton, James Alexander "Sandy"	circa 1832	1896.11.(08?)	Burton, James ?	Burton, Ann "Nancy"
Burton, Levenia (NFI)	circa 1832	circa 1900		
Burton, Lucinda "Lucy" Truslow	circa 1832	1896.02.18	Truslow, William	LNU, Elizabeth
Burton, William [William Breuton ?]	circa 1832			Gallahan, Alice ?
Burton, Mary A. Franklin	circa 1832 or circa 1833	1864.05.20	Franklin, William	LNU, Agnes
Burton, Rachel D.	circa 1832 or circa 1838	1903.11	Burton, Harris W.	LNU, Elizabeth
Burton, Seldon Wellington	1833.12.08	1913.07.25	Burton, Harris W.	LNU, Elizabeth
Burton, William J. [William J. Burton, Jr. ?] ["fifth"]	1834.03.13	1896.03.20	Burton, William (William J. Burton, Sr.?) ["fourth"]	McKenney, Catharine "Kate" [Catharine "Kate" McKenney (Burton?) Tyson]
Burton, Sarah Coakley	before 1835.03.28		Coakley, Benjamin	LNU, Margaret
Burton, Ellen Jane	before 1835		Burton, FNU	Coakley, Sarah
Burton, Daniel	before 1835	after 1881	Burton, FNU	Coakley, Sarah
Burton, Jr., William E.	circa 1835	1862	Burton, Sr., William E.	Bowler, Elizabeth
Burton, Mahala Brown	circa 1837	1915.09.04 or 1915.09.05	Brown, William	LNU, Lucy
Burton, Margaret	1837		Burton, Sr., William E.	Bowler, Elizabeth
Burton, Eliza V. Ballard	circa 1838	after 1907.02.18	Ballard, Flavius Josephus	LNU, Eliza

NAME	DOB	DOD	FATHER	MOTHER
Burton, Parker F. "Jesse"	circa 1838	1901.03.10	Burton, Harris W.	LNU, Elizabeth
Burton, Sarah Williams [Sarah "Sallie" Berton / Burton Williams Burton?]	circa 1840 or circa 1844	after 1880	Burton, John [John or Robert Berton/Burton ?]	Simpson, Missouri
Burton, Ann Eliza "Annie" [Ann Eliza "Annie" Burton Brooks]	1840.02.14	1923.11.27	Burton, Harris W.	LNU, Elizabeth
Burton, Wesley	circa 1840	1884.05.18	Burton, Richard	LNU, Mary ?
Burton, Ann Eliza [Ann Eliza Burton Conner/Connor/O'Conner/O'Connor]	circa 1842		Burton, Marshall	Bettis, Jane F.? [Jane F. Dunnington ?]
Burton, Dulcibella "Dulcie"	circa 1842	1907.08.27		
Burton, Mary H. [Mary H. Burton Brown]	before 1843		Burton, Harris W.	LNU, Elizabeth
Burton, Elizabeth H. "Bettie / Betty" [Elizabeth H. "Bettie / Betty" Burton Harding]	1843.08.14	1916.08.22	Burton, Harris W.	LNU, Elizabeth
Burton, Arthur A.	circa 1843		Burton, Joseph S.	LNU, Maria A.
Burton, Susan A. [Susan A. Burton Sullivan]	circa 1843 or circa 1847	1909.11.(27?)	Burton, William J.	Chilton, Elizabeth
Burton, Virginia "Jennie" Webb	by 1844	1887.01.28	Webb, John	LNU, Lucy Ann
Burton, Jane	circa 1844	1870.07.16		
Burton, William Henry	circa 1844	circa 1896	Burton, Marshall	Bettis, Jane F.? [Jane F. Dunnington ?]
Burton, Cornelia T.	circa 1845		Burton, Joseph S.	LNU, Maria A.
Burton, Richard	1845	1919.02.07	Burton, James A.	Dunnington, Ellen

NAME	DOB	DOD	FATHER	MOTHER
Burton, Robert L.	1846.01.20	1923.04.14	Burton, Marshall	Bettis, Jane F.? [Jane F. Dunnington ?]
Burton, Drucilla B. Knight	circa 1846	1888.06.15	Knight, Austin	Cloe, Elizabeth
Burton, Laura F.	circa 1847		Burton, Joseph S.	LNU, Maria A.
Burton, John (or Robert?)	circa 1848		Burton, William J.	Chilton, Elizabeth
Burton, Robert (or John?)	circa 1849		Burton, William J.	Chilton, Elizabeth
Burton, Sarah	circa 1849		Burton, Joseph S.	LNU, Maria A.
Burton, Beverly [Beverly C. Burton?]	circa 1849	after 1882 (circa 1912.01.03)	Burton, Marshall	Bettis, Jane F.? [Jane F. Dunnington ?]
Burton, William Jesse	1850.07.03 or 1851.07.03	1922.01.28	Burton, Fielding B.	Webb, Virginia "Jennie"
Burton, Clemma (*sic*)	circa 1850		Burton, William J.	Chilton, Elizabeth
Burton, Elijah J.	circa 1850	1895.11.25	Burton, James A.	Dunnington, Ellen
Burton, Thomas (L. or M.)	circa 1851		Burton, Marshall	Bettis, Jane F.? [Jane F. Dunnington ?]
Burton, Pemiley [Pemiley G. Burton Kelley/Kelly]	circa 1851	1927.07.01	Burton, Richard	Monroe, Willie Ann
Burton, Letha / Lethe Anne Bettis	circa 1852 or circa 1854	1889.12.08	Bettis, Thomas	LNU, Sarah
Burton, Isabella [Isabella Burton Monroe]	1852.05.27	1919.01.25	Burton, Richard	Monroe, Willie Ann
Burton, James B.	circa 1852	circa 1941 ?	Burton, James A.	Dunnington, Ellen
Burton, Haswell	1854.01.20	1940.08.04	Burton, Richard	Monroe, Willie Ann
Burton, Georgeanna / Georgianna "Anna / Annie" Patton	1854.02.09	1934.02.06	Patton, Elliot/Elliott	LNU, Delia
Burton, Mary E. (Ellen ?) Boutyard	1854.01.31	1936.06.07	Boutyard, William James	Snellings, Jane Sarah
Burton, Wellington W.	1855.04.16 or 1856.02.28	1930.04.08	Burton, Richard	Monroe, Willie Ann

NAME	DOB	DOD	FATHER	MOTHER
Burton, Thompson	circa 1855	1902.08.05	Burton, Fielding B.	Webb, Virginia "Jennie"
Burton, Sr., John Broaddus	1855.07.17 or 1857.05.12	1925.05.07	Burton, James A.	Dunnington, Ellen
Burton, Clementine [Clementina / Clementine Burton Walker]	1855.04.15	1916.12.17	Burton, William J.	Chilton, Elizabeth
Burton, Mary F. [Mary F. Burton Littrell]	1856.07.28 ?		Burton, Richard	Monroe, Willie Ann
Burton, Almeta Jane "Virginia / Jennie / Jenny"	circa 1857	1910.01.02 or 1910.01.03	Burton, William J.	Chilton, Elizabeth
Burton, Catharine	circa 1857		Burton, Marshall	Bettis, Jane F.? [Jane F. Dunnington ?]
Burton, Mary	circa 1857		Burton, Fielding B.	Webb, Virginia "Jennie"
Burton, Sarah E. Portch [Sarah E. Portch Burton Mankey]	1857.01.14	1933.10.25	Portch, John	LNU, Susan
Burton, Willie Ann [Willie Ann Burton Burgess]	1857.09.04 or 1857.12.04	1931.11.06 ?	Burton, Richard	Monroe, Willie Ann
Burton, James B. "J. B."	1857.12.09	1897.02.23	Burton, Marshall	Bettis, Jane F.? [Jane F. Dunnington ?]
Burton, Annie Laura Downs	1858.12.16	1926.10.18	Downs, Thomas	Smith, Amanda
Burton, Wilson	1858.10.02 or 1858.10.03	1924.07.27	Burton, Jr., William E.	Truslow, Lucinda "Lucy"
Burton, Milton H.	circa 1858	after 1893	Burton, William J. (William J. Burton, Jr. ?) ["fifth"]	Franklin, Mary A.
Burton, Leatha Ann Moxley	1858.10.09 or 1859.10.09	1939.07.26	Moxley, James	Monroe, Roberta
Burton, Mary W. "Mollie / Molly" West	1858.06.09	1937.11.25	West, James	O'Bryhim, Annette

NAME	DOB	DOD	FATHER	MOTHER
Burton, Alvena "Allie" [Alvena "Allie" Burton Mills]	1858.11.20	1942.10.21	Burton, Richard	Monroe, Willie Ann
Burton, Alma	circa 1859	1889.11.08 or 1889.11.09	Burton, William J. (William J. Burton, Jr. ?) ["fifth"]	Franklin, Mary A.
Burton, Melvin Strother	1859	after 1925	Burton, Marshall	Bettis, Jane F.? [Jane F. Dunnington ?]
Burton, Delia [1860 slave owner; NFI]	1860 before			
Burton, William Franklin ["sixth"]	1861.05.30	after 1893	Burton, William J. (William J. Burton, Jr. ?) ["fifth"]	Franklin, Mary A.
Burton, Thomas R.	1861.11.27	1919.02.26	Burton, Jr., William E.	Truslow, Lucinda "Lucy"
Burton, Lucy P. [Lucy P. Burton Jones]	circa 1862 or circa 1864	after 1917	Burton, Parker F. "Jesse"	Brown, Mahala
Burton, Mary J. [Mary J. Burton Brandenburg]	circa 1862	after 1925	Burton, Marshall	Bettis, Jane F.? [Jane F. Dunnington ?]
Burton, Alice L. Dickerson / Dickinson	1863	1952.04.01	Dickinson, William	LNU, Ellen
Burton, Ida R. [Ida R. Burton Hewitt]	1863.08.03	1926.07.17	Burton, Fielding B.	Webb, Virginia "Jennie"
Burton, George B.	circa 1865 or 1868.04.15 ?	1944.04.04 ?	Burton, Richard	LNU, Dulcibella "Dulcie"
Burton, William F.	1866 or 1868.07.05 or 1868.07.06	1939.04.13	Burton, Parker F. "Jesse"	Brown, Mahala
Burton, Margaret "Maggie" Lowry	1867	1949.01.06 or 1949.01.07	Lowry, Thomas	LNU, Harriet
Burton, Olga Belle [Olga Belle Burton Franklin]	1868.12.20	after 1893	Burton, William J. (William J. Burton, Jr. ?) ["fifth"]	Knight, Drucilla B.
Burton, Charles	circa 1868	1892.08.(16?)	Burton, Richard	LNU, Dulcibella "Dulcie"
Burton, Susan [NFI]	before 1869.11.18			

NAME	DOB	DOD	FATHER	MOTHER
Burton, Ida Bell / Belle Humphries [Ida Bell / Belle Humphries Burton McGhee]	1869.01.26	1943.07.28	Humphries, William H.	LNU, Charlotte
Burton, Mary "Mollie"	circa 1869, circa 1870 or 1874.04.18	1922.02.15 or 1922.04.14	Burton, Richard	LNU, Dulcibella "Dulcie"
Burton, John	circa 1869	1919.02.26 ?	Burton, Elijah J.	Bettis, Letha / Lethe Anne
Burton, Hester A. Limbrick / Limerick	circa 1869	after 1919	Limbrick, Lanius (?)	LNU, Margaret
Burton, Ida V. [Ida V. Burton Skidmore]	1870.08.03 ?	after 1910	Burton, Parker F. "Jesse"	Brown, Mahala
Burton, John Wesley [Spotsy/Stafford]	circa 1871	1911.07.15	Burton, George W. [Spotsy]	Johnson, Virginia S. [Spotsy]
Burton, unnamed infant	1871	1871	Burton, Richard	LNU, Fanny
Burton, Nettie M. Portch	1871.11.24	1948.12.28	Portch, John	LNU, Susan
Burton, Fielding (F. or T.?)	1872.02.28	1893.04.01	Burton, William J. (William J. Burton, Jr. ?) ["fifth"]	Knight, Drucilla B.
Burton, Minnie V. (Virginia?) Stephens / Stevens	circa 1872 or circa 1875	1956.06.18	Stephens, Wm.	LNU, Jennie
Burton, William M.	1873.03.26	1942.04.10	Burton, Elijah J.	Bettis, Letha / Lethe Anne
Burton, Julian	circa 1875	1911.06.17 ?	Burton, Elijah J.	Bettis, Letha / Lethe Anne
Burton, Rosa B. [Rosa B. Burton Sullivan]	1875.04.06	1965.06.09	Burton, Thompson	Burton, Almeta Jane "Virginia / Jennie / Jenny"
Burton, Ella [Ella Burton Payne]	circa 1876, 1881 or 1886	1933	Burton, Elijah J.	Bettis, Letha / Lethe Anne

NAME	DOB	DOD	FATHER	MOTHER
Burton, Mary Virginia "Virgie" [Mary Virginia "Virgie" Burton Harris]	1877.09.17	1963.03.10	Burton, William Jesse	Boutyard, Mary E. (Ellen?)
Burton, Clarence	1877.05.11	after 1930	Burton, Wellington W.	Downs, Annie Laura
Burton, Archibald B. "Archie"	1878.03.03 or 1879.08.09	1962.12.06	Burton, Elijah J.	Bettis, Letha / Lethe Anne
Burton, Frank [black] [the elder black Frank Burton]	1879	1949.04.19	Burton, Wm. [black?]	LNU, Susan [black?]
Burton, Maurice Walter	1879.08.04	1912.06.30	Burton, William Jesse	Boutyard, Mary E. (Ellen?)
Burton, William T.	1880.07.09	1910.02.28	Burton, Thompson	Burton, Almeta Jane "Virginia / Jennie / Jenny"
Burton, Alfred E. (?) [NFI]	1880.12.23		Burton, Jr., William J. (sic)	Burton, Mary V. (sic)
Burton, Carrie Irene [Carrie Irene Burton Knight]	1880.11.15	1953.07	Burton, Robert L.	Patton, Georgeanna / Georgianna "Anna / Annie"
Burton, Lizzie M.	1880.11.15	1897.02.22 or 1897.02.23	Burton, James B. "J. B."	West, Mary W. "Mollie / Molly"
Burton, Alfred Eugene	1881.12.08	1903.08.23	Burton, William Jesse	Boutyard, Mary E. (Ellen?)
Burton, Annette J. "Nettie"[Annette J. "Nettie" Burton Cooper]	1881.12.04	after 1933	Burton, James B. "J. B."	West, Mary W. "Mollie / Molly"
Burton, Kimmie (or Kennie?) A. [Kimmie A. Burton (Schofield?) Reed ?]	1881	1925.06.04	Burton, Haswell	Moxley, Leatha Ann
Burton, Julia A. [Stafford or Louisa?]	before 1881.06.11	after 1881.06.11		
Burton, Addie T. [Addie T. Burton Harding]	1881.01.13	between 1921 and 1926.10.18 ?	Burton, Wellington W.	Downs, Annie Laura

NAME	DOB	DOD	FATHER	MOTHER
Burton, Dora Lee [Dora Lee Burton Edwards]	1882.08.08 ?		Burton, Haswell	Moxley, Leatha Ann
Burton, Arthur M.	circa 1882 or circa 1883	1970.10.08	Burton, James B. "J. B."	West, Mary W. "Mollie / Molly"
Burton, Fielding B.	1882.12.26	1896.08.20	Burton, Thompson	Burton, Almeta Jane "Virginia / Jennie / Jenny"
Burton, Iva Davis Monroe	1882.12.02	1964.11.30	Monroe, George E.	LNU, Mary
Burton, Alphonso "Fonsie/Fonzie"	1882	1940.10.25	Burton, Elijah J.	Bettis, Letha / Lethe Anne
Burton, Anne E. "Annie" [Anne E. "Annie" Burton Way Berry]	circa 1882	after 1942	Burton, Elijah J.	Bettis, Letha / Lethe Anne
Burton, Carrie L. Jones [Spotsy/Stafford]	1882.04.03	1927.08.26	Jones, E. F.	Burton, Lucy P.
Burton, Levenia J. ? [Levenia J. Harding Wine ?]	circa 1883	after 1900	Harding, E. P. ?	Burton, Elizabeth H. "Bettie / Betty" ?
Burton, Sr., Benjamin Lewis / Louis "Bennie / Benny"	1883.08.08	1977.03.01	Burton, Robert L.	Patton, Georgeanna / Georgianna "Anna / Annie"
Burton, John H. [Washington, DC / Stafford]	circa 1883			
Burton, Virginia B. "Virgie" [Virginia B. "Virgie" Burton Ennis]	circa 1884	between 1906.04.25 and 1921.03.26	Burton, Elijah J.	Bettis, Letha / Lethe Anne
Burton, James Grover	circa 1884 or 1885.05.08 ?	1915.12	Burton, James B. "J. B."	West, Mary W. "Mollie / Molly"
Burton, Gilbert Cecil	circa 1884 ?	after 1905	Burton, William J. (William J. Burton, Jr. ?) ["fifth"]	Knight, Drucilla B.

NAME	DOB	DOD	FATHER	MOTHER
Burton, Columbus Ashby	1884.10.23 ?	after 1955.02.08	Burton, Haswell	Moxley, Leatha Ann
Burton, Susan (B.?) "Susie" Payne	1884.02.11	1956.01.30	Payne, George Washington	LNU, (Sarah?) "Sallie"
Burton, Mae Ballard Cooper [Stafford ?]	1885.11.04	1968.03.08	Ballard, James	
Burton, Judson Marshall	1885.10.07	1933.08.11	Burton, Robert L.	Patton, Georgeanna / Georgianna "Anna / Annie"
Burton, Frances Eunice "Fannie / Fanny" Cooper [Frances Eunice "Fannie / Fanny" Cooper Burton Berry]	1885.10.05	1960.11.26	Cooper, Henry L.	Fritter, Emma Ideler / Idella "Della / Dellie"
Burton, George ?	1885.05.08 ?		Burton, James (sic) [James B. "J. B." Burton ?]	LNU, Mary (sic) [Mary W. "Mollie / Molly" West?]
Burton, Marietta "Flossie" Curtis	circa 1885	1976.04.30	Curtis, E. L. [Edwin L. Curtis ?]	Downs, Maggie ?
Burton, Abner	circa 1885 or circa 1886	1950.09	Burton, James B. "J. B."	West, Mary W. "Mollie / Molly"
Burton, Maurice V.	circa 1885	1980.12.17	Burton, William Henry	Portch, Sarah E.
Burton, Joseph Lee	1886.06.10	1981.05.27	Burton, Sr., John Broaddus	Lowry, Margaret "Maggie"
Burton, Lucy Kate Pullen / Puller [black ?]	circa 1886	1937.04.01	Pullen / Puller, Eugene [black ?]	Coleman, Margaret ? [black ?]
Burton, Nora V. [Nora V. Burton Humphries Burton?]	1887.05.03	1919.01.30 or 1919.01.31	Burton, Wellington W.	Downs, Annie Laura
Burton, Nannie Lee [Nannie Lee Burton Berry]	1887.01.11	1932.08.09	Burton, Thompson	Burton, Almeta Jane "Virginia / Jennie / Jenny"
Burton, James Edward	1887.03.25 or 1887.03.31	1959 ?	Burton, Haswell	Moxley, Leatha Ann

NAME	DOB	DOD	FATHER	MOTHER
Burton, Leona M. [Leona M. ("Lizzie"?) Burton Mills]	1887.07.27 ?	after 1959	Burton, Robert L.	Patton, Georgeanna / Georgianna "Anna / Annie"
Burton, FNU [infant son]	1888.06.09 or 1889.06.09	1888.07.01 or 1889.07.01	Burton, James B. "J. B."	West, Mary W. "Mollie / Molly"
Burton, Anne "Annie" Lee [black] [Anne "Annie" Lee Burton (Dawson or Dorsey)] [Fredericksburg ?]	before 1888.06.28			
Burton, Thomas J.	circa 1888 or circa 1889	1938	Burton, James B. "J. B."	West, Mary W. "Mollie / Molly"
Burton, Lizzie May [Lucy May Burton?]	1888.05.08	1888.06.10 or 1888.06.13	Burton, William J. (William J. Burton, Jr. ?) ["fifth"]	Knight, Drucilla B.
Burton, Fannie D. Guy	circa 1889		Guy, Robert ?	
Burton, Sarah [Sarah Burton Way]	1889	1959	Burton, Elijah J.	Bettis, Letha / Lethe Anne
Burton, Minnie C.	1889.03.01 or 1889.04.07	1979.03.12	Burton, Sr., John Broaddus	Lowry, Margaret "Maggie"
Burton, Ira Richard	1889.03.08	1965.05.05	Burton, Haswell	Moxley, Leatha Ann
Burton, Leonard	1889.03.03	1955.09.03	Burton, Wellington W.	Downs, Annie Laura
Burton, Henry Bernard	1890.03.28	1918.07.28	Burton, William Henry	Portch, Sarah E.
Burton, Edward M. "Eddie"	1890.09.20	1930.01.25	Burton, Sr., John Broaddus	Lowry, Margaret "Maggie"
Burton, Dr. Robert Elmore	1890.06.12	1959.01.24	Burton, Robert L.	Patton, Georgeanna / Georgianna "Anna / Annie"
Burton, John ?	1890.02.25		Burton, John [John Broaddus Burton, Sr. ?]	LNU, Margaret [Margaret "Maggie" Lowry ?]

NAME	DOB	DOD	FATHER	MOTHER
Burton, Lucy Virginia [Lucy Virginia Burton Berry ?]	1890.11.16	after 1942 ?	Burton, Charles	Burton, Ida V.
Burton, Sr., Arthur James	1891	1985.05.19	Burton, Sr., John Broaddus	Lowry, Margaret "Maggie"
Burton, Mary	1891.12.27		Burton, Thomas R.	Limbrick / Limerick, Hester A.
Burton, Stonewall J.	1891.12 ?	1892.08.04	Burton, Haswell	Moxley, Leatha Ann
Burton, Winnie Davis	1891.06.22	1984.01.14	Burton, William Henry	Portch, Sarah E.
Burton, FNU [son]	1892.04.12		Burton, Wilson	Dickerson / Dickinson, Alice L.
Burton, Gilmer / Gilmore W.	1892.04.12 ? or 1894.05.19 ?	1939.09.26 or 1939.09.27	Burton, Wilson	Dickerson / Dickinson, Alice L.
Burton, Mary G. [Mary G. Burton Bullock]	1892.05.15	1968.02.19	Burton, James B. "J. B."	West, Mary W. "Mollie / Molly"
Burton, Minnie Elizabeth Humphries	1892	1970	Humphries, James	Monroe, Elizabeth Gordon
Burton, Edith [Edith Burton Umphrey]	circa 1893	1920.04.15 ?	Burton, Thomas R.	Limbrick / Limerick, Hester A.
Burton, Winnie	circa 1893	before 1914 ?	Burton, Robert L.	Patton, Georgeanna / Georgianna "Anna / Annie"
Burton, Ernest William	1894.07.09	1970.09.28	Burton, Wilson	Dickerson / Dickinson, Alice L.
Burton, Charles "Charlie"	1894.06.04	1964.08.03	Burton, William F.	Burton, Mary "Mollie"
Burton, Nina Annabelle	1894.09.22	1975.02.18	Burton, John [son of Elijah J. Burton]	Portch, Nettie M.
Burton, Major	circa 1895	1972.01.09	Burton, Haswell	Moxley, Leatha Ann
Burton, Julian [Julia Burton ?]	1895.09.27		Burton, Thomas R.	Limbrick / Limerick, Hester A.
Burton, Hugh M.	circa 1895	after 1933	Burton, William Henry	Portch, Sarah E.

NAME	DOB	DOD	FATHER	MOTHER
Burton, Raymond E.	1895.04.16	1986.02.04	Burton, William Henry	Portch, Sarah E.
Burton, Renald / Reynold Vinson	1895	1964.02.22	Burton, John [son of Elijah J. Burton]	Portch, Nettie M.
Burton, Jr., John Broaddus	1896.03.13	1960.03.12	Burton, Sr., John Broaddus	Lowry, Margaret "Maggie"
Burton, Jane McKinley "Janie" [Jane McKinley "Janie" Burton Marlow/Marlowe]	1896.11.31	after 1933	Burton, William Henry	Portch, Sarah E.
Burton, Flossie Almeda [Flossie Almeda Burton Plaskett]	circa 1896	after 1970.10.08	Burton, James B. "J. B."	West, Mary W. "Mollie / Molly"
Burton, Noel Robert	1894.03.07 or 1896.03.07	1985.03.04	Burton, Sr., John Broaddus	Lowry, Margaret "Maggie"
Burton, Lillian Embrey	1897.02.19	1985.09.04	Embrey, James	LNU, Emma
Burton, Bertha M. Yeatman [Fredericksburg / Stafford]	1897	1980.07.21	Yeatman, Fitzhugh	LNU, Dolly
Burton, Katherine E. "Katie" [Katherine E. "Katie" Burton Hudson]	circa 1897	1948 ? (by 1948.12.28)	Burton, John [son of Elijah J. Burton]	Portch, Nettie M.
Burton, Lillian Bell "Lillie / Lilly" Monroe	1897.11.06	1983.09.15	Monroe, James D.	LNU, Sis ? [LNU, Willetta L. ?]
Burton, Eddie	circa 1898		Burton, Thomas R.	Limbrick / Limerick, Hester A.
Burton, Stella E.	circa 1898 or 1899.09.10	1918.02.25	Burton, Wilson	Dickerson / Dickinson, Alice L.
Burton, Blanche May Craig	1898	1962	Craig, Henry D.	unknown first wife
Burton, Pauline M. [Pauline M. Burton Lee]	circa 1898	after 1964	Burton, John [son of Elijah J. Burton]	Portch, Nettie M.

NAME	DOB	DOD	FATHER	MOTHER
Burton, Oliver R. "Ollie"	1898.06.01	1980.08.02	Burton, William F.	Burton, Mary "Mollie"
Burton, Fleda C. Curtis	1899	1981.03.07	Curtis, E. L. [Edwin L. Curtis ?]	Downs, Maggie ?
Burton, Florence Mary Boutyard / Boutchyard	1899.02.05	1994.05.29	Boutyard, Ashton Sanford	Bryant, Elizabeth G. "Lizzie"
Burton, Eugene [black]	1902.10.20	1923.03.04 ?	Burton, Frank [black]	Pullen / Puller, Lucy Kate [black]
Burton, Frank Edwin	1903.04.10	1980.03.06	Burton, John [son of Elijah J. Burton]	Portch, Nettie M.
Burton, Carrie [Carrie Burton Hoover]	between 1903.10.04 and 1927.08.26	after 1969.12	Burton, Clarence	Jones, Carrie L.
Burton, Thelma H. [Thelma H. Burton Coghill]	circa 1904	1965.08.17	Burton, Sr., Benjamin Lewis / Louis "Bennie / Benny"	Monroe, Iva Davis
Burton, Elwood Winston [the elder]	1904.06.06	1948.08.05 or 1948.08.08	Burton, Sr., Benjamin Lewis / Louis "Bennie / Benny"	Monroe, Iva Davis
Burton, Frank [black]	circa 1905	1923.03.03 ?	Burton, Frank [black]	Pullen / Puller, Lucy Kate [black]
Burton, Glendie S. [Glendie S. Burton Johnson]	circa 1905	after 1964.02.24	Burton, John [son of Elijah J. Burton]	Portch, Nettie M.
Burton, Inez Marguerite [Inez Marguerite Burton Payne]	1905 or 1906	1963.03.20	Burton, Maurice Walter	Cooper, Frances Eunice "Fannie / Fanny"
Burton, David E.	circa 1906 or circa 1908	1955.02.08	Burton, Columbus Ashby	Curtis, Marietta "Flossie"
Burton, Merritt Dickinson "Dippy"	circa 1906	1990.02.06	Burton, Wilson	Dickerson / Dickinson, Alice L.
Burton, Fielding W.	circa 1906	after 1969.12	Burton, Clarence	Jones, Carrie L.
Burton, Lady Mazella Trigger	circa 1907		Trigger, B. J. ?	LNU, Lucy

NAME	DOB	DOD	FATHER	MOTHER
Burton, Edward James [black]	circa 1907 or circa 1910	1984.03.30 ?	Burton, Frank [black]	Pullen / Puller, Lucy Kate [black]
Burton, Pearl Vivian [Pearl Vivian Burton Jett]	circa 1907	after 1980	Burton, John [son of Elijah J. Burton]	Portch, Nettie M.
Burton, Media V. [Media V. Burton Patton]	1907	1943	Burton, William F.	Burton, Mary "Mollie"
Burton, Myrtle V. Harding [Myrtle V. Harding Burton Dallman]	1907	1989.03.23	Harding, Archie	LNU, Jennie
Burton, Walter Eugene	1907.10.27	1969.06.09	Burton, Maurice Walter	Cooper, Frances Eunice "Fannie / Fanny"
Burton, Archibald Lee "Archie" "Buck"	1908	1985	Burton, Archibald B. "Archie"	Payne, Susan (B.?) "Susie"
Burton, Agnes Margaret	1908.03.24	2003.12.07	Burton, Joseph Lee	Humphries, Nora V. Burton
Burton, Theodore R. T.	1908.11.13	1936.01.09 or 1936.01.10	Burton, Sr., Benjamin Lewis / Louis "Bennie / Benny"	Monroe, Iva Davis
Burton, Archie [black]	circa 1908		Burton, Frank [black]	Pullen / Puller, Lucy Kate [black]
Burton, J. Alvin	1909.09.25	1979.03.12	Burton, Leonard	Burton, Minnie C.
Burton, Clifton [NFI]	before 1909.09.17			
Burton, Leathea / Leathie Virginia [Leathea / Leathie Virginia Burton Blaisdell]	1909	2003.07.27	Burton, Archibald B. "Archie"	Payne, Susan (B.?) "Susie"
Burton, Pauline Kurz	1909.11.28	1993.05.06	Kurz, Sr., Gustave "Gus"	Berry, Fannie
Burton, Bessie Larkin Jones	circa 1909	1973.09.21		
Burton, Robert Franklin "Bobbie"	1910	1969.12	Burton, Clarence	Jones, Carrie L.

NAME	DOB	DOD	FATHER	MOTHER
Burton, Clifford Emory	1910.01.15	1961.02.21	Burton, John [son of Elijah J. Burton]	Portch, Nettie M.
Burton, Annie Virginia [Annie Virginia Burton Way]	circa 1910	after 1998	Burton, Joseph Lee	Humphries, Nora V. Burton
Burton, Ruby Jane Ellington [Ruby Jane Ellington Burton Allen]	circa 1910		Ellington, James M.	Heflin, Cora L.
Burton, Marie [Marie Burton Grinnan]	1911	1999	Burton, Sr., Benjamin Lewis / Louis "Bennie / Benny"	Monroe, Iva Davis
Burton, Virgie	1911.11.20	1915.12.10	Burton, Archibald B. "Archie"	Payne, Susan (B.?) "Susie"
Burton, Margaret Lloyd ?	1911	after 1957.06.14		
Burton, Maude Virginia Hummer [Loudoun ?]	before 1912			
Burton, Harold L.	1912.01.04	after 1979.03.12	Burton, Leonard	Burton, Minnie C.
Burton, Norman "Chip"	1912.09.27	1998.12.05	Burton, Joseph Lee	Humphries, Nora V. Burton
Burton, Nancy E. Madison Stevens ? [Fredericksburg ?]	1913	1973.06.20	Madison, Ollie C.	
Burton, Jr., Benjamin Lewis / Louis	1913.08.17	1984.10.30	Burton, Sr., Benjamin Lewis / Louis "Bennie / Benny"	Monroe, Iva Davis
Burton, Dollie / Dolly M. Garner [King George / Stafford ?]	1913.02.03 or 1914.02.03	1938.12.19	Garner, Lucien ?	Montieth, Dollie ?
Burton, Joseph Eustace "Josie"	1914.03.23	1958.10.26	Burton, Joseph Lee	Humphries, Nora V. Burton
Burton, Margaret Mae Carneal	1915	1991.11.11		

NAME	DOB	DOD	FATHER	MOTHER
Burton, Grace [Stafford ?]	before 1915.12	after 1929.11.16		
Burton, Leslie Hall	1915.08.18	1972.04.30	Burton, Sr., Benjamin Lewis / Louis "Bennie / Benny"	Monroe, Iva Davis
Burton, Irene Lee Grinnan	1916.01.06	1973.01.22	Grinnan, Edward	Monroe, Katherine
Burton, Elizabeth Williams	before 1917 ?			
Burton, Sr., Oliver Stansbury "Ollie"	1917.03.22	2010.03.08	Burton, Oliver R. "Ollie"	Monroe, Lillian Bell "Lillie / Lilly"
Burton, Charles Ford	1917.08.15 or circa 1918	1986.11.13	Burton, Archibald B. "Archie"	Payne, Susan (B.?) "Susie"
Burton, Ernestine Florence / Florence Ernestine [Ernestine Florence / Florence Ernestine Burton Payne]	1918	1993	Burton, Ernest William	Boutyard / Boutchyard, Florence Mary
Burton, James William	1918.06.16	1945.05.08	Burton, James Edward	Humphries, Minnie Elizabeth
Burton, FNU [Mrs. George Burton]	before 1919.02.07	after 1919.02.07		
Burton, John Pershing "Percy"	circa 1919	1961.01.04	Burton, Joseph Lee	Humphries, Nora V. Burton
Burton, Everett E.	1919.09.19	1944.06.08	Burton, Oliver R. "Ollie"	Monroe, Lillian Bell "Lillie / Lilly"
Burton, Esther [Esther Burton Grinnan]	circa 1920	2010.01.24	Burton, Sr., Benjamin Lewis / Louis "Bennie / Benny"	Monroe, Iva Davis
Burton, Edward Henry	circa 1920	1989.08.27	Burton, Archibald B. "Archie"	Payne, Susan (B.?) "Susie"
Burton, Pauline Bernice Powell [Pauline Bernice Powell Burton Daniels]	1920.12.09		Powell, Eugene Franklin	

NAME	DOB	DOD	FATHER	MOTHER
Burton, Cecil Preston	1921	2005.07.28	Burton, Oliver R. "Ollie"	Monroe, Lillian Bell "Lillie / Lilly"
Burton, Marie Elizabeth [Marie Elizabeth Burton Mitchell]	1921	2007.08.15	Burton, Ernest William	Boutyard / Boutchyard, Florence Mary
Burton, George Farrar [Albemarle? / Stafford]	1921.04.15	2008.12.13		
Burton, Elsie Mae / May [Elsie Mae / May Burton Hove] [Fredericksburg]	1921.05.21	after 1981.03.07	Burton, Major	Curtis, Fleda C.
Burton, Agnes Elizabeth Miniclier	1921.11.13	1991.04.27		
Burton, Mae Lawhorne ? [Stafford ?]	circa 1921	1986.04.28		
Burton, Robert L.	1922.01.22	1994.03.16	Burton, Sr., Benjamin Lewis / Louis "Bennie / Benny"	Monroe, Iva Davis
Burton, Dorothy Virginia Sisk [Dorothy Virginia Sisk Burton Seay]	1922.06.16	2010.11.22	Sisk, James A. (Ashby?)	Leake, Bertha
Burton, Jr., Arthur James "Junior"	1922.09.06	1977.10.10	Burton, Sr., Arthur James	Craig, Blanche May
Burton, Mary M. [Mary M. Burton Templeman] [Stafford ?]	before 1922.12			
Burton, Dorothy Virginia [Dorothy Virginia Burton Ellington] [Fredericksburg / Stafford]	1922.12.14	2009.05.07	Burton, Renald / Reynold Vinson	Yeatman, Bertha M.
Burton, Eula Meadows	1922	1988		

NAME	DOB	DOD	FATHER	MOTHER
Burton, Alfred Wilson	1923	1976.06.30	Burton, Ernest William	Boutyard / Boutchyard, Florence Mary
Burton, Ralph Monroe	1923.09.08	1957.06.22	Burton, Sr., Benjamin Lewis / Louis "Bennie / Benny"	Monroe, Iva Davis
Burton, Sr., Carroll Eugene [Fredericksburg]	1923.11.27	1979.01.07	Burton, Sr., Arthur James	Craig, Blanche May
Burton, Helen Elizabeth Newton [Elizabeth Helen Newton Burton ?]	1923	2007.06.22	Newton, Richard	LNU, Effie
Burton, Julian	1924.01.07	1956.12.29 or 1956.12.30	Burton, Archibald B. "Archie"	Payne, Susan (B.?) "Susie"
Burton, Mae Bryant [Mae Bryant Burton Boutchyard]	1924.01.08	2006.03.25	Bryant, James Murray	Withers, Gloria
Burton, Cecil Melvin	1925	2001.03.17	Burton, Elwood Winston [the elder]	Harding, Myrtle V.
Burton, Mildred [Mildred Burton Cassiday] [Stafford?]	by 1925	after 1929.11.16	Burton, James Grover	LNU, Grace
Burton, Estelle [Stafford?]	by 1925	after 1929.11.16	Burton, James Grover	LNU, Grace
Burton, Lester Clifton	1925.11.25	1954.09.30	Burton, James Edward	Humphries, Minnie Elizabeth
Burton, James Lester	between 1925.11.25 and 1954.09.25	after 2006.03.25	Burton, Lester Clifton	Bryant, Mae
Burton, Erva V. "Billie" "Sis" [Erva V. "Billie" "Sis" Burton Murphy]	1925.12.16	2008.11.09	Burton, Oliver R. "Ollie"	Monroe, Lillian Bell "Lillie / Lilly"
Burton, Sr., Sidney / Sydney Ellsworth	1926.08.09	1974.05.15	Burton, Elwood Winston [the elder]	Harding, Myrtle V.

NAME	DOB	DOD	FATHER	MOTHER
Burton, Sarah E. [Sarah E. "Nannie" Burton Green Dye]	1926.03.07	2009.04.07	Burton, Archibald B. "Archie"	Payne, Susan (B.?) "Susie"
Burton, Charlotte Bourne	circa 1926		Bourne, Henry S.	Newton, Gladys H.
Burton, FNU [Margaret A. "Margie" Burton Fitzhugh ?]	circa 1926 ?	after 1976.04.30 ?	Burton, David E. [son of Columbus Ashby Burton]	LNU, Margaret A.
Burton, Alma May [Alma May Burton Johnson] [Fredericksburg ?]	1927.04.09	after 1980	Burton, Renald / Reynold Vinson	Yeatman, Bertha M.
Burton, Lucy H.	1927.03.16	1927.06.28	Burton, Fielding W.	Trigger, Lady Mazella
Burton, Sr., Linwood Ashby "Dober"	1928.12.08	1996.06.08	Burton, Frank Edwin	Burton, Agnes Margaret
Burton, Thelma Samuel [Caroline / Stafford]	1928.10.15	2000.04.16		
Burton, Edna C. Way [Edna C. Way Burton Dallman]	1928.10.09	2007.01.31	Way, Ashton Cleveland	Burton, Annie Virginia
Burton, Jr., Sidney Ellsworth	between 1928 and 1974 ?	after 1988	Burton, Sr., Sidney / Sydney Ellsworth	Way, Edna C.
Burton, Robert Gilbert	1929.10.17		Burton, Ernest William	Boutyard / Boutchyard, Florence Mary
Burton, Christine [Flossie ? Christine Burton Sealy]	circa 1929	after 2008.11.09	Burton, Oliver R. "Ollie"	Monroe, Lillian Bell "Lillie / Lilly"
Burton, Margaret A.	before 1929.06.07	after 1955.02.08		
Burton, Arnita Ellen [Arnita Ellen Burton Beach]	circa 1929	2006.04.12	Burton, Sr., Benjamin Lewis / Louis "Bennie / Benny"	Monroe, Iva Davis

NAME	DOB	DOD	FATHER	MOTHER
Burton, Mary I. [Mary I. Burton Jefferson]	before 1929	1983.10.30	Burton, Sr., Benjamin Lewis / Louis "Bennie / Benny"	Monroe, Iva Davis
Burton, Thelma [Thelma Burton Miller] [Stafford ?]	before 1929.06.07		Burton, Ira Richard	
Burton, Helen [granddaughter of Haswell Burton ?]	before 1929.06.07			
Burton, Ruth Gallahan	1920s ?	after 2010.01.24		
Burton, Edith [Stafford ?]	before 1930.01.25	after 1930.01.25	Burton, Edward M. "Eddie"	Williams, Elizabeth
Burton, Lucille [Stafford ?]	before 1930.01.25	after 1930.01.25	Burton, Edward M. "Eddie"	Williams, Elizabeth
Burton, Mary Curtis [Mary Dodd Burton ?] [Fredericksburg ?]	1930	1972.12.12		Dodd, Ethel Desrosiers
Burton, Catherine [black]	circa 1930	2003.01.14	Burton, Edward James [black]	Buckner, Mildred Virginia [black]
Burton, Joyce Ann Shepherd	1931.09.16	1956.03.24	Shepherd, Charles F.	
Burton, Edna E. [Edna E. Burton Leake]	1932.06.02		Burton, William M.	Burton, Winnie Davis
Burton, Edwin Emory "Ed"	1933.07.28	2011.11.21	Burton, Frank Edwin	Burton, Agnes Margaret
Burton, Doris	before 1933.08.11		Burton, Judson Marshall	
Burton, Warren	before 1933.08.11	after 1933.08.11	Burton, Judson Marshall	
Burton, Aline McGill Payne	circa 1934	2011.08.28	Payne, Oliver	LNU, Pearl

Selected Marriages

Chronological

DATE	NAME	CONSORT
1690 circa	Burton, William ["first"]	Foley / Folio, Martha (Bryant?)
1725.12.14	Burton, William ["second"]	Spicer, Sarah
1741.09.30	Burton, Lettice	Jefferies, Alexander
1750s?	Burton, Nathaniel [the elder]	unknown consort
1753.10.07	Burton, William ["third"]	Porch, Rachel
1780s by ?	Burton, James [James B. Burton, Sr.?]	Taylor, FNU ?
1787 by	Burton, Samuel ["second" Samuel]	LNU, Mary
1794 by	Burton, William [William J. Burton, Sr.?] ["fourth"] (1ˢᵗ marrisge ?)	Jett, Susannah "Sukey"
1800 by	Burton, George	LNU, Mary
1801 by	Burton, Isaac	Marquess, Mary
1809 by ?	Burton, William [William John Burton / John William Burton ?]	LNU, Susan
1809 before ?	Burton, John [John William Burton / William John Burton ?]	LNU, Susan
1809 after	Burton, Jesse [Jesse Burden/Burton]	Brummett, Elizabeth Musselman (2ⁿᵈ marriage)
1810 by	Burton, Nathaniel [the younger]	LNU, Jane
1812 before	Burton, Cary (1ˢᵗ marriage)	Walker, Susanna

DATE	NAME	CONSORT
1820 by	Burton, William [William (L. or S.) Burton]	Pollard, Margaret (A. ?)
1820 by ?	Burton, Thomas S.	unknown consort
1826 ?	Burton, William [William J. Burton, Sr.?] ["fourth"] (2nd marrisge?)	McKenney, Catharine "Kate" [Catharine "Kate" McKenney (Burton?) Tyson] (1ˢᵗ marriage?)
1826.04.11 by	Burton, FNU	Limbrick, Sarah
1830s ?	Burton, Ann "Nancy" [the younger] (unmarried consort?)	Burton, James (unmarried consort?)
1830s ?	Burton, James (unmarried consort?)	Burton, Ann "Nancy" [the younger] (unmarried consort?)
1830 by	Burton, Harris W.	LNU, Elizabeth
1832 circa	Burton, Cary (2ⁿᵈ marriage)	Burns (or Pollard?), Nancy
1833 and 1840 between	Burton (?), Catharine "Kate" McKenney [Catharine "Kate" McKenney (Burton?) Tyson] (2ⁿᵈ marriage?)	Tyson, William
1835 by	Burton, Sr., William E. (1ˢᵗ marriage)	Bowler, Elizabeth "Betsy"
1838.10.08 before	Burton, FNU	Coakley, Sarah
1840 by	Burton, Richard [son of John Burton] (suspected 1ˢᵗ marriage)	LNU, Mary (suspected)
1840s by	Burton, Joseph S.	LNU, Maria A.
1841 ?	Burton, Elijah M. [Elijah Marquess Burton ?]	Hearn, Margaret ?
1841 before	Burton, Eliza A.	Petit, FNU ?
1842 by	Burton, Marshall	Bettis ?, Jane F. (or Jane F. Dunnington?)
1843 by ?	Burton, Catharine	Southard, Harrison
1843 by	Burton, Mary	Rodgers, James M.
1843 after	Burton, Emily M.	Brown, FNU
1845 by	Burton, James A.	Dunnington, Ellen
1846 by	Burton, William J. [son of Thomas S. Burton ?]	Chilton, Elizabeth

DATE	NAME	CONSORT
1846 circa	Burton, Mary E. (Elizabeth?) (suspected marriage)	Bloxton, Jr., William Ashby ? (2nd marriage)
1848.10.19	Burton, Terrissa M.	Guy, FNU
1849.07.28	Burton, Arthur A. (1st marriage)	Ballard, Mary A.
1850 by	Burton, Richard [son of John Burton] (2nd marriage?)	Monroe, Willie Ann
1850 by	Burton, Lucinda / Lucindy "Lucy"	Turner, Newton A.
1850 by	Burton, Jr., James [James B. Burton, Jr.?]	LNU, Elizabeth
1850 circa	Burton, Fielding (B.?)	Webb, Virginia "Jennie"
1853.12.12	Burton, Virginia F.	Ellington, John
1854.12.16 or 1855.12.16	Burton, William J. [William J. Burton, Jr. ?] ["fifth"] (1st marriage)	Franklin, Mary A.
1856.08.14	Burton, Mary H.	Brown, Richard
1857.10.15	Burton, Jr., William E.	Truslow, Lucinda "Lucy"
1858.03.20	Burton, Elizabeth Musselman Brummett (3rd marriage)	Reed, Gustavus (2nd marriage)
1860 by	Burton, James Alexander "Sandy"	LNU, Mary A. (Ann?)
1861.12.27	Burton, Parker F. "Jesse"	Brown, Mahala
1866.04.17 or 1866.04.19	Burton, Ann Eliza	Conner / Connor / O'Conner / O'Connor, Jr., William Henry
1866.11.04	Burton, William [William E. Burton, Sr. ?] (2nd marriage?)	Williams, Sarah [Sarah "Sallie" Berton / Burton Williams ?] (2nd marriage?)
1867.06.16	Burton (or Tyson?), Sarah "Sallie / Sally"	Southard, James Samuel
1867.10.24	Burton, Susan A.	Sullivan, George W.
1867.12.30 or 1868.01.02	Burton, William J. [William J. Burton, Jr. ?] ["fifth"] (2nd marriage)	Knight, Drucilla B.
1869.06.24	Burton, Martha A.	Bradshaw, John F.
1870 by	Burton, Richard	LNU, Dulcibella "Dulcie"
1870.07.16 by	Burton, Richard	LNU, Jane
1870.09.17	Burton, Ann Eliza "Annie"	Brooks, Henry H.

DATE	NAME	CONSORT
1872.01.17	Burton, Isabella	Monroe, Joseph A.
1873.01.19	Burton, Clementina / Clementine	Walker, William Henry
1875.03.04	Burton, Almeta Jane "Virginia / Jennie / Jenny"	Burton, Thompson
1875.03.04	Burton, Thompson	Burton, Almeta Jane "Virginia / Jennie / Jenny"
1876.05.14	Burton, William Jesse	Boutyard, Mary E. (Ellen?)
1877.02.19	Burton, Wellington W.	Downs, Annie Laura
1877.04.26	Burton, Robert L.	Patton, Georgeanna / Georgianna "Anna / Annie"
1878.08.28 or 1878.08.29	Burton, Ida R.	Hewitt, Peter
1878.09.11	Burton, Beverly C.	Octavia B. Fleming [Octavia B. Fleming Burton Kendig] (1ˢᵗ marriage)
1879.12.16 or 1879.12.17	Burton, James B. "J. B."	West, Mary W. "Mollie / Molly"
1880.06.03	Burton, Haswell	Moxley, Leatha Ann
1880.12.26 or 1881.01.03	Burton, Elizabeth H. "Bettie / Betty"	Harding, E. P.
1881.06.11 by	Burton, Daniel B.	LNU, Julia A.
1881.04.06 or 1881.04.13	Burton, Lucy P.	Jones, E. F.
1882.10.06 or 1882.10.08 ?	Burton, Elijah J.	Bettis, Letha / Lethe Anne
1883.02.13 or 1883.02.15	Burton, Alvena "Allie"	Mills, Robert Wyatt
1883.05.29 or 1883.05.31	Burton, Willie Ann	Burgess, John A.
1883.12.19	Burton, Mary J.	Brandenburg, C. M. [Clarence M. Brandenburg?]
1885.02.18 or 1885.02.18	Burton, Arthur A. (2ⁿᵈ marriage)	Ballard, Eliza V.
1885.09.10	Burton, Sr., John Broaddus	Lowry, Margaret "Maggie"
1886.10.17	Burton, Mary F.	Littrell, Charles
1888.06.27 or 1888.06.28	Burton, Anne "Annie" Lee [black] [Fredericksburg ?]	Dawson or Dorsey, John Henry [black]
1889.02.05 or 1890.02.05	Burton, Mary "Mollie"	Burton, William F.
1889.02.05 or 1890.02.05	Burton, William F.	Burton, Mary "Mollie"
1889.04.17	Burton, Charles	Burton, Ida V. [Ida V. Burton Skidmore] (1ˢᵗ marriage)

DATE	NAME	CONSORT
1889.04.17	Burton, Ida V. [Ida V. Burton Skidmore] (1st marriage)	Burton, Charles
1889.11.06	Burton, William Washington [Culpeper/Fredericksburg]	Humphries, Ida Bell / Belle [Ida Bell / Belle Humphries Burton McGhee] (1st marriage)
1889.12.05	Burton, William Henry	Portch, Sarah E. [Sarah E. Portch Burton Mankey] (1st marriage)
1891.01.03 or 1891.01.04	Burton, Thomas R.	Limbrick / Limerick, Hester A.
1891.09.29 or 1891.09.30	Burton, Wilson	Dickerson / Dickinson, Alice L.
1891.11.04	Burton, Olga Belle	Franklin, John R.
1893.11.22	Burton, John [son of Elijah J. Burton]	Portch, Nettie M.
1899.07.09	Burton, Ida V. [Ida V. Burton Skidmore] (2nd marriage)	Skidmore, Robert H.
1900 and 1920.04.15 between	Burton, Edith	Umphrey, FNU
1901.01.28	Burton, Addie T.	Harding, McDuff
1902	Burton, Carrie Irene	Knight, Clarence Newman
1902.06.01	Burton, Ella	Payne, Gustavus "Gus / Gusty"
1903.08.12	Burton, Anne E. "Annie" [Anne E. "Annie" Burton Way Berry] (1st marriage)	Way, L. L.
1903.09.25	Burton, Nora V. [Nora V. Burton Humphries Burton ?] (1st marriage)	Humphries, Samuel D.
1903.10.04	Burton, Clarence	Jones, Carrie L.
1904.03.06	Burton, Sr., Benjamin Lewis / Louis "Bennie / Benny"	Monroe, Iva Davis
1904.06.07 license	Burton, Pemiley G.	Kelley/Kelly, James M.
1904.11.23	Burton, Mary Virginia "Virgie"	Harris, John Thomas
1904.12.27	Burton, Maurice Walter	Cooper, Frances Eunice "Fannie / Fanny" [Frances Eunice "Fannie / Fanny" Cooper Burton Berry] (1st marriage)
1905.01.11	Burton, James B.	Stephens / Stevens, Minnie V. (Virginia?)

DATE	NAME	CONSORT
1905.06.03 by	Burton, Kimmie (or Kennie?) A. [Kimmie A. Burton (Schofield?) Reed ?] (1" marriage ?)	Schofield, Oliver Carlton ?
1905.09.26	Burton, Sarah	Way, R. W. [Rhonie W. Way]
1906.04.25	Burton, Virginia B. "Virgie"	Ennis, John E.
1906.05.06	Burton, Columbus Ashby	Curtis, Marietta "Flossie"
1906.11.14	Burton, Sarah E. Portch [Sarah E. Portch Burton Mankey] (2nd marriage)	Mankey, Francis (2nd marriage)
1906.12.26 or 1906.12.27	Burton, Archibald B. "Archie"	Payne, Susan (B.?) "Susie"
1907.02.25	Burton, Annette J. "Nettie"	Cooper, Melvin E.
1907.03.25	Burton, John H. [Washington, DC/Stafford]	Guy, Fannie D.
1907.09.04 ?	Burton, Joseph Lee (1" marriage)	Humphries, Nora V. Burton (2nd marriage)
1908.06.(29?)	Burton, Leonard	Burton, Minnie C.
1908.06.(29?)	Burton, Minnie C.	Burton, Leonard
1910.10.04	Burton, Rosa B.	Sullivan, Hunter
1912.06.27 or 1912.07.04	Burton, Judson Marshall	Hummer, Maude Virginia
1912.12.19	Burton, Nannie Lee	Berry, Sr., John William
1914.12.07 by	Burton, Frank [the elder black Frank Burton] (1" marriage)	Pullen / Puller, Lucy Kate [black]
1915.10.06	Burton, Oliver R. "Ollie"	Monroe, Lillian Bell "Lillie / Lilly"
1915.12 by	Burton, James Grover	LNU, Grace
1916.09.19	Burton, Leona M. ("Lizzie"?)	Mills, Alfred
1917	Burton, Dr. Robert Elmore	Baxter, Nannie
1917.04.26	Burton, William M.	Burton, Winnie Davis
1917.04.26	Burton, Winnie Davis	Burton, William M.
1917.05.01 and 1930.01.25 between	Burton, Edward M. "Eddie"	Williams, Elizabeth
1917.09.13	Burton, James Edward	Humphries, Minnie Elizabeth
1917.11.24	Burton, Ernest William	Boutyard, Florence Mary
1919.02.07 by	Burton, George B.	LNU, FNU ("Mrs. George Burton")

DATE	NAME	CONSORT
1919.09.05 or 1919.09.06	Burton, Major	Curtis, Fleda C.
1921 after	Burton, Warren	Lawhorne, Mae ?
1921.09.28	Burton, Renald / Reynold Vinson	Yeatman, Bertha M.
1921.11.03	Burton, Charles "Charlie"	Embrey, Lillian
1922.01.11	Burton, Sr., Arthur James	Craig, Blanche May
1922.12	Burton, Mary M. [Stafford ?]	Templeman, James Nelson
1923.12.(04?)	Burton, Katherine E. "Katie"	Hudson, Sidney Bradford
1924.06.26	Burton, Pauline M.	Lee, Richard Henry
1924.07.05	Burton, Elwood Winston [the elder]	Harding, Myrtle V. [Myrtle V. Harding Burton Dallman] (1st marriage)
1925.02.15	Burton, Thelma H.	Coghill, Rudolph [Edgar Rudolph Coghill, Sr. ?]
1925.06.04 by	Burton, Kimmie (or Kennie?) A. [Kimmie A. Burton (Schofield?) Reed ?] (2nd marriage ?)	Reed, FNU
1925.07.30 by	Burton, Melvin Strother	LNU, Mary C.
1925.11.25 and 1954.09.30 between	Burton, Lester Clifton	Bryant, Mae [Mae Bryant Burton Boutchyard] (1st marriage)
1926.01.09	Burton, Fielding W.	Trigger, Lady Mazella
1926.05.01	Burton, Leathea / Leathie Virginia	Blaisdell, Clarence George
1926.07.03	Burton, Frances Eunice "Fannie / Fanny" Cooper (2nd marriage)	Berry, Norman
1927	Burton, Glendie S.	Johnson, Sidney
1927.04.16	Burton, Media V.	Patton, Erland L.
1928.05.22 before	Burton, Mildred [Stafford?]	Cassiday, FNU
1928.10.20	Burton, Theodore R. T.	Ellington, Ruby Jane [Ruby Jane Ellington Burton Allen] (1st marriage)
1929 by	Burton, Ira Richard	unknown consort
1929.06.07 before	Burton, David E. [son of Columbus Ashby Burton]	LNU, Margaret A.
1929.09.26	Burton, Flossie Almeda	Plaskett, John M.
1929.11.27	Burton, Marie	Grinnan, Sr., Arnold P.

DATE	NAME	CONSORT
1930	Burton, Julian	LNU, Loraine
1930.12.26	Burton, Annie Virginia	Way, Ashton Cleveland
1930 by	Burton, Jane McKinley "Janie"	Marlow / Marlowe, John
1930 by	Burton, Noel Robert	Jones, Bessie Larkin
1930 after	Burton, Alfred Wilson	Newton, Helen Elizabeth [Elizabeth Helen Newton ?]
1930 after ?	Burton, Archibald Lee "Archie" "Buck" (suspected 1st marriage)	Lloyd, Margaret ?
1930 and 1973.06.20 between	Burton, Archibald Lee "Archie" "Buck" (2nd marriage?)	Burton, Nancy E. Madison Stevens ? [Fredericksburg ?]
1930 after	Burton, Charles Ford	Whited, Irma M.
1930 after	Burton, Edward Henry	Welch, Laura
1931	Burton, Pearl Vivian	Jett, John Sidney
1931.01.14	Burton, Frank Edwin	Burton, Agnes Margaret
1931.01.14	Burton, Agnes Margaret	Burton, Frank Edwin
1931.12.19	Burton, Walter Eugene	Kurz, Pauline
1932.08.27	Burton, Edward James [black] [son of the black Frank Burton]	Buckner, Mildred Virginia [black]
1933	Burton, Robert Franklin "Bobbie"	Carneal, Margaret Mae
1934.05.19	Burton, Ernestine Florence / Florence Ernestine	Payne, Warren Edward
1935 after	Burton, Joseph Lee (2nd marriage)	Cooper, Mae Ballard (2nd marriage)
1935.12.12	Burton, Inez Marguerite	Payne, Sr., Laney George
1936	Burton, Ruby Jane Ellington (2nd marriage)	Allen, Marion Haden
1936 and 1972 between	Burton, Esther	Grinnan, David L.
1937.05.01	Burton, Jr., Benjamin Lewis / Louis	Grinnan, Irene Lee
1937.12.31 or 1938.01.02	Burton, Marie Elizabeth	Mitchell, Jr., William Thomas
1938	Burton, James William	Powell, Pauline Bernice [Pauline Bernice Powell Burton Daniels] (1st marriage)
1938.06.15	Burton, Mary G.	Bullock, Charles N.
1938.12.19 before	Burton, Sr., Oliver Stansbury "Ollie" (1st marriage)	Garner, Dollie / Dolly M.

DATE	NAME	CONSORT
1939.07.26 by	Burton, Dora Lee	Edwards, FNU
1941.10.25	Burton, Sr., Oliver Stansbury "Ollie" (2nd marriage)	Miniclier, Agnes Elizabeth
1941.06.09	Burton, Frank [the elder black Frank Burton] (2nd marriage)	Coleman, Nancy [black]
1941.09.20	Burton, Mary I.	Jefferson, Joseph Rudolph [Rudolph Joseph Jefferson ?]
1942 ?	Burton, Lucy Virginia (suspected marriage)	Berry, James Allen ?
1942	Burton, Cecil Preston	Meadows, Eula
1942.04.10 after	Burton, Edna E.	Leake, Clarence M.
1943.06.03	Burton, Jr., Arthur James "Junior"	Bourne, Charlotte
1944 and 1947 between	Burton, Erva V. "Billie" "Sis"	Murphy, FNU ?
1944 and 1947 between	Burton, (Flossie?) Christine	Sealy, R. Mason
1944	Burton, Elsie Mae / May [Fredericksburg]	Hove, Helmer M.
1944.03.25	Burton, Dorothy Virginia [Fredericksburg / Stafford]	Ellington, Linwood H.
1944.08.24	Burton, Ralph Monroe	Sisk, Dorothy Virginia [Dorothy Virginia Sisk Burton Seay] (1st marriage)
1945.06.09 or 1945.06.15	Burton, Sarah E. [Sarah E. "Nannie" Burton Green Dye] (1st marriage)	Green, Sr., Milton
1947.06.13	Burton, Arnita Ellen	Beach, Daniel Lewis / Louis
1947.06.13 before ?	Burton, Sr., Sidney / Sydney Ellsworth	Way, Edna C. [Edna C. Way Burton Dallman] (1st marriage)
1948.05 or 1949	Burton, Sr., Linwood Ashby "Dober" (1st marriage)	Shepherd, Joyce Ann
1951.04.28 by	Burton, George Farrar [Albemarle? / Stafford]	Samuel, Thelma [Caroline / Stafford]
1951.10.23 before	Burton, Sr., Carroll Eugene [Fredericksburg] (1st marriage)	LNU, Agnes Marie
1951.10.23 and 1972.12.12 between	Burton, Sr., Carroll Eugene [Fredericksburg] (2nd marriage)	Curtis, Mary (or Mary Dodd ?)
1954 or 1954.07.10	Burton, Robert Gilbert	Payne, Aline McGill

DATE	NAME	CONSORT
1954.09.30 after	Burton, James Lester	LNU, Shirley
1954.09.30 after	Burton, Mae Bryant (2nd marriage)	Boutchyard, FNU
1955.02.08 before	Burton, Margaret A. "Margie" ?	Fitzhugh, Howard
1955.09.03	Burton, Cecil Melvin	Parker, Margie
1955.09.03 and 1974.05.15 between	Burton, Myrtle V. Harding (2nd marriage)	Dallman, Marvin D.
1956.03.24 and 1967.01.08 between	Burton, Sr., Linwood Ashby "Dober" (2nd marriage)	Hall or Meade, Lillian Mae
1957.06.22 after	Burton, Dorothy Virginia Sisk (2nd marriage)	Seay, Charlie P.
1962 circa	Burton, Pauline Bernice Powell (2nd marriage)	Daniels, Howard Russell "Casey"
1964 by	Burton, Alma May [Fredericksburg?]	Johnson, FNU
1965.05.05 after	Burton, Thelma [Stafford ?]	Miller, FNU
1969.12 before	Burton, Carrie	Hoover, FNU
1974.05.15 after	Burton, Edna C. Way (2nd marriage)	Dallman, Marvin D.
1982.08.19 before	Burton, Jr., Sidney Ellsworth (1st marriage)	Lunsford, Betty Jean
1982.08.19 after	Burton, Jr., Sidney Ellsworth (2nd marriage)	LNU Geneva (or Sue ?)
1988.06.01 by	Burton, Robert L. [son of Benjamin Burton, Sr.]	Gallahan, Ruth
1990.02.06 before	Burton, Merritt Dickinson "Dippy"	LNU, Gernie R.

SELECTED MARRIAGES

Alphabetical by Burton

IN THIS particular list, I have included non-Burton brides not only in the "consort" column for their respective husbands, but also in the "name" column as Burtons themselves. Although this creates redundant entries, it allows readers to look up a non-Burton bride whether they know her husband's name or not. The primary drawback to this approach, however, is that it might create confusion over which women had the surname "Burton" as their maiden name and which did not. If a reader is in doubt concerning an entry for a Burton bride, I recommend looking up the marriage under the groom's name, too, to determine the bride's maiden name.

NAME	CONSORT	DATE
Burton, Addie T.	Harding, McDuff	1901.01.28
Burton, Agnes Elizabeth Miniclier	Burton, Sr., Oliver Stansbury "Ollie" (2nd marriage)	1941.10.25
Burton, Agnes Margaret	Burton, Frank Edwin	1931.01.14
Burton, Alfred Wilson	Newton, Helen Elizabeth [Elizabeth Helen Newton ?]	1930 after
Burton, Alice L. Dickerson / Dickinson	Burton, Wilson	1891.09.29 or 1891.09.30
Burton, Aline McGill Payne	Burton, Robert Gilbert	1954 or 1954.07.10
Burton, Alma May [Fredericksburg?]	Johnson, FNU	1964 by

NAME	CONSORT	DATE
Burton, Almeta Jane "Virginia / Jennie / Jenny"	Burton, Thompson	1875.03.04
Burton, Alvena "Allie"	Mills, Robert Wyatt	1883.02.13 or 1883.02.15
Burton, Ann "Nancy" [the younger]	Burton, James (unmarried consort?)	1830s ?
Burton, Ann Eliza "Annie"	Brooks, Henry H.	1870.09.17
Burton, Ann Eliza	Conner / Connor / O'Conner / O'Connor, Jr., William Henry	1866.04.17 or 1866.04.19
Burton, Anne "Annie" Lee [black] [Fredericksburg ?]	Dawson or Dorsey, John Henry [black]	1888.06.27 or 1888.06.28
Burton, Anne E. "Annie" (1ˢᵗ marriage)	Way, L. L.	1903.08.12
Burton, Annette J. "Nettie"	Cooper, Melvin E.	1907.02.25
Burton, Annie Laura Downs	Burton, Wellington W.	1877.02.19
Burton, Annie Virginia	Way, Ashton Cleveland	1930.12.26
Burton, Archibald B. "Archie"	Payne, Susan (B.?) "Susie"	1906.12.26 or 1906.12.27
Burton, Archibald Lee "Archie" "Buck" (suspected 1ˢᵗ marriage)	Lloyd, Margaret ?	1930 after ?
Burton, Archibald Lee "Archie" "Buck" (suspected 2ⁿᵈ marriage)	Stevens, Nancy E. Madison ?	1973.06.20 before
Burton, Arnita Ellen	Beach, Daniel Lewis / Louis	1947.06.13
Burton, Arthur A. (1ˢᵗ marriage)	Ballard, Mary A.	1849.07.28
Burton, Arthur A. (2ⁿᵈ marriage)	Ballard, Eliza V.	1885.02.18
Burton, Jr., Arthur James "Junior"	Bourne, Charlotte	1943.06.03
Burton, Sr., Arthur James	Craig, Blanche May	1922.01.11
Burton, Jr., Benjamin Lewis / Louis	Grinnan, Irene Lee	1937.05.01
Burton, Sr., Benjamin Lewis / Louis "Bennie / Benny"	Monroe, Iva Davis	1904.03.06
Burton, Bertha M. Yeatman [Fredericksburg / Stafford]	Burton, Renald / Reynold Vinson	1921.09.28
Burton, Bessie Larkin Jones	Burton, Noel Robert	1930 by
Burton, Blanche May Craig	Burton, Sr., Arthur James	1922.01.11
Burton, Beverly C.	Fleming, Octavia B.	1878.09.11
Burton, Carrie Irene	Knight, Clarence Newman	1902

NAME	CONSORT	DATE
Burton, Carrie L. Jones [Spotsy / Stafford]	Burton, Clarence	1903.10.04
Burton, Carrie	Hoover, FNU	1969.12 before
Burton, Sr., Carroll Eugene [Fredericksburg] (1st marriage)	LNU, Agnes Marie	1951.10.23 before
Burton, Sr., Carroll Eugene [Fredericksburg] (2nd marriage)	Curtis, Mary (or Mary Dodd ?)	1951.10.23 and 1972.12.12 between
Burton, Cary (1st marriage)	Walker, Susanna	1812 before
Burton, Cary (2nd marriage)	Burns (or Pollard?), Nancy	1832 circa
Burton, Catharine	Southard, Harrison	1843 by ?
Burton (?), Catharine "Kate" McKenney [Catharine "Kate" McKenney (Burton?) Tyson] (1st marriage)	Burton, William [William J. Burton, Sr.?] ["fourth"]	1826
Burton (?), Catharine "Kate" McKenney [Catharine "Kate" McKenney (Burton?) Tyson] (2nd marriage)	Tyson, William	1833 and 1840 between
Burton, Cecil Melvin	Parker, Margie	1955.09.03
Burton, Cecil Preston	Meadows, Eula	1942
Burton, Charles	Burton, Ida V.	1889.04.17
Burton, Charles "Charlie"	Embrey, Lillian	1921.11.03
Burton, Charles Ford	Whited, Irma M.	1930 after
Burton, Charlotte Bourne	Burton, Jr., Arthur James "Junior"	1943.06.03
Burton, Christine [Flossie (?) Christine Burton ?]	Sealy, R. Mason	1944 and 1947 between
Burton, Clarence	Jones, Carrie L.	1903.10.04
Burton, Clementina / Clementine	Walker, William Henry	1873.01.19
Burton, Columbus Ashby	Curtis, Marietta "Flossie"	1906.05.06
Burton, Daniel	LNU, Julia A.	1881 before
Burton, David E.	LNU, Margaret A.	1929.06.07 before
Burton, Dollie / Dolly M. Garner [King George / Stafford ?]	Burton, Sr., Oliver Stansbury "Ollie"	1938.12.19 before
Burton, Dora Lee	Edwards, FNU	1939.07.26 by

NAME	CONSORT	DATE
Burton, Dorothy Virginia [Fredericksburg / Stafford]	Ellington, Linwood H.	1944.03.25
Burton, Dorothy Virginia Sisk (1st marriage)	Burton, Ralph Monroe	1944.08.24
Burton, Dorothy Virginia Sisk (2nd marriage)	Seay, Charlie P.	1957.06.22 after
Burton, Dr. Robert Elmore	Baxter, Nannie	1917
Burton, Drucilla B. Knight	Burton, Jr., William J. ["fifth"]	1867.12.30 or 1868.01.02
Burton, Dulcibella "Dulcie"	Burton, Richard	1870 by
Burton, Edith	Umphrey, FNU	1900 and 1920.04.15 between
Burton, Edna C. Way (1st marriage)	Burton, Sr., Sidney / Sydney Ellsworth	1955.09.03 before
Burton, Edna C. Way (2nd marriage)	Dallman, Marvin D.	1974.05.15 after
Burton, Edna E.	Leake, Clarence M.	1942.04.10 after
Burton, Edward Henry	Welch, Laura	1930 after
Burton, Edward James [black] [son of the black Frank Burton]	Buckner, Mildred Virginia [black]	1932.08.27
Burton, Edward M. "Eddie"	Williams, Elizabeth	1917.05.01 and 1930.01.25 between
Burton, Elijah J.	Bettis, Letha / Lethe Anne	1882.10.06 or 1882.10.08 ?
Burton, Elijah M. [Elijah Marquess Burton ?]	Hearn, Margaret ?	1841 ?
Burton, Eliza A.	Petit, FNU ?	1841 before
Burton, Eliza V. Ballard	Burton, Arthur A.	1885.02.12 or 1885.02.18
Burton, Elizabeth	Burton, Jr., James B.	1850 before
Burton, Elizabeth	Burton, Harris W.	1830 by
Burton, Elizabeth "Betsy" Bowler	Burton, Sr., William E.	1835 by
Burton, Elizabeth Chilton	Burton, William J. [son of Thomas S. Burton?]	1846 by
Burton, Elizabeth H. "Bettie / Betty"	Harding, E. P.	1880.12.26 or 1881.01.03
Burton, Elizabeth Musselman Brummett (2nd marriage)	Burden/Burton, Jesse	1809 after

NAME	CONSORT	DATE
Burton, Elizabeth Musselman Brummett (3rd marriage)	Reed, Gustavus	1858.03.20
Burton, Elizabeth Williams	Burton, Edward M. "Eddie"	1917.05.01 and 1930.01.25 between
Burton, Ella	Payne, Gustavus "Gus/Gusty"	1902.06.01
Burton, Ellen Dunnington	Burton, James A.	1845 by
Burton, Elsie Mae / May [Fredericksburg]	Hove, Helmer M.	1944
Burton, Elwood Winston [the elder]	Harding, Myrtle V.	1924.07.05
Burton, Emily M.	Brown, FNU	1843 after
Burton, Ernest William	Boutyard, Florence Mary	1917.11.24
Burton, Ernestine Florence / Florence Ernestine	Payne, Warren Edward	1934.05.19
Burton, Erva V. "Billie" "Sis"	Murphy, FNU ?	1944 and 1947 between
Burton, Esther	Grinnan, David L.	1936 and 1972 between
Burton, Eula Meadows	Burton, Cecil Preston	1942
Burton, Fannie D. Guy	Burton, John H.	1907.03.25
Burton, Fielding B.	Webb, Virginia "Jennie"	1850 circa
Burton, Fielding W.	Trigger, Lady Mazella	1926.01.09
Burton, Fleda C. Curtis	Burton, Major	1919.09.05 or 1919.09.06
Burton, Florence Mary Boutyard / Boutchyard	Burton, Ernest William	1917.11.24
Burton, Flossie Almeda	Plaskett, John M.	1929.09.26
Burton, FNU [Mrs. George Burton] [NFI]	Burton, George B. [son of Richard Burton]	1919.02.07 before
Burton, Frances Eunice "Fannie / Fanny" Cooper (1st marriage)	Burton, Maurice Walter	1904.12.27
Burton, Frances Eunice "Fannie / Fanny" Cooper (2nd marriage)	Berry, Norman	1926.07.03
Burton, Frank Edwin	Burton, Agnes Margaret	1931.01.14
Burton, Frank [the elder black Frank Burton] (1st marriage)	Pullen / Puller, Lucy Kate [black]	1914.12.07 by

NAME	CONSORT	DATE
Burton, Frank [the elder black Frank Burton] (2nd marriage)	Coleman, Nancy [black]	1941.06.09
Burton, George	LNU, Mary	1800 by
Burton, George B.	LNU, FNU ("Mrs. George Burton")	1919.02.07 by
Burton, George Farrar [Albemarle? / Stafford]	Samuel, Thelma	1951.04.28 by
Burton, Georgeanna / Georgianna "Anna / Annie" Patton	Burton, Robert L.	1877.04.26
Burton, Glendie S.	Johnson, Sidney	1927
Burton, Grace [Stafford?]	Burton, James Grover	1915.12 by
Burton, Harris W.	LNU, Elizabeth	1830 by
Burton, Haswell	Moxley, Leatha Ann	1880.06.03
Burton, Helen Elizabeth Newton [Elizabeth Helen Newton Burton?]	Burton, Alfred Wilson	1930 after
Burton, Hester A. Limbrick / Limerick	Burton, Thomas R.	1891.01.03 or 1891.01.04
Burton, Ida Bell / Belle Humphries (1st marriage)	Burton, William Washington	1889.11.06
Burton, Ida Bell / Belle Humphries (2nd marriage)	McGhee, Sr., Reuben H.	1903.09.02 or 1903.09.09
Burton, Ida R.	Hewitt, Peter	1878.08.28 or 1878.08.29
Burton, Ida V. (1st marriage)	Burton, Charles	1889.04.17
Burton, Ida V. (2nd marriage)	Skidmore, Robert H.	1899.07.09
Burton, Inez Marguerite	Payne, Sr., Laney George	1935.12.12
Burton, Ira Richard	unknown consort	1929 by
Burton, Irene Lee Grinnan	Burton, Jr., Benjamin Lewis / Louis	1937.05.01
Burton, Isaac	Marquess, Mary	1801 by
Burton, Isabella	Monroe, Joseph A.	1872.01.17
Burton, Iva Davis Monroe	Burton, Sr., Benjamin Lewis / Louis "Bennie / Benny"	1904.03.06
Burton, James [James B. Burton, Sr.?]	Taylor, FNU ?	1780s by ?

NAME	CONSORT	DATE
Burton, Jr., James [James B. Burton, Jr.?]	LNU, Elizabeth	1850 by
Burton, James A.	Dunnington, Ellen	1845 by
Burton, James Alexander "Sandy"	LNU, Mary A. (Ann?)	1860 by
Burton, James B.	Stephens/Stevens, Minnie V. (Virginia?)	1905.01.11
Burton, James B. "J. B."	West, Mary W. "Mollie / Molly"	1879.12.16 or 1879.12.17
Burton, James Edward	Humphries, Minnie Elizabeth	1917.09.13
Burton, James Grover	LNU, Grace	1915.12 by
Burton, James Lester	LNU, Shirley	1954.09.30 after
Burton, James William	Powell, Pauline Bernice	1938
Burton, Jane	Burton, Richard	1870.07.16 by
Burton, Jane	Burton, Nathaniel [the younger]	1810 by
Burton, Jane F. Bettis (or Dunnington?)	Burton, Marshall	1842 by
Burton, Jane McKinley "Janie"	Marlow / Marlowe, John	1930 by
Burton, Jesse [Jesse Burden / Burton]	Brummett, Elizabeth Musselman	1809 after
Burton, John [John William Burton / William John Burton ?]	LNU, Susan	1809 before ?
Burton, John [son of Elijah J. Burton]	Portch, Nettie M.	1893.11.22
Burton, Sr., John Broaddus	Lowry, Margaret "Maggie"	1885.09.10
Burton, John H. [Washington, DC / Stafford]	Guy, Fannie D.	1907.03.25
Burton, Joseph Lee (1st marriage)	Humphries, Nora V. Burton	1907.09.04 ?
Burton, Joseph Lee (2nd marriage)	Cooper, Mae Ballard	1935 after
Burton, Joseph S.	LNU, Maria A.	1840s by
Burton, Joyce Ann Shepherd	Burton, Sr., Linwood Ashby "Dober"	1948.05 or 1949
Burton, Judson Marshall	Hummer, Maude Virginia	1912.06.27 or 1912.07.04
Burton, Julia A. [Stafford or Louisa?]	Burton, Daniel B.	1881.06.11 by
Burton, Julian	LNU, Loraine	1930

NAME	CONSORT	DATE
Burton, Katherine E. "Katie"	Hudson, Sidney Bradford	1923.12.(04?)
Burton, Kimmie (or Kennie?) A. [Kimmie A. Burton (Schofield?) Reed ?] (1ˢᵗ marriage ?)	Schofield, Oliver Carlton ?	1905.06.03 by
Burton, Kimmie (or Kennie?) A. [Kimmie A. Burton (Schofield?) Reed ?] (2ⁿᵈ marriage ?)	Reed, FNU	1925.06.04 by
Burton, Lady Mazella Trigger	Burton, Fielding W.	1926.01.09
Burton, Leatha Ann Moxley	Burton, Haswell	1880.06.03
Burton, Leathea / Leathie Virginia	Blaisdell, Clarence George	1926.05.01
Burton, Leona M. ("Lizzie"?)	Mills, Alfred	1916.09.19
Burton, Leonard	Burton, Minnie C.	1908.06.(29?)
Burton, Lester Clifton	Bryant, Mae	1925.11.25 and 1954.09.30 between
Burton, Letha / Lethe Anne Bettis	Burton, Elijah J.	1882.10.06
Burton, Lettice	Jefferies, Alexander	1741.09.30
Burton, Lillian Bell "Lillie / Lilly" Monroe	Burton, Oliver R. "Ollie"	1915.10.06
Burton, Lillian Embrey	Burton, Charles "Charlie"	1921.11.03
Burton, Sr., Linwood Ashby "Dober" (1ˢᵗ marriage)	Shepherd, Joyce Ann	1948.05 or 1949
Burton, Sr., Linwood Ashby "Dober" (2ⁿᵈ marriage)	Hall or Meade, Lillian Mae	1956.03.24 and 1967.01.08 between
Burton, Lucinda "Lucy" Truslow	Burton, Jr., William E.	1857.10.15
Burton, Lucinda / Lucindy "Lucy"	Turner, Newton A.	1850 by
Burton, Lucy Kate Pullen / Puller [black?]	Burton, Frank [black]	1914.12.09 before
Burton, Lucy P.	Jones, E. F.	1881.04.06 or 1881.04.13
Burton, Lucy Virginia (suspected marriage)	Berry, James Allen ?	1942 ?
Burton, Mae Ballard Cooper [Stafford ?] (1ˢᵗ marriage)	Cooper, Edward Howard	1905.09.03
Burton, Mae Ballard Cooper [Stafford ?] (2ⁿᵈ marriage)	Burton, Joseph Lee	1935.02.22 after

NAME	CONSORT	DATE
Burton, Mae Bryant (1ˢᵗ marriage)	Burton, Lester Clifton	1925.11.25 and 1954.09.30 between
Burton, Mae Bryant (2ⁿᵈ marriage)	Boutchyard, FNU	1954.09.30 after
Burton, Mae Lawhorne ? [Stafford ?]	Burton, Warren	1921 after
Burton, Mahala Brown	Burton, Parker F. "Jesse"	1861.12.27
Burton, Major	Curtis, Fleda C.	1919.09.06
Burton, Margaret "Maggie" Lowry	Burton, Sr., John Broaddus	1885.09.10
Burton, Margaret (A.?) Pollard	Burton, William (L. or S.?)	1820 by
Burton, Margaret A.	Burton, David E. [son of Columbus Ashby Burton]	1929.06.07 before
Burton, Margaret A. "Margie" ?	Fitzhugh, Howard	1955.02.08 before
Burton, Margaret Hearn ?	Burton, Elijah M. [Elijah Marquess Burton ?]	1841 ?
Burton, Margaret Lloyd ?	Burton, Archibald Lee "Archie" "Buck"	1930 after ?
Burton, Margaret Mae Carneal	Burton, Robert Franklin "Bobbie"	1933
Burton, Maria A.	Burton, Joseph S.	1840s by
Burton, Marie	Grinnan, Sr., Arnold P.	1929.11.27
Burton, Marie Elizabeth	Mitchell, Jr., William Thomas	1937.12.31 or 1938.01.02
Burton, Marietta "Flossie" Curtis	Burton, Columbus Ashby	1906.05.06
Burton, Marshall	Bettis ?, Jane F. (or Jane F. Dunnington?)	1842 by
Burton, Martha (Bryant?) Foley / Folio	Burton, William ["first"]	1690 circa
Burton, Martha A.	Bradshaw, John F.	1869.06.24
Burton, Mary	Burton, George	1800 by
Burton, Mary	Burton, Samuel ["second" Samuel]	1787 by
Burton, Mary	Rodgers, James M.	1843 by
Burton, Mary "Mollie"	Burton, William F.	1889.02.05 or 1890.02.05
Burton, Mary A. (Ann?)	Burton, James Alexander "Sandy"	1860 by
Burton, Mary A. Ballard	Burton, Arthur A.	1849.07.28

NAME	CONSORT	DATE
Burton, Mary A. Franklin	Burton, Jr., William J.	1854.12.16 or 1855.12.16
Burton, Mary Curtis [Mary Dodd Burton ?] [Fredericksburg ?]	Burton, Sr., Carroll Eugene	1951.10.23 after
Burton, Mary E. (Ellen ?) Boutyard	Burton, William Jesse	1876.05.14
Burton, Mary E. (Elizabeth?) (suspected marriage)	Bloxton, Jr., William Ashby ? (2ⁿᵈ marriage)	1846 circa
Burton, Mary F.	Littrell, Charles	1886.10.17
Burton, Mary G.	Bullock, Charles N.	1938.06.15
Burton, Mary H.	Brown, Richard	1856.08.14
Burton, Mary I.	Jefferson, Joseph Rudolph [Rudolph Joseph Jefferson ?]	1941.09.20
Burton, Mary J.	Brandenburg, C. M. [Clarence M. Brandenburg?]	1883.12.19
Burton, Mary M. [Stafford ?]	Templeman, James Nelson	1922.12
Burton, Mary Marquess	Burton, Isaac	1801 by
Burton, Mary Virginia "Virgie"	Harris, John Thomas	1904.11.23
Burton, Mary W. "Mollie / Molly" West	Burton, James B. "J. B."	1879.12.16 or 1879.12.17
Burton, Maude Virginia Hummer [Loudoun ?]	Burton, Judson Marshall	1912.06.27 or 1912.07.04
Burton, Maurice Walter	Cooper, Frances "Fannie / Fanny" Eunice (1ˢᵗ marriage)	1904.12.27
Burton, Media V.	Patton, Erland L.	1927.04.16
Burton, Melvin Strother	LNU, Mary C.	1925.07.30 by
Burton, Merritt Dickinson "Dippy"	LNU, Gernie R.	1990.02.06 before
Burton, Mildred [Stafford?]	Cassiday, FNU	1928.05.22 before
Burton, Minnie C.	Burton, Leonard	1908.06.(29?)
Burton, Minnie Elizabeth Humphries	Burton, James Edward	1917.09.13
Burton, Minnie V. (Virginia?) Stephens / Stevens	Burton, James B. [son of James A. Burton]	1905.01.11
Burton, Myrtle V. Harding (1ˢᵗ marriage)	Burton, Elwood Winston [the elder]	1924.07.07

NAME	CONSORT	DATE
Burton, Myrtle V. Harding (2nd marriage)	Dallman, Marvin D.	1955.09.03 and 1974.05.15 between
Burton, Nancy Burns [Nancy Pollard Burton ?]	Burton, Cary	1833 by ?
Burton, Nancy E. Madison Stevens ? [Fredericksburg ?]	Burton, Archibald Lee "Archie" "Buck"	1930 and 1973.06.20 between
Burton, Nannie Lee	Berry, Sr., John William	1912.12.19
Burton, Nathaniel [the elder]	unknown consort	1750s?
Burton, Nathaniel [the younger]	LNU, Jane	1810 by
Burton, Nettie M. Portch	Burton, John [son of Elijah J. Burton]	1893.11.22
Burton, Noel Robert	Jones, Bessie Larkin	1930 by
Burton, Nora V. [Nora V. Burton Humphries Burton ?] (1st marriage)	Humphries, Samuel D.	1903.09.25
Burton, Nora V. [Nora V. Burton Humphries Burton ?] (2nd marriage)	Burton, Joseph Lee (1st marriage)	1907.09.04
Burton, Olga Belle	Franklin, John R.	1891.11.04
Burton, Oliver R. "Ollie"	Monroe, Lillian Bell "Lillie / Lilly"	1915.10.06
Burton, Sr., Oliver Stansbury "Ollie" (1st marriage)	Garner, Dollie / Dolly M.	1938.12.19 before
Burton, Sr., Oliver Stansbury "Ollie" (2nd marriage)	Miniclier, Agnes Elizabeth	1941.10.25
Burton, Parker F. "Jesse"	Brown, Mahala	1861.12.27
Burton, Pauline Bernice Powell (1st marriage)	Burton, James William	1938
Burton, Pauline Bernice Powell (2nd marriage)	Daniels, Howard Russell "Casey"	1962 circa
Burton, Pauline Kurz	Burton, Walter Eugene	1931.12.19
Burton, Pauline M.	Lee, Richard Henry	1924.06.26
Burton, Pearl Vivian	Jett, John Sidney	1931
Burton, Pemiley G.	Kelley/Kelly, James M.	1904.06.07 license
Burton, Rachel Porch	Burton, William ["third"]	1753.10.07
Burton, Ralph Monroe	Sisk, Dorothy Virginia	1944.08.24

NAME	CONSORT	DATE
Burton, Renald / Reynold Vinson	Yeatman, Bertha M.	1921.09.28
Burton, Richard	LNU, Dulcibella "Dulcie"	1870 by
Burton, Richard [son of John Burton] (suspected 1" marriage)	LNU, Mary (suspected)	1840 by
Burton, Richard [son of John Burton] (2nd ? marriage)	Monroe, Willie Ann	1850 by
Burton, Robert Franklin "Bobbie"	Carneal, Margaret Mae	1933
Burton, Robert Gilbert	Payne, Aline McGill	1954 or 1954.07.10
Burton, Robert L.	Patton, Georgeanna / Georgianna "Anna / Annie"	1877.04.26
Burton, Robert L. [son of Benjamin Burton, Sr.]	Gallahan, Ruth	1988.06.01 by
Burton, Rosa B.	Sullivan, Hunter	1910.10.04
Burton, Ruby Jane Ellington (1st marriage)	Burton, Theodore R. T.	1928.10.20
Burton, Ruby Jane Ellington (2nd marriage)	Allen, Marion Haden	1936
Burton, Ruth Gallahan	Burton, Robert L. [son of Benjamin Burton, Sr.]	1988.06.01 by
Burton, Samuel ["second" Samuel]	LNU, Mary	1787 by
Burton (or Tyson?), Sarah "Sallie / Sally"	Southard, James Samuel	1867.06.16
Burton, Sarah Coakley	Burton, FNU	1838.10.08 before
Burton, Sarah E. Portch (1st marriage)	Burton, William Henry	1889.12.06
Burton, Sarah E. Portch (2nd marriage)	Mankey, Francis	1906.11.14
Burton, Sarah E. "Nannie" [Sarah E. "Nannie" Burton Green Dye] (1st marriage)	Green, Sr., Milton	1945.06.09 or 1945.06.15
Burton, Sarah E. "Nannie" [Sarah E. "Nannie" Burton Green Dye] (2nd marriage)	Dye, William Gaines	1985 by
Burton, Sarah Limbrick	Burton, FNU	1826.04.11 by
Burton, Sarah Spicer	Burton, William ["second"]	1725.12.14

NAME	CONSORT	DATE
Burton, Sarah Williams [Sarah "Sallie" Berton / Burton Williams Burton ?] (2nd marriage)	Burton, William [William E. Burton, Sr. ?] (2nd marriage)	1866.11.04
Burton, Sarah	Way, R. W. [Rhonie W. Way]	1905.09.26
Burton, Jr., Sidney Ellsworth (1st marriage)	Lunsford, Betty Jean	1982.08.19 before
Burton, Jr., Sidney Ellsworth (2nd marriage)	LNU Geneva (or Sue ?)	1982.08.19 after
Burton, Sr., Sidney / Sydney Ellsworth	Way, Edna C. [Edna C. Way Burton Dallman] (1st marriage)	1947.06.13 before ?
Burton, Susan	Burton, John ?	1809 by ?
Burton, Susan	Burton, William [son of James Burton] or John Burton ?	1809 by ?
Burton, Susan A.	Sullivan, George W.	1867.10.24
Burton, Susan (B.?) "Susie" Payne	Burton, Archibald B. "Archie"	1906.12.26 or 1906.12.27
Burton, Susanna Walker [Culpeper ?]	Burton, Cary	1812 by ?
Burton, Susannah "Sukey" Jett	Burton, William (William J. Burton, Sr.?) ["fourth"]	1794 by ?
Burton, Terrissa M.	Guy, FNU	1848.10.19
Burton, Thelma H.	Coghill, Rudolph [Edgar Rudolph Coghill, Sr. ?]	1925.02.15
Burton, Thelma Samuel [Caroline / Stafford]	Burton, George Farrar	1951.04.28 by
Burton, Thelma [Stafford ?]	Miller, FNU	1965.05.05 after
Burton, Theodore R. T.	Ellington, Ruby Jane (1st marriage)	1928.10.20
Burton, Thomas R.	Limbrick, Hester A. (or Limerick?)	1891.01.03 or 1891.01.04
Burton, Thomas S.	unknown consort	1820 by ?
Burton, Thompson	Burton, Almeta Jane "Virginia / Jennie / Jenny"	1875.03.04
Burton, Virginia "Jennie" Webb	Burton, Fielding (B.?)	1850 circa
Burton, Virginia B. "Virgie"	Ennis, John E. (1st marriage ?)	1906.04.25
Burton, Virginia F.	Ellington, John	1853.12.12
Burton, Walter Eugene	Kurz, Pauline	1931.12.19

NAME	CONSORT	DATE
Burton, Warren	Lawhorne, Mae ?	1921 after
Burton, Wellington W.	Downs, Annie Laura	1877.02.19
Burton, William ["first"]	Foley / Folio, Martha (Bryant?)	1690 circa
Burton, William ["second"]	Spicer, Sarah	1725.12.14
Burton, William ["third"]	Porch, Rachel	1753.10.07
Burton, William [William J. Burton, Sr.?] ["fourth"]	Jett, Susannah "Sukey"	1794 by
Burton, William [William John Burton / John William Burton ?]	LNU, Susan	1809 by ?
Burton, Jr., William E.	Truslow, Lucinda "Lucy"	1857.10.15
Burton, Sr., William E. (1ˢᵗ marriage)	Bowler, Elizabeth "Betsy"	1835 by
Burton, Sr., William E. (2ⁿᵈ marriage)	Williams, Sarah [Sarah "Sallie" Berton / Burton Williams Burton ?] (2ⁿᵈ marriage)	1866.11.04
Burton, William F.	Burton, Mary "Mollie"	1889.02.05 or 1890.02.05
Burton, William Henry	Portch, Sarah E. [Sarah E. Portch Burton Mankey] (1ˢᵗ marriage)	1889.12.05
Burton, William J.	Chilton, Elizabeth	1846 by
Burton, William J. [William J. Burton, Jr. ?] ["fifth"] (1ˢᵗ marriage)	Franklin, Mary A.	1854.12.16 or 1855.12.16
Burton, William J. [William J. Burton, Jr. ?] ["fifth"] (2ⁿᵈ marriage)	Knight, Drucilla B.	1867.12.30 or 1868.01.02
Burton, William Jesse	Boutyard, Mary E. (Ellen?)	1876.05.14
Burton, William [William (L. or S.) Burton]	Pollard, Margaret	1820 by
Burton, William M.	Burton, Winnie Davis	1917.04.26
Burton, Willie Ann Monroe	Burton, Richard	1850 by
Burton, Willie Ann	Burgess, John A.	1883.05.29 or 1883.05.31
Burton, Wilson	Dickerson / Dickinson, Alice L.	1891.09.29 or 1891.09.30
Burton, Winnie Davis	Burton, William M.	1917.04.26

Selected Marriages

Alphabetical by Consort

CONSORT	NAME	DATE
Allen, Marion Haden	Burton, Ruby Jane Ellington (2nd marriage)	1936
Ballard, Eliza V.	Burton, Arthur A. (2nd marriage)	1885.02.18
Ballard, Mary A.	Burton, Arthur A. (1st marriage)	1849.07.28
Baxter, Nannie	Burton, Dr. Robert Elmore	1917
Beach, Daniel Lewis / Louis	Burton, Arnita Ellen	1947.06.13
Berry, James Allen ?	Burton, Lucy Virginia (suspected marriage)	1942 ?
Berry, Sr., John William	Burton, Nannie Lee	1912.12.19
Berry, Norman	Burton, Frances Eunice "Fannie / Fanny" Cooper (2nd marriage)	1926.07.03
Bettis ?, Jane F. (or Jane F. Dunnington?)	Burton, Marshall	1842 by
Bettis, Letha / Lethe Anne	Burton, Elijah J.	1882.10.06 or 1882.10.08 ?
Blaisdell, Clarence George	Burton, Leathea / Leathie Virginia	1926.05.01
Bloxton, Jr., William Ashby ?	Burton, Mary E. (Elizabeth ?)	1846 circa
Bourne, Charlotte	Burton, Jr., Arthur James "Junior"	1943.06.03
Boutchyard, FNU	Burton, Mae Bryant (2nd marriage)	1954.09.30 after
Boutyard, Florence Mary	Burton, Ernest William	1917.11.24
Boutyard, Mary E. (Ellen?)	Burton, William Jesse	1876.05.14

CONSORT	NAME	DATE
Bowler, Elizabeth "Betsy"	Burton, Sr., William E. (1ˢᵗ marriage)	1835 by
Bradshaw, John F.	Burton, Martha A.	1869.06.24
Brandenburg, C. M. [Clarence M. Brandenburg?]	Burton, Mary J.	1883.12.19
Brooks, Henry H.	Burton, Ann Eliza "Annie"	1870.09.17
Brown, FNU	Burton, Emily M.	1843 after
Brown, Mahala	Burton, Parker F. "Jesse"	1861.12.27
Brown, Richard	Burton, Mary H.	1856.08.14
Brummett, Elizabeth Musselman [Elizabeth Musselman Brummett Burton Reed] (2ⁿᵈ marriage)	Burton, Jesse [Jesse Burden/Burton]	1809 after
Bryant, Mae	Burton, Lester Clifton	1925.11.25 and 1954.09.30 between
Buckner, Mildred Virginia [black]	Burton, Edward James [black] [son of the black Frank Burton]	1932.08.27
Bullock, Charles N.	Burton, Mary G.	1938.06.15
Burgess, John A.	Burton, Willie Ann	1883.05.29 or 1883.05.31
Burns (or Pollard?), Nancy	Burton, Cary (2ⁿᵈ marriage)	1832 circa
Burton, Agnes Margaret	Burton, Frank Edwin	1931.01.14
Burton, Almeta Jane "Virginia / Jennie / Jenny"	Burton, Thompson	1875.03.04
Burton, Charles	Burton, Ida V. [Ida V. Burton Skidmore] (1ˢᵗ marriage)	1889.04.17
Burton, Frank Edwin	Burton, Agnes Margaret	1931.01.14
Burton, Ida V.	Burton, Charles	1889.04.17
Burton, James (unmarried consort?)	Burton, Ann "Nancy" [the younger]	1830s ?
Burton, Joseph Lee (1ˢᵗ marriage)	Burton, Nora V. [Nora V. Burton Humphries Burton ?] (2ⁿᵈ marriage)	1907.09.04
Burton, Leonard	Burton, Minnie C.	1908.06.(29?)
Burton, Mary "Mollie"	Burton, William F.	1889.02.05 or 1890.02.05
Burton, Minnie C.	Burton, Leonard	1908.06.(29?)

CONSORT	NAME	DATE
Burton, Thompson	Burton, Almeta Jane "Virginia / Jennie / Jenny"	1875.03.04
Burton, William F.	Burton, Mary "Mollie"	1889.02.05 or 1890.02.05
Burton, William M.	Burton, Winnie Davis	1917.04.26
Burton, Winnie Davis	Burton, William M.	1917.04.26
Carneal, Margaret Mae	Burton, Robert Franklin "Bobbie"	1933
Cassiday, FNU	Burton, Mildred [Stafford?]	1928.05.22 before
Chilton, Elizabeth	Burton, William J.	1846 by
Coghill, Rudolph [Edgar Rudolph Coghill, Sr. ?]	Burton, Thelma H.	1925.02.15
Coleman, Nancy [black]	Burton, Frank [the elder black Frank Burton] (2nd marriage)	1941.06.09
Conner / Connor / O'Conner / O'Connor, Jr., William Henry	Burton, Ann Eliza	1866.04.17 or 1866.04.19
Cooper, Frances Eunice "Fannie / Fanny" [Frances Eunice "Fannie / Fanny" Cooper Burton Berry] (1st marriage)	Burton, Maurice Walter	1904.12.27
Cooper, Mae Ballard (2nd marriage)	Burton, Joseph Lee (2nd marriage)	1935 after
Cooper, Melvin E.	Burton, Annette J. "Nettie"	1907.02.25
Craig, Blanche May	Burton, Sr., Arthur James	1922.01.11
Curtis, Fleda C.	Burton, Major	1919.09.06
Curtis, Marietta "Flossie"	Burton, Columbus Ashby	1906.05.06
Curtis, Mary (or Mary Dodd ?)	Burton, Sr., Carroll Eugene [Fredericksburg] (2nd marriage)	1951.10.23 and 1972.12.12 between
Dallman, Marvin D. (1st marriage)	Burton, Myrtle V. Harding (2nd marriage)	1955.09.03 and 1974.05.15 between
Dallman, Marvin D. (2nd marriage)	Burton, Edna C. Way (2nd marriage)	1974.05.15 after
Daniels, Howard Russell "Casey"	Burton, Pauline Bernice Powell (2nd marriage)	1962 circa
Dawson or Dorsey, John Henry	Burton, Anne "Annie" Lee [black] [Fredericksburg ?]	1888.06.27 or 1888.06.28
Dickerson / Dickinson, Alice L.	Burton, Wilson	1891.09.29 or 1891.09.30

CONSORT	NAME	DATE
Downs, Annie Laura	Burton, Wellington W.	1877.02.19
Dunnington, Ellen	Burton, James A.	1845 by
Edwards, FNU	Burton, Dora Lee	1939.07.26 by
Ellington, John	Burton, Virginia F.	1853.12.12
Ellington, Linwood H.	Burton, Dorothy Virginia [Fredericksburg / Stafford]	1944.03.25
Ellington, Ruby Jane [Ruby Jane Ellington Allen] (1st marriage)	Burton, Theodore R. T.	1928.10.20
Embrey, Lillian	Burton, Charles "Charlie"	1921.11.03
Ennis, John E. (1st marriage ?)	Burton, Virginia B. "Virgie"	1906.04.25
Fitzhugh, Howard	Burton, Margaret A. "Margie" ?	1955.02.08 before
Fleming, Octavia B. [Octavia B. Fleming Burton Kendig] (1st marriage)	Burton, Beverly C.	1878.09.11
Foley / Folio, Martha (Bryant?) (2nd marriage)	Burton, William ["first"]	1690 circa
Franklin, John R.	Burton, Olga Belle	1891.11.04
Franklin, Mary A.	Burton, William J. [William J. Burton, Jr. ?] ["fifth"] (1st marriage)	1854.12.16 or 1855.12.16
Gallahan, Ruth	Burton, Robert L. [son of Benjamin Burton, Sr.]	1988.06.01 by
Garner, Dollie / Dolly M.	Burton, Sr., Oliver Stansbury "Ollie" (1st marriage)	1938.12.19 before
Green, Sr., Milton	Burton, Sarah E. "Nannie" [Sarah E. "Nannie" Burton Green Dye] (1st marriage)	1945.06.09 or 1945.06.15
Grinnan, David L.	Burton, Esther	1936 and 1972 between
Grinnan, Irene Lee	Burton, Jr., Benjamin Lewis / Louis	1937.05.01
Grinnan, Sr., Arnold P.	Burton, Marie	1929.11.27
Guy, Fannie D.	Burton, John H. [Washington, DC / Stafford]	1907.03.25
Guy, FNU	Burton, Terrissa M.	1848.10.19
Hall or Meade, Lillian Mae	Burton, Sr., Linwood Ashby "Dober" (2nd marriage)	1956.03.24 and 1967.01.08 between

CONSORT	NAME	DATE
Harding, E. P.	Burton, Elizabeth H. "Bettie / Betty"	1880.12.26 or 1881.01.03
Harding, McDuff	Burton, Addie T.	1901.01.28
Harding, Myrtle V. [Myrtle V. Harding Burton Dallman] (1ˢᵗ marriage)	Burton, Elwood Winston [the elder]	1924.07.05
Harris, John Thomas	Burton, Mary Virginia "Virgie"	1904.11.23
Hearn, Margaret ?	Burton, Elijah M. [Elijah Marquess Burton ?]	1841 ?
Hewitt, Peter	Burton, Ida R.	1878.08.28 or 1878.08.29
Hoover, FNU	Burton, Carrie	1969.12 before
Hove, Helmer M.	Burton, Elsie Mae / May [Fredericksburg]	1944
Hudson, Sidney Bradford	Burton, Katherine E. "Katie"	1923.12.(04?)
Hummer, Maude Virginia	Burton, Judson Marshall	1912.06.27 or 1912.07.04
Humphries, Minnie Elizabeth	Burton, James Edward	1917.09.13
Humphries, Nora V. Burton (2ⁿᵈ marriage)	Burton, Joseph Lee (1ˢᵗ marriage)	1907.09.04 ?
Humphries, Samuel D.	Burton, Nora V. [Nora V. Burton Humphries Burton ?] (1ˢᵗ marriage)	1903.09.25
Jefferies, Alexander	Burton, Lettice	1741.09.30
Jefferson, Joseph Rudolph [Rudolph Joseph Jefferson ?]	Burton, Mary I.	1941.09.20
Jett, John Sidney	Burton, Pearl Vivian	1931
Jett, Susannah "Sukey"	Burton, William [William J. Burton, Sr.?] ["fourth"]	1794 by
Johnson, FNU	Burton, Alma May [Fredericksburg?]	1964 by
Johnson, Sidney	Burton, Glendie S.	1927
Jones, Bessie Larkin	Burton, Noel Robert	1930 by
Jones, Carrie L.	Burton, Clarence	1903.10.04
Jones, E. F.	Burton, Lucy P.	1881.04.06 or 1881.04.13
Kelley/Kelly, James M.	Burton, Pemiley G.	1904.06.07 license

CONSORT	NAME	DATE
Knight, Clarence Newman	Burton, Carrie Irene	1902
Knight, Drucilla B.	Burton, William J. [William J. Burton, Jr. ?] ["fifth"] (2nd marriage)	1867.12.30 or 1868.01.02
Kurz, Pauline	Burton, Walter Eugene	1931.12.19
Lawhorne, Mae ?	Burton, Warren	1921 after
Leake, Clarence M.	Burton, Edna E.	1942.04.10 after
Lee, Richard Henry	Burton, Pauline M.	1924.06.26
Limbrick / Limerick, Hester A.	Burton, Thomas R.	1891.01.03 or 1891.01.04
Littrell, Charles	Burton, Mary F.	1886.10.17
Lloyd, Margaret ?	Burton, Archibald Lee "Archie" "Buck" (suspected 1st marriage)	1930 after ?
LNU, Agnes Marie	Burton, Sr., Carroll Eugene [Fredericksburg] (1st marriage)	1951.10.23 before
LNU, Dulcibella "Dulcie"	Burton, Richard	1870 by
LNU, Elizabeth	Burton, Jr., James [James B. Burton, Jr.?]	1850 by
LNU, Elizabeth	Burton, Harris W.	1830 by
LNU, FNU ("Mrs. George Burton") [NFI]	Burton, George B.	1919.02.07 by
LNU Geneva (or Sue ?)	Burton, Jr., Sidney Ellsworth (2nd marriage)	1982.08.19 after
LNU, Gernie R.	Burton, Merritt Dickinson "Dippy"	1990.02.06 before
LNU, Grace	Burton, James Grover	1915.12 by
LNU, Jane	Burton, Nathaniel [the younger]	1810 by
LNU, Julia A.	Burton, Daniel B.	1881 before
LNU, Loraine	Burton, Julian	1930
LNU, Margaret A.	Burton, David E.	1929.06.07 before
LNU, Maria A.	Burton, Joseph S.	1840s by
LNU, Mary	Burton, Samuel ["second" Samuel]	1787 by
LNU, Mary	Burton, George	1800 by
LNU, Mary (suspected)	Burton, Richard [son of John Burton] (suspected 1st marriage)	1840 by

CONSORT	NAME	DATE
LNU, Mary A. (Ann?)	Burton, James Alexander "Sandy"	1860 by
LNU, Mary C.	Burton, Melvin Strother	1925.07.30 by
LNU, Shirley	Burton, James Lester	1954.09.30 after
LNU, Susan	Burton, John [John William Burton / William John Burton ?]	1809 by ?
LNU, Susan	Burton, William [William John Burton / John William Burton ?]	1809 by ?
Lowry, Margaret "Maggie"	Burton, Sr., John Broaddus	1885.09.10
Lunsford, Betty Jean	Burton, Jr., Sidney Ellsworth (1st marriage)	1982.08.19 before
Mankey, Francis	Burton, Sarah E. Portch (2nd marriage)	1906.11.14
Marlow / Marlowe, John	Burton, Jane McKinley "Janie"	1930 by
Marquess, Mary	Burton, Isaac	1801 by
Meade or Hall, Lillian Mae	Burton, Sr., Linwood Ashby "Dober" (2nd marriage)	1956.03.24 and 1967.01.08 between
Meadows, Eula	Burton, Cecil Preston	1942
Miller, FNU	Burton, Thelma [Stafford ?]	1965.05.05 after
Mills, Alfred	Burton, Leona M. ("Lizzie"?)	1916.09.19
Mills, Robert Wyatt	Burton, Alvena "Allie"	1883.02.13 or 1883.02.15
Miniclier, Agnes Elizabeth	Burton, Sr., Oliver Stansbury "Ollie" (2nd marriage)	1941.10.25
Mitchell, Jr., William Thomas	Burton, Marie Elizabeth	1937.12.31 or 1938.01.02
Monroe, Iva Davis	Burton, Sr., Benjamin Lewis / Louis "Bennie / Benny"	1904.03.06
Monroe, Joseph A.	Burton, Isabella	1872.01.17
Monroe, Lillian Bell "Lillie / Lilly"	Burton, Oliver R. "Ollie"	1915.10.06
Monroe, Willie Ann	Burton, Richard [son of John Burton] (2nd ? marriage)	1850 by
Moxley, Leatha Ann	Burton, Haswell	1880.06.03
Murphy, FNU ?	Burton, Erva V. "Billie" "Sis"	1944 and 1947 between
Newton, Helen Elizabeth [Elizabeth Helen Newton ?]	Burton, Alfred Wilson	1930 after
Parker, Margie	Burton, Cecil Melvin	1955.09.03

CONSORT	NAME	DATE
Patton, Erland L.	Burton, Media V.	1927.04.16
Patton, Georgeanna / Georgianna "Anna / Annie"	Burton, Robert L.	1877.04.26
Payne, Aline McGill	Burton, Robert Gilbert	1954 or 1954.07.10
Payne, Gustavus "Gus/Gusty"	Burton, Ella	1902.06.01
Payne, Sr., Laney George	Burton, Inez Marguerite	1935.12.12
Payne, Susan (B.?) "Susie"	Burton, Archibald B. "Archie"	1906.12.26 or 1906.12.27
Payne, Warren Edward	Burton, Ernestine Florence / Florence Ernestine	1934.05.19
Petit, FNU ?	Burton, Eliza A.	1841 before
Plaskett, John M.	Burton, Flossie Almeda	1929.09.26
Pollard, Margaret	Burton, William [William (L. or S.) Burton]	1820 by
Porch, Rachel	Burton, William ["third"]	1753.10.07
Portch, Nettie M.	Burton, John [son of Elijah J. Burton]	1893.11.22
Portch, Sarah E. [Sarah E. Portch Burton Mankey] (1st marriage)	Burton, William Henry	1889.12.05
Powell, Pauline Bernice [Pauline Bernice Powell Burton Daniels] (1st marriage)	Burton, James William	1938
Pullen / Puller, Lucy Kate [black]	Burton, Frank [the elder black Frank Burton] (1st marriage)	1914.12.07 by
Reed, FNU	Burton, Kimmie (or Kennie?) A. [Kimmie A. Burton (Schofield?) Reed ?] (2nd marriage ?)	1925.06.04 by
Reed, Gustavus	Burton, Elizabeth Musselman Brummett (3rd marriage)	1858.03.20
Rodgers, James M.	Burton, Mary	1843 by
Samuel, Thelma	Burton, George Farrar [Albemarle? / Stafford]	1951.04.28 by
Schofield, Oliver Carlton ?	Burton, Kimmie (or Kennie?) A. [Kimmie A. Burton (Schofield?) Reed ?] (1st marriage ?)	1905.06.03 by
Sealy, R. Mason	Burton, Christine [Flossie ? Christine Burton Sealy]	1944 and 1947 between

CONSORT	NAME	DATE
Seay, Charlie P.	Burton, Dorothy Virginia Sisk (2nd marriage)	1957.06.22 after
Shepherd, Joyce Ann	Burton, Sr., Linwood Ashby "Dober" (1st marriage)	1948.05 or 1949
Sisk, Dorothy Virginia [Dorothy Virginia Sisk Burton Seay] (1st marriage)	Burton, Ralph Monroe	1944.08.24
Skidmore, Robert H.	Burton, Ida V. [Ida V. Burton Skidmore] (2nd marriage)	1899.07.09
Southard, Harrison	Burton, Catharine	1843 by ?
Southard, James Samuel	Burton (or Tyson?), Sarah "Sallie / Sally"	1867.06.16
Spicer, Sarah	Burton, William ["second"]	1725.12.14
Stephens / Stevens, Minnie V. (Virginia?)	Burton, James B.	1905.01.11
Stevens, Nancy E. Madison ?	Burton, Archibald Lee "Archie" "Buck" (suspected 2nd marriage)	1973.06.20 before
Sullivan, George W.	Burton, Susan A.	1867.10.24
Sullivan, Hunter	Burton, Rosa B.	1910.10.04
Taylor, FNU ?	Burton, James [James B. Burton, Sr.?]	1780s by ?
Templeman, James Nelson	Burton, Mary M. [Stafford ?]	1922.12
Trigger, Lady Mazella	Burton, Fielding W.	1926.01.09
Truslow, Lucinda "Lucy"	Burton, Jr., William E.	1857.10.15
Turner, Newton A.	Burton, Lucinda / Lucindy "Lucy"	1850 by
Tyson, William	Burton (?), Catharine "Kate" McKenney (2nd marriage)	1833 and 1840 between
Umphrey, FNU	Burton, Edith	1900 and 1920.04.15 between
unknown consort	Burton, Nathaniel [the elder]	1750s?
unknown consort	Burton, Ira Richard	1929 by
unknown consort	Burton, Thomas S.	1820 by ?
Walker, Susanna	Burton, Cary (1st marriage)	1812 before
Walker, William Henry	Burton, Clementina / Clementine	1873.01.19
Way, Ashton Cleveland	Burton, Annie Virginia	1930.12.26

CONSORT	NAME	DATE
Way, Edna C. [Edna C. Way Burton Dallman] (1ˢᵗ marriage)	Burton, Sr., Sidney / Sydney Ellsworth	1947.06.13 before ?
Way, L. L.	Burton, Anne E. "Annie" [Anne E. "Annie" Burton Way Berry] (1ˢᵗ marriage)	1903.08.12
Way, R. W. [Rhonie W. Way]	Burton, Sarah	1905.09.26
Webb, Virginia "Jennie"	Burton, Fielding (B.?)	1850 circa
Welch, Laura	Burton, Edward Henry	1930 after
West, Mary W. "Mollie / Molly"	Burton, James B. "J. B."	1879.12.16 or 1879.12.17
Whited, Irma M.	Burton, Charles Ford	1930 after
Williams, Elizabeth	Burton, Edward M. "Eddie"	1917.05.01 and 1930.01.25 between
Williams, Sarah [Sarah "Sallie / Sally" Berton / Burton Williams Burton ?] (2ⁿᵈ marriage)	Burton, Sr., William E. (2ⁿᵈ marriage ?)	1866.11.04
Yeatman, Bertha M.	Burton, Renald / Reynold Vinson	1921.09.28

A PRE-STAFFORD CHRONOLOGY

T HERE WERE Burtons in Virginia long before Stafford County existed. And, according to some sources, there have been Burtons in England since at least the Middle Ages, when the surname reportedly first came into use. There were even Burtons who served in the Court and army of famed English king Henry V. Regrettably, as I mention above, I was unable to determine the pre-Stafford origins of the Stafford Burton family and, hence, was unable to trace the family lineage back to the Old Country.

More detailed research into the pre-1664 records of Stafford's predecessor districts might yield valuable information about Stafford Burton origins, but that was simply too great an endeavor for me to undertake on top of all the other research I was doing. Still, I cannot ignore the issue completely, so I present here some cursory information about pre-Stafford Burtons in Virginia, followed by a Pre-Stafford Chronology of documented references to Burtons who might have been land owners or residents in or near Stafford predecessor districts.

Early Virginia Burtons

The first Burton in North America might have been John Burden, who was among the members of Sir Walter Raleigh's "Lost Colony" that arrived in 1587 on the outer banks of what is now North Carolina. [Melvin Robinson, *Riddle of the Lost Colony* (New Bern, North Carolina: Owen G. Dunn Co., Publishers, 1946), 64.]

Another source lists him as John Burdon, indicating that the original document was difficult to read. [Conway Whittle Sams, *The Conquest of Virginia: The First Attempt* (Norfolk, Virginia: Keyser-Doherty Printing Corporation, 1924) (Reprinted in 1973 by The Reprint Company, Spartanburg, South Carolina), 507.]

But even though the Burton surname was sometimes spelled "Burden" back then, does John Burden/Burdon really count as a "Burton"? And even though the Outer Banks might have been referred to as "Virginia" at the time, should that area be included in Virginia history today?

The first person with a surname spelled "B-U-R-T-O-N" in Virginia (and, apparently, in North America) was George Burton, who arrived in Jamestown in October 1608 as part of the "Second Supply." (According to Sams, the Second Supply was so named because they were considered the second addition to the First Planters, but they were actually the third company of settlers to arrive.)

George had left England in July 1608, sailing on the ship *Mary and Margaret* under Captain Newport. He was presumably the same George Burton listed in the Second Charter for the Virginia Company, issued by King James I. [Conway Whittle Sams, *The Conquest of Virginia: The Second Attempt* (Norfolk, Virginia: Keyser-Doherty Printing Corporation, 1929) (Reprinted in 1973 by The Reprint Company, Spartanburg, South Carolina), 820-821.]

George accompanied Captain John Smith on some of his travels in Virginia. Although some secondary sources list George as a "gentleman," a facsimile copy of Smith's account lists George Burton among the soldiers, *not* among the "gentleman." [John Smith, *The Generall Historie of Virginia, New England, and the Summer Isles*, Book III, Chapter VIII, "Captain Smith's Journey to Pamavnkee" (London, 1624) (Reprinted in 1966 by Readex Microprint Corporation), 74.]

George's name was not followed by the word "gentleman" in the Virginia Company's Second Charter, either, yet more than one secondary source lists him as "gent." or "gentleman." For example, George Burton is listed among the "Gent." in the Second Supply in Thelma W. Bastow's *Additional Windows, Volume I: Early Virginia and its Peoples.* On the very next page, however, he is not listed among the "gent." but is instead listed among the "souldiers" in the ship *Pinnance*, the second of two ships that Captain John Smith took on a journey to obtain food and provisions from Powhatan in the winter of 1608-1609. [Thelma W. Bastow, *Additional Windows, Volume I: Early Virginia and its Peoples* (Richmond, Virginia: Whittet, Shepperson, Inc., 1980), 37, 38.]

George is also the only Burton included in Alexander Brown's "Brief Biographies of Persons Connected with the Founding of Virginia," and the sparse information provided includes the abbreviation "gent." followed by "paid £12, 10s." [Alexander Brown, *The Genesis of the United States, Vol. II* (New York: Russell & Russell, Inc., 1964), 836.]

The payment was presumably for one share in the Virginia Company. (According to another source, one share cost 12 pounds, 10 shillings. Those who went to Virginia in person, by the way, were known as "planters," whereas "adventurers" were those who only "adventured" their money as an investment in the company, but did not necessarily go to Virginia.) [Nell Marion Nugent, ed., *Cavaliers and Pioneers: Abstracts of Virginia Land Patents and Grants, 1623-1800, in Five Volumes, Volume One, 1623-1666* (Richmond, Virginia: Press of the Dietz Printing Co., 1934), xii.]

Regardless of his social standing, it is very likely that George was the first Burton to ever lay eyes on the area of land that would one day become Stafford County, given Smith's explorations up the Potomac and Rappahannock rivers. This raises the intriguing possibility that the first Burton in North America, the first Burton in Virginia and the first Burton to see what would later become Stafford County, were one and the same man.

A George Burton is also listed multiple times in later records of the Virginia Company of London. I do not know, however, if all such occurrences refer to the same man who came to Virginia in 1608, or if one or more refer to a different George Burton. For example, "George Burton 12 10" is included in "A Complete List in Alphabetical Order of the 'Adventurers to Virginia' with the Several Amounts of their Holding," (dated 1618 or 1619). A similar entry is also included in "The Names of the Aduenturers, with their seuerall summes aduentured, paid to Sir Thomas Smith, Knight, late Treasurer of the Company for Virginia" (dated 22 June 1620). [Susan Myra Kingsbury, ed., *The Records of the Virginia Company of London, Volume III* (Washington, D.C.: Government Printing Office, 1933), 81, 319.]

In addition, George Burton is on a list of names of members of the company in a record of the proceedings of the Court of King's Bench (i.e., King James I) (dated 4 November 1623 to 24 May 1624). [Susan Myra Kingsbury, ed., *The Records of the Virginia Company of London, Volume IV* (Washington, D.C.: Government Printing Office, 1935), 295, 364.]

After George, at least one Burden and two Burtons came to Virginia before the 1621/1622 Indian massacre, but it seems unlikely that either came as far north as the area that would become Stafford. According to one source, a Luke Burden was in Virginia by 1620, but he might not have stayed. More specifically, "Att a Generall Courte Helde in the Afternoone for Virginia the 12ᵗʰ Iulie 1620…Vppon the request of Captaine Warde for the returne of Luke Burden into England now deteyned in Virginia for takinge a way certaine goods from the Indians there The Court was pleased to order that a letter should be write to Sʳ George Yeardly Gouernor of

Virginia to pmitt the said Luke Burden to come ouer if hee be onely deteyned for that ffact (and no other) wth wch Capt Warde stood himselfe charged and was by fauore acquited." [Susan Myra Kingsbury, ed., *The Records of the Virginia Company of London, Volume I* (Washington, D.C.: Government Printing Office, 1906), 399,400.]

According to another source, Christopher Burton was among 35 people who arrived in James City on the ship *Margaret* on 4 (or 14?) December 1619. They were the first settlers in the town and "hundred" of Berkeley on the James River. [Alexander Brown, *The First Republic in America* (Cambridge: The Riverside Press, 1898), 371.]

Other sources indicate that "a John Burton was killed at Edward Bennett's plantation in 1622 in the great Indian Massacre." [Francis Burton Harrison, *Burton Chronicles of Colonial Virginia* (privately published in 1933) (Reprinted in 1979 by Cook & McDowell Publications, Hartford, Kentucky), 15.]

More specifically, "Here following is set downe a true list of the names of all those that were massacred by the treachery of the sauages in VIRGINIA, the 22 March last, To the end that their lawful heyres may take speady order for the inheriting of their lands and estates there...At Mr. Edward Bennets Plantation...John Burton." [Susan Myra Kingsbury, ed., *The Records of the Virginia Company of London, Volume III* (Washington, D.C.: Government Printing Office, 1933), 564-565, 571.]

By the way, the Pilgrims had arrived in Massachusetts in 1620, just prior to the massacre in Virginia, but there were no Burtons among them. Passenger lists for the 1620 voyage of the *Mayflower*, the 1621 voyage of the *Fortune* and the voyages of the *Ann* and *Little James* did not include any Burtons. [John Camden Hotten, ed., *Lists of Emigrants to America, 1600-1700* (a.k.a., *The Original Lists of Persons of Quality*....) (Baltimore: Genealogical Publishing Co., Inc., 1974), xxiv-xxx.]

Apparently, the first Burton to come to Virginia *after* the Indian Massacre (and after the arrival of the Pilgrims in Massachusetts) was Richard Burton. More specifically, according to a 1624 muster of Virginia residents, ordered by King James I just prior to his making Virginia a Royal Colony, Richard Burton came to America on the ship *Swan* in 1623 and probably lived in Elizabeth Cittie County near the confluence of the James River and Waters Creek. [Ware Crowell Callaway, *The Muster of the Inhabitants of the Virginia Colony, 1624/1625 A. D.*, (Jonesboro, Georgia, 1994), 139-139A, 141.]

Another source confirms that Richard Burton embarked from the port of London for Virginia in the *Swan*, but states that it was in 1624 and that Richard was 28 years old. [John Camden Hotten, ed., *Lists of Emigrants to America, 1600-1700* (a.k.a., *The*

Original Lists of Persons of Quality….) (Baltimore: Genealogical Publishing Co., Inc., 1974), 254.] (Calloway indicates that Richard was 38, but his age appeared to me to be 23 or 28 in Calloway's facsimile copy of the original muster. Also, the discrepancy regarding the year of his departure/arrival might be a result the British Empire's switch to the Gregorian calendar in the 18th century, but I don't know for sure.)

Harrison also indicates that in 1635, Thomas Burton, 19, embarked from London for Virginia in the ship *Ann and Elizabeth*, and William Burton, 24, embarked from London for Virginia in the ship *Thomas*. [Francis Burton Harrison, *Burton Chronicles of Colonial Virginia* (privately published in 1933) (Reprinted in 1979 by Cook & McDowell Publications, Hartford, Kentucky), 14. From *The Original Lists &c. of Emigrants &c.* by John Camden Hotten.]

I checked the Hotten book and it mentions *two* Wm. Burtons coming to Virginia in 1635. According to a (7?) August 1635 passenger list, Wm. Burton, age 20, embarked for Virginia in the ship *Globe* of London. According to a 21 August 1635 passenger list, Wm. Burton, age 24, embarked for Virginia in the ship *Thomas*. I don't know, however, where either of them ended up in Virginia. [John Camden Hotten, ed., *Lists of Emigrants to America, 1600-1700* (a.k.a., *The Original Lists of Persons of Quality….*) (Baltimore: Genealogical Publishing Co., Inc., 1974), 119,126.]

Harrison correctly points out that many Burtons came to Virginia as "headrights." As Harrison explains it: "In the early days of the colony one who transported or paid for the passage of a settler coming to Virginia was entitled to a patent for fifty acres of land for each person whom he brought over; the dates given in the land records, however, are those of the patents and give no clue as to the exact date of arrival of the headright."

Some other early Virginia Burtons mentioned in Harrison's book include the following: In 1633, Sam'll Burton was a headright of Thomas Hodkin "in a bay of Carolina River;" in 1636, Christopher Burton was a headright of John Gater in Elizabeth City County; in 1640, a John Burton of unknown county was fined by the Virginia Council for killing an Indian, but an Indian leader interceded on his behalf; in 1652, a John Burton was in Isle of Wight County; and in 1657, George Burton was a headright of John Wood in Westmoreland County. [Francis Burton Harrison, *Burton Chronicles of Colonial Virginia* (privately published in 1933) (Reprinted in 1979 by Cook & McDowell Publications, Hartford, Kentucky), 14-15.]

In his book *Early Virginia Immigrants, 1623-1666*, George Cabell Greer lists eight Burtons coming to Virginia: John Burton and William Burton (1643, Upper Norfolk Co.); Bryan Burton (1646); Ann (1650, Yorke Co.); Robt. Burton (1651, Yorke Co.);

Issabell Burton (1652, Northampton Co.); Anne Burton (1652, Gloucester Co.); and Ralph Burton (1653, James City Co.). Greer also lists several Burdens. (As previously noted, Burden was often a variation of Burton.) [George Cabell Greer, *Early Virginia Immigrants, 1623-1666*, (Baltimore: Genealogical Publishing Co., Inc., 1973), 53, 55.]

By the way, Greer's listing for Bryan Burton, who was brought to Virginia by Sir William Berkeley, does not mention in which county he arrived. Another source, however, includes Bryan Burton on a 6 June 1646 list of 35 people who apparently settled a 1,090 acre tract of Governor Berkeley's land in James City County. [Louise Pledge Heath Foley, *Early Virginia Families Along the James River, Vol. III* (Baltimore: Genealogical Publishing Co., Inc., 1990), 40.]

I should point out, though, that none of these sources focus especially on Stafford or its predecessor districts. Even Harrison's *Burton Chronicles of Colonial Virginia* has a misleading title. As Harrison himself notes,

> Other Burton families were to be found at an early date in Rappahanock (*sic*) County and on the eastern shore of Virginia, and there are scattered references to Burtons in the early records of York and Gloucester, but the line of which we write is associated solely with the valley of the James. [Francis Burton Harrison, *Burton Chronicles of Colonial Virginia* (privately published in 1933) (Reprinted in 1979 by Cook & McDowell Publications, Hartford, Kentucky), 19.]

Regrettably, I am not aware of any one book that chronicles the many Burtons who settled in the Rappahannock River valley in Colonial Virginia. I did, however, find a few sources of information that listed various Burtons in connection with early Stafford and its predecessor districts.

One of the best of these sources is an extensive list of headrights and land patentees in early Virginia, compiled in the multi-volume work *Cavaliers and Pioneers: Abstracts of Virginia Land Patents and Grants,* the first eight volumes of which cover the period 1623-1782. (As of 2005, additional volumes were apparently planned but I do not know if they were ever published.)

This publication was initiated in the 1930s by Nell Marion Nugent, who edited the first three volumes. Later volumes were edited by Dennis Ray Hudgins and published by the Virginia Genealogical Society.

Nugent provides some interesting information in the introduction to Volume One. For example, on page xxiv, she cautions researchers that "headrights may have arrived in the Colony long before the patentee had entered claim for the land thereby due." Also, not all headrights were new immigrants. Some might have traveled back and forth to England or other locations.

In addition, Nugent points out the explosive growth in the white population of Virginia between 1621 and 1649. On page xviii, she notes that on 22 March 1621/1622, Indians under the leadership of Opechancenough (Powhatan's brother), massacred 347 of the 1,240 white inhabitants of the Colony. And it might have been worse, had the Christian Indian Chanco not warned the colonists of the impending attack.

By 1649, according to the "Perfect Description of Virginia," there were about 15,000 English colonists in Virginia, plus about 300 "negros," in 12 counties with 20 churches (p. xx). So the white population grew from 893 after the 1621/1622 massacre to about 15,000 in less than 30 years.

The influx of immigrants to Virginia in the 17th century included dozens of Burtons. For example, at least 65 Burtons are listed as headrights in just the first three volumes of *Cavaliers and Pioneers*, which cover the period 1623-1732. There are additional references to Burdens and others with similarly spelled surnames.

Later volumes mention very few Burtons as headrights, but Burtons continue to be listed as patentees or referenced in non-Burton patents as adjacent land owners. Most of the Burton-related entries in the third through eighth volumes, however, concern land patents that were nowhere near Stafford and, thus, are not useful for the purposes of this Chronology. Still, I was able to find 30 references to Burtons, as headrights or patentees, in the first two volumes (covering 1623-1695) that were related to patents in Stafford and its predecessor districts.

Explanatory Remarks Regarding the Chronologies

My pre-Stafford research was complicated because the predecessor districts of northern Stafford are not the same as the predecessor districts of southern Stafford. As a result, there is a somewhat confusing chronological overlap between the Pre-Stafford Chronology and the Main Chronology, from 1664 to 1776, because what is now southern Stafford did not become part of Stafford until 1777.

I have therefore restricted entries in my Pre-Stafford Chronology, with a few exceptions, to those that reference one of Stafford's predecessor districts prior to Stafford's formation in 1664 (i.e., Northumberland and Westmoreland), or that reference pre-1777 predecessor districts of what is now southern Stafford (i.e.,

Lancaster, Old Rappahannock, Richmond and King George). (I have chosen not to include early Charles River/York County references because the chances that any of them refer to the Stafford area seem remote at that early stage of colonization.)

In addition, I decided not to include these references to "pre-Stafford" Burtons in the Main Chronology because, technically, they were not actually in Stafford back then. Furthermore, in most cases, I don't know for sure which of these "pre-Stafford" Burtons, if any, actually lived in areas that came to be known as Stafford County.

Nevertheless, I think the pre-Stafford references are worth mentioning, in part because the details might, in some cases, help American Burtons trace their ancestry back to England. I have, therefore, compiled the shorter, Pre-Stafford Chronology as a supplement to the Main Chronology.

Readers should note that the information in the Pre-Stafford Chronology is often much more speculative in nature than the information in the Main Chronology because the earlier sources typically do not provide sufficient information for more definite assessments. In both this and the Main Chronology, however, I have tried to keep my comments separate from my summary of the source information.

For the most part, I have confined comments to clearly marked paragraphs that not only begin with the word COMMENT in all caps, but are *italicized* to further differentiate them from the source summaries. On occasion, however, I have inserted short comments in parentheses or brackets within the cited information.

Source citations are enclosed in square brackets and are embedded within the text. In some cases, a source citation immediately follows the cited information. In other cases, such as those where I have mixed information from multiple sources into one summary, the citations are placed one after another at the end of the cited information.

When I make cross-references to other Chronology entries in my comments, I generally do not repeat the source citation. The reader will need to look up the cross-referenced entry to see its source.

*   *   *   *   *

1608
(Pre-Stafford)

ENTRY PS-1. George Burton, a charter member of the Virginia Company, was among those who accompanied John Smith on some of his expeditions in Virginia in 1608. [John Smith, *The Generall Historie of Virginia, New England, and the Summer Isles*, Book III, Chapter VIII, "Captain Smith's Journey to Pamavnkee" (London, 1624) (Reprinted in 1966 by Readex Microprint Corporation), 74.]

COMMENT: Given Smith's explorations of the Potomac and Rappahannock rivers, it is possible that George was not only the first Burton in North America and the first Burton in Virginia, but also the first Burton to lay eyes on the area that would later become Stafford County.

Interestingly, a hill or ridge was apparently named after Burton during one Smith's expeditions and was included on Smith's 1612 map. (See 1612 Pre-Stafford entry, below.) - MB

1612
(Pre-Stafford)

ENTRY PS-2. John Smith's 1612 map of his 1608 expeditions in Virginia is possibly the first map ever made that included the area that would become Stafford County. This map included a landmark designated "Burton's Mount."

The designated hill or ridge appears on the map to be located in what today is either northern Stafford County or Prince William County. (Prince William, however, was originally part of Stafford, so Burton's Mount was definitely located within that area that would become Stafford County.) [John Smith, *A Map of Virginia*, 1612. Facsimile viewed by the author in 2011 at the headquarters branch of the Central Rappahannock Regional Library.]

A modern, reformatted version of the map includes a commentary by Edward Wright Haile. Haile asks in his commentary "Was Burton's Mount the Bull Run Mountains or merely the 400 foot ridge behind Aquia Creek and Quantico Marine Base?" [Edward Wright Haile, *Virginia Discovered and Described by Captayn John Smith*. Viewed by the author in 2011 at the headquarters branch of the Central Rappahannock Regional Library.]

Burton's Mount is also noted on a modern map, based on multiple sources, that depicts the Chesapeake Bay region from 1607 to 1634. This map places Burton's Mount clearly in what would today be Prince William County.

This map also includes a note stating that Smith's party boated from Quiyough [Aquia?] and "…marched several miles overland to an antimony mine in Burton's Mount." [*England in America: The Chesapeake Bay from Jamestown to St. Mary's City, 1607-1634*. Viewed by the author in 2011 at the headquarters branch of the Central Rappahannock Regional Library.]

COMMENT: Burton's Mount was presumably named after the George Burton who accompanied John Smith on his expeditions in Virginia in 1608. (See 1608 Pre-Stafford entry, above.)

To my knowledge, this was the first landmark named after a Burton in Virginia or, for that matter, all of North America. Smith's map was also, presumably, the first map of Virginia, or of North America, or possibly even of the New World, to include a reference to a Burton.

If the note about the overland trek to the antimony mine in the 1607-1634 map is correct, it probably means that George Burton was not merely the first Burton to lay eyes on the land that would become Stafford, but was the first Burton to actually step foot on it.

By the way, I seriously doubt that Burton's Mount was located in today's Prince William County because I doubt that Smith and his men would have ventured that far on foot in an unknown wilderness populated by potentially hostile natives. And the Bull Run area is far more than "several miles" from tidal Aquia Creek. - MB

1640
(Pre-Stafford)

Entry PS-3. According to Conway Robinson's "Notes and Excerpts from the Records of Colonial Virginia," John Burton was fined 20 pounds sterling, circa 14 December 1640, for killing an Indian. Burton appealed, however, and "Opashankanow and his great men" intervened on Burton's behalf, so the fine was rescinded. [Conway Robinson, "Notes and Excerpts from the Records of Colonial Virginia," in *Minutes of the Council and General Court of Colonial Virginia, 1622-1632, 1670-1676*, ed. H. R. McIlwaine (Richmond, Virginia: Virginia State Library, 1924), 478, 483.]

COMMENT: If I remember correctly, the source document did not reveal where Burton lived or where he killed the Indian. Furthermore, John Burton was a very popular name, even in mid-17th century Virginia.

I do not know, then, if this John Burton was the same man as, or was in any way related to, the John Burton(s) who owned land in Northumberland in 1655, who received a land patent in Lancaster in 1656, or who owned cattle in Old Rappahannock County in 1672. (See entries below). I include this entry only because of the chance of a possible connection, however slim, between them, and also because there was a John Burton farming in Stafford by 1680.

By the way, "Opashankanow" appears to be the phonetic equivalent of the Indian "king" Opechancanough encountered by John Smith 32 years earlier. [John Smith, *The Generall Historie of Virginia, New England, and the Summer Isles*, Book III, Chapter VIII, "Captain Smith's Journey to Pamavnkee" (London, 1624) (Reprinted in 1966 by Readex Microprint Corporation), 78.]

I am not an expert on the subject, however, and do not know if it was the same man encountered by Smith, or the one who was responsible for the 1621/1622 massacre. It might provide a clue, however, regarding the general region in which the incident occurred. - MB

1653
(Pre-Stafford)

ENTRY PS-4. William Burton was listed as a headright of Thomas Hankins for a 26 February 1653 patent of land in Northumberland County near Herringe Creek. [Nell Marion Nugent, ed., *Cavaliers and Pioneers: Abstracts of Virginia Land Patents and Grants, 1623-1800, in Five Volumes, Volume One, 1623-1666* (Richmond, Virginia: Press of the Dietz Printing Co., 1934), 284.]

1654
(Pre-Stafford)

ENTRY PS-5. Rich. Burton was listed as a headright of Wm. Beach for a 10 June 1654 patent of land located on the north side of Potomeck Creek. [Nell Marion Nugent, ed., *Cavaliers and Pioneers: Abstracts of Virginia Land Patents and Grants, 1623-1800, in Five Volumes, Volume One, 1623-1666* (Richmond, Virginia: Press of the Dietz Printing Co., 1934), 297.]

1655
(Pre-Stafford)

ENTRY PS-6. John Burton was listed as owning land adjacent to that of Gervace (?) Dodson's 4 June 1655 patent in Northumberland County, north of great Wicomoco River. Jeremy Dodson also owned land adjacent to the patent. [Nell Marion Nugent, ed., *Cavaliers and Pioneers: Abstracts of Virginia Land Patents and Grants, 1623-1800, in Five Volumes, Volume One, 1623-1666* (Richmond, Virginia: Press of the Dietz Printing Co., 1934), 308.]

ENTRY PS-7. According to a secondary source, an entry on page 231 of *Lancaster County Court Orders, 1652-1655*, dated 7 December 1655, indicates that Robt. Burton was admitted guardian for Jo Johnson and Jo's brothers and sisters. Wm. Copeland was listed as security for Burton.

Multiple entries in the secondary source refer to a single entry in the original. The phrase "comm of admr to Burton" is used in one of them, but it is not clear if this was the wording used in the original.

One entry in the secondary sources notes that the original does not specify whose estate was to be administered. Other secondary source entries, however, indicate that Bertram Obert and Mr. Willis/Wyllis were to appraise the estate of Jo Johnson and his brothers and sisters. [Beverley Fleet, *Virginia Colonial Abstracts, Volume I* (Baltimore: Genealogical Publishing Co., Inc., 1988), 179, 185, 202, 215, 232.]

COMMENT: Presumably, the estate in question belonged to a deceased parent or guardian of Jo Johnson and his siblings. The secondary source had separate entries on different pages for each name mentioned in the single original entry, but the secondary source entries included varying levels of detail. - MB

ENTRY PS-8. According to a secondary source, an entry on page 237 of *Lancaster County Court Orders, 1652-1655*, dated 7 December 1655, indicates that Sam Burton was to pay a levy on "1 tytheabled" to Abra Weeks, as was Robt. Burton, who was listed separately. [Beverley Fleet, *Virginia Colonial Abstracts, Volume I* (Baltimore: Genealogical Publishing Co., Inc., 1988), 179, 235.]

COMMENT: Another entry in the same source indicates that Abra Weeks was Abraham Weeks. - MB

1656
(Pre-Stafford)

ENTRY PS-9. On 3 March 1656, Jno. Burton received a patent for 900 acres in Lancaster County on a branch of the Corotomen River "upon land of Thomas Harrisse," for transporting 18 unspecified people. [Nell Marion Nugent, ed., *Cavaliers and Pioneers: Abstracts of Virginia Land Patents and Grants, 1623-1800, in Five Volumes, Volume One, 1623-1666* (Richmond, Virginia: Press of the Dietz Printing Co., 1934), 343.]

COMMENT: *Could this Thomas "Harrisse" be the Thomas Harris mentioned 36 years later in a 1692 Stafford deed as owning land near William Burton's cornfield, or perhaps a father or uncle? If so, could that William Burton be a son or relative of the John Burton mentioned here? (See 1692 entry in the Main Chronology.) With such common names, I am reluctant to even speculate. - MB*

1657
(Pre-Stafford)

ENTRY PS-10. Anne Burton was listed as a headright of Nicholas Jernow for a 22 March 1657 patent of land near the "Potomeck freshes, beyond Doegs Island." [Nell Marion Nugent, ed., *Cavaliers and Pioneers: Abstracts of Virginia Land Patents and Grants, 1623-1800, in Five Volumes, Volume One, 1623-1666* (Richmond, Virginia: Press of the Dietz Printing Co., 1934), 362.]

COMMENT: *The original source does not mention in which county the patent was located. I mention this, nevertheless, because I vaguely recall reading that Doegs Island might have been near what is now Stafford. - MB*

ENTRY PS-11. Geo. Burton was listed as a headright of John Wood for a 15 July 1657 patent of land near "Yosococomoco Creek in Potomeck freshes." [Nell Marion Nugent, ed., *Cavaliers and Pioneers: Abstracts of Virginia Land Patents and Grants, 1623-1800, in Five Volumes, Volume One, 1623-1666* (Richmond, Virginia: Press of the Dietz Printing Co., 1934), 351.]

According to the another source, the patented land was in Westmoreland County. [Francis Burton Harrison, *Burton Chronicles of Colonial Virginia* (privately published in 1933) (Reprinted in 1979 by Cook & McDowell Publications, Hartford, Kentucky), 14-15.]

ENTRY PS-12. Jno. Burton was a headright of Georg (*sic*) Seaton for a 9 October 1657 patent of land in Westmoreland County. [Nell Marion Nugent, ed., *Cavaliers and Pioneers: Abstracts of Virginia Land Patents and Grants, 1623-1800, in Five Volumes, Volume One, 1623-1666* (Richmond, Virginia: Press of the Dietz Printing Co., 1934), 355.]

1658
(Pre-Stafford)

ENTRY PS-13. Sam Burton was listed as a headright of Thomas Woodhouse and John Wood for a 29 May 1658 patent of land "upon Patomeck River." No county was specified. [Nell Marion Nugent, ed., *Cavaliers and Pioneers: Abstracts of Virginia Land Patents and Grants, 1623-1800, in Five Volumes, Volume One, 1623-1666* (Richmond, Virginia: Press of the Dietz Printing Co., 1934), 375.]

COMMENT: Although no county was specified, I wonder if the John Wood mentioned here was the same one who transported Geo. Burton in 1657 for a patent of land in Westmoreland. (See Pre-Stafford entry for 1657.) - MB

1662
(Pre-Stafford)

ENTRY PS-14. Samll. Burton was listed as a headright of Mich. Hugill for a 20 February 1662 patent of land in Rappahannock County, Farnham Parish, on the north side of the Rappa. River at the head of Totoskey Creek.

Sam. Burton was listed as a headright of Wm. Moseley and John Hull on the same date for a patent of land in Rappahannock County, Farnham Parish, on the north side of "Rappa." near Totoskey. [Nell Marion Nugent, ed., *Cavaliers and Pioneers: Abstracts of Virginia Land Patents and Grants, 1623-1800, in Five Volumes, Volume One, 1623-1666* (Richmond, Virginia: Press of the Dietz Printing Co., 1934), 467-468.]

COMMENT: I have listed these two entries together because their similarities seem too great to be mere coincidence. I would not be surprised if different patentees were trying to get credit for transporting the same man.

Also, Totoskey Creek might be a reference to what is today Totuskey Creek in Richmond County (which is on the north side of the Rappahannock.) (See also 1664 Pre-Stafford entry regarding "Totescay" Creek.) - MB

ENTRY **PS-15**. An Old Rappahannock County deed, Book 1656-1664, Page 282, recorded in 1663 but dated 3 November 1662, lists Richd. Burton as a witness regarding a power of attorney from Allen to Catlett. [*Embrey's General Index to Deeds and Wills, Old Rappahannock County, 1654-1692 and 1692-1700.*]

COMMENT: *It is possible that Catletts lived at that time in the area that would later become southern Stafford. For example, according to King George Deed 1-54, recorded 2 March 1721 but dated 2 June 1666, Col. Jno. Catlett was granted a 2,000-acre patent of land on the Rappahannock River one mile below the Falls. This is no guarantee that the Catlett mentioned in 1662 was from the same family, nor that this Richard Burton lived in the area that would become Stafford, but both are possible. - MB*

ENTRY **PS-16**. Ellinor Burton and Thomas Burton were listed as headrights of Daniell (*sic*) Hutt for a 9 December 1662 land patent in Northumberland County. [Nell Marion Nugent, ed., *Cavaliers and Pioneers: Abstracts of Virginia Land Patents and Grants, 1623-1800, in Five Volumes, Volume One, 1623-1666* (Richmond, Virginia: Press of the Dietz Printing Co., 1934), 500.]

1663
(Pre-Stafford)

ENTRY **PS-17**. An Old Rappahannock County deed, Book 1656-1664, Page 342, dated 20 July 1663, mentions that Edwd. Burton of England was the uncle of Wm. Underwood, Jr. [*Embrey's General Index to Deeds and Wills, Old Rappahannock County, 1654-1692 and 1692-1700.*] An extract of the deed indicates that this was Edward Burton of Kederminster in the County of Worcester (*sic*) in England and that he was apparently a gentleman. Underwood was "of Rappa. Virga." [Ruth and Sam Sparacio, eds., *Deed Abstracts of Old Rappahannock County, Virginia, 1656-1664, Part II* (McLean, Virginia: 1989), 59-60.]

COMMENT: *I do not know if this Edward Burton was related in any way to the Edward Burton (or Barton) living in Stafford in 1680. (See entry for 1680 in the Main Chronology.) I only mention him because he might have had other relatives besides his nephew living in the area, or he himself might have come to Virginia to live with his nephew. - MB*

1664
(Pre-Stafford)

ENTRY PS-18. Wm. Burton was listed as a headright of Richard Webley, Robt. Davis and Thomas Freshwater for a 24 August 1664 patent of land in Rappahannock and Northumberland counties, on the eastern most branch of Totescay Creek. (The patentees transported a total of 145 people, including a Saml. Furton and a Charles Bryant.) [Nell Marion Nugent, ed., *Cavaliers and Pioneers: Abstracts of Virginia Land Patents and Grants, 1623-1800, in Five Volumes, Volume One, 1623-1666* (Richmond, Virginia: Press of the Dietz Printing Co., 1934), 430.]

COMMENT: This is only speculation on my part, but I wonder if Saml. Furton was actually Samuel Burton, given the reference to Totescay Creek. (See 1662 Pre-Stafford entry for Samll. Burton, which mentions a "Totoskey" Creek.) I also wonder if Charles Bryant might have been related to the family of Richard Bryant. Could Charles, for example, have been the mysterious Bryant who is thought to have married a Patawomeck Indian princess, and whose daughter later married a William Burton in Stafford?

Totescay Creek, by the way, might be a reference to what is today Totuskey Creek in Richmond County. - MB

1665
(Pre-Stafford)

ENTRY PS-19. Samll. Burton was listed as a headright of Tho. Harper and Robt. Clemonds for a 27 February 1665/1666 patent of land in Rappahannock County. [Nell Marion Nugent, ed., *Cavaliers and Pioneers: Abstracts of Virginia Land Patents and Grants, 1623-1800, Volume Two, 1666-1695* (Richmond, Virginia: Virginia State Library, 1977), 14.]

ENTRY PS-20. Wm. Burton was listed as a headright of Randoph Kirke for a 22 March 1665/1666 patent of land in Westmoreland County, between the Potomack and Rappa. rivers, on the branches of Nomany. [Nell Marion Nugent, ed., *Cavaliers and Pioneers: Abstracts of Virginia Land Patents and Grants, 1623-1800, in Five Volumes, Volume One, 1623-1666* (Richmond, Virginia: Press of the Dietz Printing Co., 1934), 546.]

COMMENT: Technically, I should not include this entry here because Stafford was already in existence by 1665. Still, it's possible that this William Burton later moved to

Stafford (in part because later records indicate a William Burton living in Stafford by 1680). It is also possible that Burton arrived long before the patent was recorded and, thus, before Stafford had been formed. - MB

1667
(Pre-Stafford)

ENTRY PS-21. Jno. Burton was listed as a headright of Tho. Page, Wm. Hodgson and Samll. Weilding for a 3 April 1667 patent of land in Rappahannock County, adjacent to land of Tho. Lucas. [Nell Marion Nugent, ed., *Cavaliers and Pioneers: Abstracts of Virginia Land Patents and Grants, 1623-1800, Volume Two, 1666-1695* (Richmond, Virginia: Virginia State Library, 1977), 47.]

ENTRY PS-22. Rich. Burton was listed as a headright of Tho. Chetwood and Jno. Proser for a 28 September 1667 patent of land on the north side of Rappahannock County. [Nell Marion Nugent, ed., *Cavaliers and Pioneers: Abstracts of Virginia Land Patents and Grants, 1623-1800, Volume Two, 1666-1695* (Richmond, Virginia: Virginia State Library, 1977), 47.]

   COMMENT: The reference to the north side of Rappahannock County presumably means the north side of the river. I do not know, however, if the patent was located in the area of Rappahannock County that would later become southern Stafford. The location of the patent, of course, does not indicate where the headright ended up living. - MB

1669
(Pre-Stafford)

ENTRY PS-23. Wm. Burton was listed as a headright of Thomas Pattison for a 12 June 1669 patent in Rappahannock County on the south side. [Nell Marion Nugent, ed., *Cavaliers and Pioneers: Abstracts of Virginia Land Patents and Grants, 1623-1800, Volume Two, 1666-1695* (Richmond, Virginia: Virginia State Library, 1977), 58.]

ENTRY PS-24. Richard Burton had been a servant of John Whiston's, according to Whiston's 1669 Will, recorded in Westmoreland County. Whiston, of Nominy, left "one cow calfe" to Burton. [John Frederick Dorman, ed., *Westmoreland County, Virginia, Deeds, Patents, Etc., 1665-1677, Part One* (Washington, D.C., 1973), 61.]

COMMENT: Stafford had already been formed from Westmoreland by the time this deed was recorded, but I include this entry because it is possible that Richard Burton might have lived in the area that became Stafford prior to the recording of the Will, or had descendants who lived in or moved to Stafford. - MB

1670
(Pre-Stafford)

ENTRY PS-25. John Burton was listed as a headright of Francis Furmes for a 16 August 1670 patent in Rappahannock County, on the south side. [Nell Marion Nugent, ed., *Cavaliers and Pioneers: Abstracts of Virginia Land Patents and Grants, 1623-1800, Volume Two, 1666-1695* (Richmond, Virginia: Virginia State Library, 1977), 81.]

COMMENT: Although Furmes' land was located on the south side of the river, and was therefore not in the part of the county that would later become southern Stafford, it remains possible that John Burton might have lived on the northern side of the river. - MB

1671
(Pre-Stafford)

ENTRY PS-26. According to a Westmoreland County deed, Richard Burton and Richard Walker witnessed a power of attorney circa 23 October 1671. According to the deed, which was recorded 29 November 1671, Dennis White appointed his friend Clement Spillman as his attorney to obtain all debts in Virginia or elsewhere. [John Frederick Dorman, ed., *Westmoreland County, Virginia, Deeds, Pattents, Etc., 1665-1677, Part Two* (Washington, D.C., 1973), 21.]

COMMENT: I only include this because it might refer to the same Richard mentioned in John Whiston's 1669 Will. (See 1669 Pre-Stafford entry, above.) If so, it seems to suggest that he remained in Westmoreland after his employer's death and did not live in Stafford. I wonder if it is the same Richard who witnessed another power of attorney in neighboring Old Rappahannock County in 1662. - MB

1672
(Pre-Stafford)

ENTRY PS-27. John Burton was mentioned as a cattle owner in an Old Rappahannock County court document recorded in November 1672. [Ruth and Sam Sparacio, eds., *Deed Abstracts of Old Rappahannock County, Virginia, 1672-1676, Part I* (Mclean, Virginia: The Antient Press, 1989), 37.]

COMMENT: I do not know if this John Burton lived in the area of Old Rappahannock County that would eventually become southern Stafford County. I also do not know if he is the same John Burton who was mentioned as living in Stafford County in 1680. (See the 1680 entry in the Main Chronology.) Given the small population of the area at that time, however, there is a chance that it was the same man. - MB

1673
(Pre-Stafford)

ENTRY PS-28. Jno. Burton and Jno. Austine (Austin) received a 5 November 1673 patent of 2,172 acres in Rappahannock County, on the south side, near a branch of Nasaponnocks, for transporting 43 people. [Nell Marion Nugent, ed., *Cavaliers and Pioneers: Abstracts of Virginia Land Patents and Grants, 1623-1800, Volume Two, 1666-1695* (Richmond, Virginia: Virginia State Library, 1977), 138.]

COMMENT: The reference to the south side presumably means that the land was on the south side of the Rappahannock River. This means that the land was probably not located in that area of Old Rappahannock County, north of the river, that would one day become southern Stafford. Still, it is one of several sources that mentions a John Burton in the area at the time.

Burton and Austin would later lose the land, however, after being "found to escheat"; that is, they apparently did not cultivate and improve the property quickly enough, as required by law. (See related 1682 and 1683 Pre-Stafford entries.)

By the way, this patent was mentioned several times in a book about the first settlers of Spotsylvania County and Fredericksburg. [Paula S. Felder, Forgotten Companions: The First Settlers of Spotsylvania County and Fredericksburg Town (With Notes on Early Land Use), *Second Edition (Fredericksburg, Virginia: The American History Company, 2000), 165,195.] - MB*

Entry PS-29. Tho. Burton was listed as a headright of Henry Benson for a 5 November 1673 patent of land in Rappahannock County, on the south side of the river, in the freshes above the falls, "by Motts falling br." [Nell Marion Nugent, ed., *Cavaliers and Pioneers: Abstracts of Virginia Land Patents and Grants, 1623-1800, Volume Two, 1666-1695* (Richmond, Virginia: Virginia State Library, 1977), 139.]

COMMENT: *Although the patent was for land on the south side of the river, that does not necessarily indicate where the headright ended up living. I assume the land was near today's Motts Run Reservoir. - MB*

1675
(Pre-Stafford)

Entry PS-30. According to a court record recorded 28 April 1675, Jane Burton gave a lengthy deposition in Westmoreland County Court, apparently regarding a case in which James Green had been accused of stealing hogs. [John Frederick Dorman, ed., *Westmoreland County, Virginia, Deeds, Patents, Etc., 1665-1677, Part Three* (Washington, D.C., 1974), 33.]

COMMENT: *I do not know if Jane was related to any Stafford Burtons. If nothing else, this record seems to indicate that one or more Burtons remained in Westmoreland County even after the formation of Stafford (from Westmoreland) in 1664.*

Regrettably, I was not able to conduct a thorough search of early Westmoreland County records and I do not know whether Stafford Burtons are related to any Westmoreland Burtons. Were the Stafford Burtons, prior to 1664, already living in that area of Westmoreland that became Stafford? Or did southern Westmoreland Burtons migrate into Stafford? Or did the Stafford Burtons arrive in Stafford from elsewhere after Stafford was formed? - MB

1682
(Pre-Stafford)

Entry PS-31. Robert Burton was listed as a headright of Wm. Covington for a 24 April 1682 patent in Rappahannock County. [Nell Marion Nugent, ed., *Cavaliers and Pioneers: Abstracts of Virginia Land Patents and Grants, 1623-1800, Volume Two, 1666-1695* (Richmond, Virginia: Virginia State Library, 1977), 240.]

ENTRY PS-32. Lt. Col. Isaac Allerton received a 20 November 1682 patent for 2,172 acres in Rappahannock County, on the south side, that had formerly been granted to John Burton and John Austin, who had been "found to escheat." [Nell Marion Nugent, ed., *Cavaliers and Pioneers: Abstracts of Virginia Land Patents and Grants, 1623-1800, Volume Two, 1666-1695* (Richmond, Virginia: Virginia State Library, 1977), 246-247.]

COMMENT: *This same patent appears to have been recorded in 1683, too. (See related 1673 and 1683 Pre-Stafford entries.) - MB*

1683
(Pre-Stafford)

ENTRY PS-33. Col. Isaac Allerton received a 16 April 1683 patent for 2,172 acres in Rappahannock County, on the south side, that had formerly been granted to John Burton and John Austin, who had been "found to escheat." [Nell Marion Nugent, ed., *Cavaliers and Pioneers: Abstracts of Virginia Land Patents and Grants, 1623-1800, Volume Two, 1666-1695* (Richmond, Virginia: Virginia State Library, 1977), 263.]

COMMENT: *This entry might have been a renewal, because it appears to be the same patent granted to Allerton in 1682. (See related 1673 and 1682 Pre-Stafford entries.) - MB*

1684
(Pre-Stafford)

ENTRY PS-34. A 10 February 1684 entry in Lancaster County Deed Book 6, page 60, lists William Burton as an indentured servant of John Carter II. [Christine A. Jones, ed., *John Carter II of "Corotoman," Lancaster County, Virginia* (Irvington, Virginia: Foundation for Historic Christ Church, Inc., 1978), 21.]

COMMENT: *This, presumably, was not the William Burton who was living in Stafford at that time. - MB*

1695
(Pre-Stafford)

ENTRY PS-35. According to an abstract of a Richmond County court document recorded 6 November 1695, Elinor (or Elenor) Burton was an indentured servant who petitioned the court for her freedom. Although originally indentured to Joseph Eyon for four years, he assigned her to Capt. Richard Newsom. At some point, however, she was reassigned to William Woodbridge and Mrs. Winifred Griffin. The court ordered Burton to serve Griffin an additional five weeks after the expiration of her original period of indenture as a penalty for Burton's having been "fugitively absent" from Griffin's service for three days. [Ruth and Sam Sparacio, eds., *Order Book Abstracts of Richmond County, Virginia, 1694-1697* (McLean, Virginia: The Antient Press, 1991), 63.]

COMMENT: I do not know if this was the same "Ellinor" Burton listed as a headright in 1662 (see entry above), but I doubt it. A 33-year time span seems too long for an indentured servant. - MB

1699
(Pre-Stafford)

ENTRY PS-36. According to an abstract of a Richmond County court document recorded 5 October 1699, Samuel Burton was paid a levy of 400 pounds of tobacco for "bringing Melitia (*sic*) Commissions Proclamations, etc., from his Excellency to this county." [Ruth and Sam Sparacio, eds., *Order Book Abstracts of Richmond County, Virginia, 1697-1699* (McLean, Virginia: The Antient Press, 1991), 122.]

COMMENT: I strongly suspect that this was the same Samuel Burton who probably lived in southeast Stafford near the border with that portion of Richmond County that later became King George County.

By the way, a Samuel Burton is included on a list of Stafford County "Colonial War Veterans." The only source information provided for Samuel was "Public Records Office in London." [Homer J. Musselman, Stafford County, Virginia, Veterans and Cemeteries *(Fredericksburg, Virginia: Bookcrafters, 1994), 1.] - MB*

ENTRY PS-37. According to an abstract of a Richmond County Court document recorded 1 November 1699, Katherine Peachey testified that Patrick Burton was "the true Father of the bastard Child bourn of her body." Both Katherine and Patrick were indentured servants of Manus Maclathlin. [Ruth and Sam Sparacio, eds., *Order Book Abstracts of Richmond County, Virginia, 1697-1699* (McLean, Virginia: The Antient Press, 1991), 123.]

COMMENT: If I understand the abstract correctly, Burton and Peachy were each fined 500 pounds of tobacco for the sin of fornication, but neither could apparently pay the fine. So Maclathlin paid the fines on their behalf to the church wardens of North Farnham

Parish. In return, the court ordered Burton and Peachey to serve Maclathlin for an additional six months beyond their original terms of indenture.

I do not know, however, if Patrick was related to the Sam Burton listed as a headright in 1662 for a patent of land in Farnham Parish (see entry above). - MB

1700
(Pre-Stafford)

ENTRY PS-38. According to an abstract of a Richmond County court document recorded 5 April 1700, Samll. Burton was involved in a lawsuit against Cornelius Macarty. A separate abstract of a document recorded 6 June 1700 reveals that Cornelius Macarty was ordered by the court to pay Saml. Burton 200 pounds of good tobacco. [Ruth and Sam Sparacio, eds., *Order Book Abstracts of Richmond County, Virginia, 1699-1701* (McLean, Virginia: The Antient Press, 1991), 26, 31.]

COMMENT: I strongly suspect that this is the same Samuel Burton mentioned in the 1699 Pre-Stafford entry, and that he lived in Stafford, but very close to the border with Richmond County. (Also see entries below regarding Samuel.) - MB

1720
(Pre-Stafford)

ENTRY PS-39. Samuel Burton reportedly lived in King George County in 1720. [*Virginia in 1720: A Reconstructed Census*, (Miami Beach, Florida: T. L. C. Genealogy, 1992), 33.]

COMMENT: Another source indicates that Samuel lived in Stafford, not in King George. (See, for example, the 1703 entry in the Main Chronology, below.) Perhaps Samuel moved from one county to the other, but I strongly suspect that this was the same Samuel Burton who probably lived in southeast Stafford near the border with that portion of Richmond County that later became King George County.

Regardless of this particular claim, I have serious doubts about the reliability of this source and its companion books, Virginia in 1740: A Reconstructed Census *and* Virginia in 1760: A Reconstructed Census. *None of these books lists any Burtons in Stafford (with one possible exception in 1740), but my research indicates that there were Burtons in Stafford in all three years. (See 1740 entry in the Main Chronology regarding Burten.)*

In addition, it is my understanding that King George County was not formed until 1721, so how could Samuel have lived there in 1720? Is the date in error, or does the date fall within those months affected by the Gregorian calendar change?

Furthermore, none of the books list an author, which only raises more doubts about the credibility of these sources. I do not want to be too harsh in my criticism, however, because I, personally, know that it is very difficult to find information on Burtons in Stafford during the Colonial era. - MB

1721
(Pre-Stafford)

ENTRY PS-40. Sam Burton was listed as grantor and Chas. Seal as grantee regarding an unspecified action in King George County Order Book 1721-34, Page 18, recorded 6 October 1721. [*Embrey's General Index to Deeds and Wills, King George County, 1721-1924.*] [*General Index to Deeds, Trusts, Releases, Wills, Court Orders, Etc., Grantors, A-G, 19 May 1721 - 8 October 1924*, Records Office of the Clerk of the Circuit Court, King George, Virginia.]

ENTRY PS-41. Sam Burton was listed as grantee and James Marks (*sic*) as grantor regarding an unspecified [court?] order in King George County Order Book 1721-34, Page 18, recorded 6 October 1721. [*Embrey's General Index to Deeds and Wills, King George County, 1721-1924.*] [*General Index to Deeds, Trusts, Releases, Wills, Court Orders, Etc., Grantees, A-G, 19 May 1721 - 8 October 1924*, Records Office of the Clerk of the Circuit Court, King George, Virginia.]

COMMENT: I first found the two entries above on a microfilm copy of the indexes, and the microfilm box had the shorter "Embrey's" title. I later visited the King George County courthouse and noticed that the hard copy indexes have the longer title.

By the way, Embrey's index appears to use the terms "grantor" and "grantee" in lieu of "plaintiff" and "defendant." See, for example, the two following entries. - MB

ENTRY PS-42. According to 6 October 1721 King George County court records, Samuel Burton's (action?) against Charles Seal was dismissed because Burton failed to appear. [Mary Marshall Brewer, ed., *King George County, Virginia, Orders, 1721-1724* (Lewes, Delaware: Colonial Roots, 2007), 16.]

ENTRY PS-43. According to 6 October 1721 King George County court records, the action brought against Samuel Burton by James Markham was dismissed because Markham failed to appear. [Mary Marshall Brewer, ed., *King George County, Virginia, Orders, 1721-1724* (Lewes, Delaware: Colonial Roots, 2007), 17.]

1722
(Pre-Stafford)

ENTRY PS-44. According to a 6 July 1722 King George County court record, Samuel Burton and John Traviss (*sic*) witnessed Thomas Gwibort (*sic*) and his wife Rebecca grant power of attorney to Thomas Gregsby (*sic*). [Mary Marshall Brewer, ed., *King George County, Virginia, Orders, 1721-1724* (Lewes, Delaware: Colonial Roots, 2007), 48.]

Another source reveals that the transfer was dated 30 April and recorded 6 July. It also has the following different spellings for Travis, Guibert and Grigsby. [Sue Ann Damron, *Land Records of King George County, Virginia, 1721-1743* (Westminster, Maryland: Willow Bend Books, 1999), 9.]

1724
(Pre-Stafford)

ENTRY PS-45. Sam Burton was listed as grantee and Wm. Robertson as grantor regarding a "dismissed" action in King George County (Chancery or Court?) Order Book 1721-1734, Page 210, recorded 5 September 1724. [*Embrey's General Index to Deeds and Wills, King George County, 1721-1924.*]

An abstract of the actual Order Book entry states that the attachment obtained by John Dinwiddie in behalf of Willm. Robertson, Esq., of Williamsburg, against Saml. Burton, was ordered to be dismissed. [Mary Marshall Brewer, ed., *King George County, Virginia, Orders, 1721-1724* (Lewes, Delaware: Colonial Roots, 2007), 195.]

COMMENT: Without further research, I cannot say if this John Dinwiddie was in any way related to Robert Dinwiddie, a mid-18th century governor of Virginia. - MB

1727
(Pre-Stafford)

ENTRY **PS-46.** James Burden was mentioned in a 7 October 1727 King George County court record regarding his "taking up" a servant lad named Frederick Black, who belonged to Hugh Lambert of Richmond County. [Mary Marshall Brewer, ed., *King George County, Virginia, Orders, 1724-1728* (Lewes, Delaware: Colonial Roots, 2007), 163.]

1728
(Pre-Stafford)

ENTRY **PS-47.** Robert Burten (*sic*) was listed as a witness to the Will of Simon Taylor, dated 18 August 1728, 4 February 1728/29. [Robert K. Headley, Jr., *Wills of Richmond County, Virginia, 1699-1800* (Baltimore: Genealogical Publishing Co., Inc., 1998), 64.]

COMMENT: I assume that the first date given refers to the date the Will was signed and the second refers to the date it was recorded. Given the dates, however, this was probably in that portion of Richmond County that did not become King George and, hence, did not become southern Stafford.

By the way, I only had access to the secondary source, in which the surname is spelled with an "e." I don't know how it was spelled in the original, but such spelling variations were common at the time. - MB

1729
(Pre-Stafford)

ENTRY **PS-48.** According to a 5 April 1729 King George County court record, John Long was ordered to pay John Burton for attending court for two days as a witness in a suit against Frances Woffendale and Henry Bartlett. [Mary Marshall Brewer, ed., *King George County, Virginia, Orders, 1728-1731* (Lewes, Delaware: Colonial Roots, 2007), 41.]

1733
(Pre-Stafford)

ENTRY PS-49. According to a 4 May 1733 King George County court record, Thomas Monteith won a lawsuit against William Burton for 300 pounds of tobacco with costs. [Mary Marshall Brewer, ed., *King George County, Virginia, Orders, 1731-36* (Lewes, Delaware: Colonial Roots, 2007), 99.]

COMMENT: This might be the William Burton who married Sarah Spicer in 1725 and lived in southeastern Stafford, near the border with King George. (See 1725 entry in the Main Chronology.) - MB

1734
(Pre-Stafford)

ENTRY PS-50. According to a 5 July 1734 King George County court record, Elizabeth Caton won a lawsuit against William Burton for 400 pounds of tobacco with costs. [Mary Marshall Brewer, ed., *King George County, Virginia, Orders, 1731-36* (Lewes, Delaware: Colonial Roots, 2007), 133.]

COMMENT: This might be the William Burton who married Sarah Spicer in 1725 and lived in southeastern Stafford, near the border with King George. (See 1725 entry in the Main Chronology.) - MB

1735
(Pre-Stafford)

ENTRY PS-51. According to 6 February 1735 King George County court records, an unspecified attachment obtained by William Burton against Charles Pain was ordered to be dismissed. [Mary Marshall Brewer, ed., *King George County, Virginia, Orders, 1731-36* (Lewes, Delaware: Colonial Roots, 2007), 162.]

COMMENT: This might be the William Burton who married Sarah Spicer in 1725 and lived in southeastern Stafford, near the border with King George. (See 1725 entry in the Main Chronology.) - MB

ENTRY PS-52. William Burton and Charles Jones were listed as securities for Ann Jones, widow of Henry Jones, deceased, regarding her qualification to administer Henry's estate, according to King George County Will Book A-1, 1721-1752, page

246, dated or recorded 6 June 1735. [*King George County, Virginia, Will Book A-1, 1721-1752*, ed. George Harrison Sanford King (Fredericksburg, Virginia: 1978), p. 246.]

Another source indicates that Burton and Jones put up a 100 pound bond for Ann. [Mary Marshall Brewer, ed., *King George County, Virginia, Orders, 1731-36* (Lewes, Delaware: Colonial Roots, 2007), 145.]

COMMENT: This might be the William Burton who married Sarah Spicer in 1725 and lived in southeastern Stafford, near the border with King George. (See 1725 entry in the Main Chronology.) - MB

ENTRY PS-53. According to 7 November 1735 King George County court records, William Burton was on a jury that ordered defendant Benjamin Rush to pay plaintiff William Flowers 40 shillings, plus costs and attorney's fees, for slander. [Mary Marshall Brewer, ed., *King George County, Virginia, Orders, 1731-36* (Lewes, Delaware: Colonial Roots, 2007), 153.]

COMMENT: This might be the William Burton who married Sarah Spicer and lived in southeastern Stafford, near the King George border. (See 1725 entry in the Main Chronology.) I am not sure, however, if a Stafford resident at that time could have served on a King George jury. - MB

1736
(Pre-Stafford)

ENTRY PS-54. According to 4 February 1736 King George County court records, Thomas Turner won a lawsuit for 715 pounds of tobacco against William Burton. He apparently won another 750 pounds of tobacco against William Burton and William Straton. [Mary Marshall Brewer, ed., *King George County, Virginia, Orders, 1736-1740* (Lewes, Delaware: Colonial Roots, 2007), 24.]

COMMENT: This might be the William Burton who married Sarah Spicer in 1725 and lived in southeastern Stafford, near the border with King George. (See 1725 entry in the Main Chronology.) - MB

ENTRY PS-55. Rachel Porch, future wife of William Burton, was born circa 1736 in what was then King George County. [William L. Deyo, *Porch Family: The Forgotten Legacy of White Oak, Stafford County, Virginia* (Colonial Beach, Virginia: DeJoux Publications, 2001), 21.]

COMMENT: If I understand it correctly, the same source indicates that Rachel's parents were probably Richard and Mary Porch. - MB

1770
(Pre-Stafford)

ENTRY **PS-56**. Charles Burton married Jane (Chapman?) in June 1770. [*King George County, Virginia, Marriages, Volume II: Implied Marriages.*]

COMMENT: I include this marriage because it occurred before the 1777 boundary change, but I do not know if the couple resided in the area of old King George that would become southern Stafford.

By the way, Jane might have been the daughter of Taylor and Margaret Chapman. According to Taylor Chapman's Will, his children were William, Joseph and Jane. A secondary source indicates that the Will was signed 8 November 1749 and recorded 13 February 1749. (I assume that February came after November in the pre-Gregorian calendar.) The same source indicates that Taylor Chapman resided in, or had his Will recorded in, Overwharton Parish in Stafford. [William Lindsay Hopkins, Some Wills from the Burned Counties of Virginia and Other Wills Not Listed in Virginia Wills and Administrations, 1632-1800 *(Richmond, Virginia, 1987), 126.]*

Another source also indicates that Jane had a brother named William. (See 1773 Pre-Stafford entry, below.) - MB

1773
(Pre-Stafford)

ENTRY **PS-57**. Charles Burton and Alexander Rose witnessed the signing of Mary Long (Longley?) Tankersley's Will on 1 May 1773. Mary was the widow of George Tankersley. They were married in 1718 and he died in 1758. They lived in Hanover Parish in King George County. [John Otto Yurechko, *Virginia Genealogies Along the Lower Rappahannock River, 1607-1799* (Westminster, Maryland: Family Line Publications, 1995), 198, 242.]

ENTRY **PS-58**. Chas. Burton was listed as grantee, and Wm. Chapman as grantor, regarding a Will dated 23 September 1773 and recorded 7 October 1773 in King George County Will Book W-2, Page 95. [*Embrey's General Index to Deeds and Wills, King George County, 1721-1924.*]

The entry in the actual Will Book indicates that Chapman appointed Burton as executor and directed Burton to sell his (Chapman's) lands in Stafford. Chapman refers to Burton as his "beloved brother-in-law." The Will was confirmed in court 7 September 1786. [*Wills 2, 1780-1804*, Records Office of the Clerk of the Circuit Court, King George County, Virginia, 95.]

COMMENT: This suggests that William Chapman was Jane Chapman's brother and that he died in 1786. (See 1770 Pre-Stafford entry.) - MB

ENTRY PS-59. John Burton and Marthann Burton were among those who witnessed the signing of Howson Hooe's Will on 16 December 1773. They also witnessed a codicil signed on 7 May 1777. The Will was recorded in King George County court on 4 January 1781 by Howson's son, William Hooe. [Ruth and Sam Sparacio, eds., *Will Abstracts of King George County, Virginia, 1752-1780* (McLean, Virginia: 1986), 111.]

COMMENT: I put this in the Pre-Stafford Chronology because the Burtons' initial involvement was in then-King George, not Stafford, and the Will itself was eventually recorded in King George rather than in Stafford, even though it occurred after the 1777 land swap. - MB

1778
(Pre-Stafford)

ENTRY PS-60. John Burton, William Hooe, Thomas Massey, Howson Hooe and William Steward witnessed the signing of a deed for a one-year lease on a 500-acre tract of land, recorded 3 June 1778, between Thomas Bumbury (Bunbury), Jr. of King George and John Hooe of Prince William. The same witnesses witnessed a deed of release, recorded the following day, between the same two men (Bunbury and John Hooe). [Mary Marshall Brewer, ed., *Abstracts of Land Records of King George County, Virginia, 1752-1783* (Lewes, Delaware: Colonial Roots, 2006), 153-154.]

COMMENT: Even though these deeds were recorded after the 1777 land swap between Stafford and King George, I list them here because the deeds might have been signed before the land swap. I suspect that this John Burton might have been a King George resident who became a Stafford resident because of the land swap, but I don't know for sure. - MB

MAIN CHRONOLOGY OF STAFFORD BURTONS

Part I: 17th & 18th Centuries

STAFFORD COUNTY, Virginia, was formed in 1664 from what had been the northwest portion of Westmoreland County, but it looked a lot different back then than it does now. From 1664 until 1730, Stafford County encompassed all of northern Virginia, including what are today Prince William, Fauquier, Fairfax and Loudoun counties, as well as additional land to the southeast, along the Potomac river basin, that was later traded to King George.

In subsequent years, Stafford was greatly reduced in size as other counties were formed from it's vast northwest territory, including Prince William County in 1731. From 1731 to 1777, Stafford was a relatively narrow, curved strip along the western bank of the Potomac and had no frontage along the Rappahannock River.

Then, in 1777, a land swap between Stafford and King George went into effect, giving King George frontage along the Potomac in what had been southeast Stafford, and giving Stafford land along the Rappahannock that had been in northwest King George, including the port of Falmouth. Many Stafford Burtons ended up living in that area of southern Stafford that had originally been part of King George.

Interestingly, the early Burtons of White Oak lived near the border between Stafford and King George both before and after the 1777 land swap. If my understanding is correct, the original border ran roughly east-west, close to what is today Route 218, and extended all the way up to the current border with Fauquier. After the land swap, the border ran roughly north-south, along Muddy Creek and then up to Potomac Creek.

This Main Chronology covers the period from 1666 (when the first possible Burton was mentioned in connection with Stafford County) to 1930, so readers should keep the changes in Stafford's territory in mind when reviewing the pre-1777 entries. (The first indisputable references to Burtons in Stafford, however, are from 1680.)

Also, except for some of the earlier, pre-1680 entries concerning land patents and headrights, I am generally much *less* speculative in the Main Chronology than I am in the Pre-Stafford Chronology. In addition, as in the Pre-Stafford Chronology, I have employed parenthetical notes, placing source citations in brackets at the end of the cited material.

Furthermore, as in the Pre-Stafford Chronology, I have tried to clearly distinguish my comments from the cited material by placing them at the end of each entry in *italics*, marked with the word "COMMENT" in all caps. I occasionally add comments in parentheses or brackets within the cited material, however, in cases where special clarification is needed.

*   *   *   *   *

1666

ENTRY 1. Thomas Burton and 19 others were to be brought to the Colony by John Keech. [Ruth and Sam Sparacio, eds., *Order Book Abstracts of Stafford County, Virginia, 1664-1668 and 1689-1690* (McLean, Virginia, 1987), 36.]

   COMMENT: Although this secondary source clearly lists him as a Burton, I am not sure if Thomas was a Burton or a Barton. (See 1668, 1698 and 1728 entries.) - MB

1668

ENTRY 2. Tho. Burton was listed as a headright of Jno. Palmer for a 17 April 1668 patent of 500 acres in Stafford County, granted for transporting 10 persons. (This patent had originally been granted to Robt. Alexander on 23 March 1664, but was re-granted to Palmer on grounds that Alexander had deserted the patent.) [Nell Marion Nugent, ed., *Cavaliers and Pioneers: Abstracts of Virginia Land Patents and Grants, 1623-1800, Volume Two, 1666-1695* (Richmond, Virginia: Virginia State Library, 1977), 35.]

   COMMENT: This might be the same Thomas Burton (or Barton) mentioned in 1666, but I don't know for sure. (See 1666 entry.) - MB

1669

ENTRY 3. Eliz. Burton was listed as a headright of Robt. Howsing for a 21 October 1669 patent of land in an unspecified county on the west side of the Potomack in the freshes, near Indian Cabin Creek. [Nell Marion Nugent, ed., *Cavaliers and Pioneers: Abstracts of Virginia Land Patents and Grants, 1623-1800, Volume Two, 1666-1695* (Richmond, Virginia: Virginia State Library, 1977), 67.]

COMMENT: I do not know if Indian Cabin Creek was located in or near Stafford. I only include this because, given the description of the land, it might have been near Stafford (especially because Stafford was much larger at the time than it is now). - MB

ENTRY 4. Percivall Burton was listed as a headright of Edward Rogers and Charles Hoyle for a 25 October 1669 patent of 1,500 acres in Stafford County, on the north side of Potomack Creek. [Nell Marion Nugent, ed., *Cavaliers and Pioneers: Abstracts of Virginia Land Patents and Grants, 1623-1800, Volume Two, 1666-1695* (Richmond, Virginia: Virginia State Library, 1977), 76.]

1670

ENTRY 5. During a 10 October 1670 session held at James City, the Council and General Court of Virginia granted a 3,000-acre patent of land to Willm. Harris and Thomas Baxter in Stafford County. The patent had apparently been abandoned by Coll. (*sic*) Miles Cary. During that same session, Harris was authorized to import 12 people into the Colony, including James Burton. [*Minutes of the Council and General Court of Colonial Virginia, 1622-1632, 1670-1676*, ed. H. R. McIlwaine (Richmond, Virginia: Virginia State Library, 1924), 225.]

According to another source, James Burton was listed as a headright of William Harris (Haris) and Thomas Baxtor (*sic*) for a 10 October 1670 patent for 3,000 acres in Stafford County, located southwest on the Occaquon River near the falls. [Nell Marion Nugent, ed., *Cavaliers and Pioneers: Abstracts of Virginia Land Patents and Grants, 1623-1800, Volume Two, 1666-1695* (Richmond, Virginia: Virginia State Library, 1977), 84.]

COMMENT: By 1680, there was a John Burton living in Stafford and farming some of Harris' land, but I don't know if John and James were related. (See 1680 entry.)

By the way, at least 625 of the 3,000 acres in the Stafford patent might have been north of "Ocquaon" (probably the Occaquon River), according to a deed regarding the sale of those 625 acres years later by Elizabeth Spencer. [Ruth and Sam Sparacio, eds., Deed and Will Abstracts of Stafford County, Virginia, 1689-1693 *(McLean, Virginia, 1989), 100.] In any case, a large portion of the patent was probably located in what is now Prince William County. - MB*

ENTRY 6. Nic. Burton was listed as a headright of John Mott and George Mott for a 17 October 1670 patent of 15,654 acres on the north side of the Rappahannock and over the branches of the Potomeck River. Burton was one of 313 headrights for this patent. One of the other headrights was Tho. Foley. [Nell Marion Nugent, ed., *Cavaliers and Pioneers: Abstracts of Virginia Land Patents and Grants, 1623-1800, Volume Two, 1666-1695* (Richmond, Virginia: Virginia State Library, 1977), 85.]

COMMENT: Although no county was specified, I include this in the Main Chronology, rather than the Pre-Stafford Chronology, because (1) Stafford had been formed by 1670; and (2) the description of "branches of the Potomeck" indicates that the land was wholly or partially located in what was then Stafford County, because Stafford included the Potomac watershed; and (3) I doubt that the patentees would have been granted such a large patent in the older, smaller counties of Northumberland or Westmoreland.

I also mention Tho. Foley because he might have been the Thomas Foley/Folio who married Martha (Bryant?). (See 1690 entries related to Martha.) - MB

ENTRY 7. Henry Burton and Andrew Ryan witnessed a 10 December 1670 Westmoreland County deed in which Henry Bury and his wife Hannah Bury conveyed 70 acres to planter John Small of Stafford County. The land was near a small run upon the river of Machotick, upon the common path bounding upon the land of John Partins. [John Frederick Dorman, ed., *Westmoreland County, Virginia, Deeds, Patents, Etc., 1665-1677, Part One* (Washington, D.C., 1973), 58.]

COMMENT: I am not aware of any Henry Burtons in Stafford at this time. I include this only because one of the parties to the deed was from Stafford and, therefore, it is possible that one of the witnesses might also have been from Stafford. - MB

1677

ENTRY 8. Rich. Burden was listed as a headright of Lieut. Col. Cad. Jones and David Jones for a 29 December 1677 patent for 14,114 acres in Stafford County "upon both sides of Accotynk and Pohick rivers," about four miles from Doege's Run to a branch of Occaquon. [Nell Marion Nugent, ed., *Cavaliers and Pioneers: Abstracts of Virginia Land Patents and Grants, 1623-1800, Volume Two, 1666-1695* (Richmond, Virginia: Virginia State Library, 1977), 191.]

COMMENT: *I include this because, until about the mid-19th century, the surname Burton was sometimes spelled Burden. - MB*

1678

ENTRY 9. Jno. Burton was listed as a headright of Major Andrew Gilsonn (Gilson) for a 10 October 1678 patent of land in Stafford County, on the south-southwest side of Powell's Run. [Nell Marion Nugent, ed., *Cavaliers and Pioneers: Abstracts of Virginia Land Patents and Grants, 1623-1800, Volume Two, 1666-1695* (Richmond, Virginia: Virginia State Library, 1977), 193.]

COMMENT: *I don't know if this was the same John Burton mentioned in 1680. (See 1680 entry.) - MB*

1680

ENTRY 10. Circa May 1680, John Burton signed a deed with William Harris (both of Stafford County), apparently to farm Harris' plantation near "Neapscoe" for five years (until Christmas 1684). [Ruth and Sam Sparacio, eds., *Deed and Will Abstracts of Stafford County, Virginia, 1809-1810* (McLean, Virginia: The Antient Press, 1992), 30. Includes court records for 1680.]

COMMENT: *According to a 1770 map of Virginia, Neapsco was the name of a creek in what was then northern Stafford County (but today would likely be part of Marine Corps Base Quantico).* [A New and Accurate Map of Virginia, *Surveyed by John Henry of Hanover County (London, 1770). Viewed by the author in the Fredericksburg Area Museum in 2010.]*

I do not know, however, if the plantation to be farmed by Burton was in Stafford or Westmoreland, because Harris owned land in both counties. For example, William Harris and Lewis Markham had a 1,600 acre patent in Westmoreland County near Neapscoe Creek, granted to them 26 February 1690. [Ruth and Sam Sparacio, eds., Deed and Will Abstracts of Stafford County, Virginia, 1699-1709 *(McLean, Virginia, 1987), 142.] (This was in addition to the 3,000 acre patent in Stafford that William Harris and Thomas Baxter received in 1670.)*

The date of the Westmoreland patent, if accurate, was more than 25 years after the formation of Stafford County from Westmoreland, so perhaps there were two Neapscoe Creeks (one in northern Stafford and one in Westmoreland). The 1680 deed, however, pre-dates the 1690 Westmoreland patent; therefore, I suspect that the plantation was in northern Stafford.

By the way, I do not know if Lewis Markham was related to the James Markham who filed a lawsuit against Samuel Burton in King George in 1721. (See 1721 Pre-Stafford entry.) - MB

ENTRY 11. William Burton was about 30 years old when he gave a sworn deposition, recorded 11 November 1680, regarding JNO (John?) Dry. [Ruth and Sam Sparacio, eds., *Deed and Will Abstracts of Stafford County, Virginia, 1809-1810* (McLean, Virginia: The Antient Press, 1992), 24. Includes court records for 1680.]

ENTRY 12. Edward ("EDWD") Burton was paid a "leavy" for a "Wolfe" circa November 1680. [Ruth and Sam Sparacio, eds., *Deed and Will Abstracts of Stafford County, Virginia, 1809-1810* (McLean, Virginia: The Antient Press, 1992), 28. Includes court records for 1680.]

COMMENT: I am not sure if Edward was a Burton or a Barton. Another source indicates that there was an Edward Barton in Stafford during the late 1600s. [Court Records, 1664-1668, 1689-1693, Records Office of the Clerk of the Circuit Court, Stafford County, Virginia, 165.] Perhaps they were two different men. - MB

1690

ENTRY 13. William Burton "became Security" to "perform what the Law requires" regarding an estate, circa 11 June 1690. [Ruth and Sam Sparacio, eds., *Order Book Abstracts of Stafford County, Virginia, 1664-1668 and 1689-1690* (McLean, Virginia, 1987), 90-91.]

ENTRY 14. William Burton served on either one jury regarding two separate cases, or on two separate juries, circa 11-12 June 1690. [Ruth and Sam Sparacio, eds., *Order Book Abstracts of Stafford County, Virginia, 1664-1668 and 1689-1690* (McLean, Virginia, 1987), 94, 96.]

ENTRY 15. William Burton served on a jury circa 12 June 1690 regarding Richard Bryant's accusation that Thomas Folio had killed one of Bryant's hogs. [Ruth and Sam Sparacio, eds., *Order Book Abstracts of Stafford County, Virginia, 1664-1668 and 1689-1690* (McLean, Virginia, 1987), 97.]

COMMENT: I cannot help but think that William Burton might have had a conflict of interest in serving on this particular jury. For example, it appears that Richard Bryant might have been Burton's landlord (see 1701, 1703 and 1726 entries, below, regarding Burtons and Bryants). In addition, Burton would marry Folio's widow later that same year. (See 1690 entry, below.)

By the way, I do not know if Folio was still alive as of 12 June 1690. Perhaps Bryant was suing Folio's estate. - MB

ENTRY 16. In what might be one of the first prenuptial agreements in Stafford County history, the widowed Martha Folio had William Burton agree in writing on 5 November 1690 to provide specified items to each of Martha's children by Folio as they came of age.

The agreement was recorded 8 November 1690, and included the statement that "…the said William Burton doth grant & promise with ye said Martha before Matrimony to pay her Children as they come of age as followeth."

The children named in the deed were Brian Folio, John, Thomas, Richard and Anne. They were each to receive one mare, one cow and one calf. In addition, Brian and John were each to receive a gun. [Ruth and Sam Sparacio, eds., *Deed and Will Abstracts of Stafford County, Virginia, 1689-1693* (McLean, Virginia, 1989), 32.]

COMMENT: According to one researcher, Martha might have been Martha Bryant Foley (a.k.a. Folio), the daughter of a Potomac Indian princess named Keziah Aroyah and an Englishman known only as Mr. Bryant. Keziah Aroyah, in turn, was purportedly the daughter of Wahanganoche, king of Patawomeck (Potomac). Wahanganoche was the cousin of Pocahontas and the nephew of Powhatan.

According to this theory, Keziah Aroyah's children included Martha; Dr. Richard Bryant, Sr.; Thomas Bryant; Silent Bryant; and another son who was the father of Elinor (Bryant?) Gallop Owens.

This same source indicates that Martha's son, Brian Folio (a.k.a. Bryant Foley), married Mary Jones. [William L. Deyo, The Monteith Family and the Potomac Indians (Colonial Beach, Virginia: DeJoux Publications, 2001.) Based on details found on page 36 and in a chart near the back of the publication on an unnumbered page.]

If Martha Folio really was the sister of Dr. Richard Bryant, Sr., it would help explain the apparent close relationship between the Bryant and Burton families. (See 1690, 1701, 1703 and 1726 entries regarding Bryants, Elkins and Burtons.)

Furthermore, if Martha was half-Indian, it might mean that hundreds of Burton descendants in southern Stafford could claim Potomac Indian ancestry, but only if Martha and William had children of their own. I will need a bit more evidence, however, before I claim to be related to Pocahontas.

By the way, the same researcher indicates in another publication that Keziah Aroyah's father, Wahanganoche, was the son of Japasaw and one of Japasaw's two wives (possibly Paupauwiske). [William L. Deyo, A Brief Outline of Recorded History of the Patawomeck Tribe *(Colonial Beach, Virginia: DeJoux Publications, 2000), 6.]*

In addition, I have been unable to confirm or refute claims on the Internet that Martha married Thomas Foley/Folio in 1671 in Stafford. For what it's worth, however, a Tho. Foley was listed as a headright in 1670 regarding a patent in the Stafford area. (See 1670 entry for Nic. Burton, above.)

Some of those same sources include claims that Thomas, or both Thomas and Martha, died 9 September 1690, perhaps based on the 8 November 1690 recording date of the "pre-nup" mentioned here. It would be more accurate to say that Thomas, not Martha, had died by 5 November 1690.

I also could not confirm or refute online claims that (1) Thomas Foley was born in 1650 in Elizabeth City, Virginia, or born before 1650 in the U.K. (sic); or (2) Martha was born in 1652 or 1655 in Westmoreland or Stafford (sic). [I do not know the source(s) of these dates.] - MB

ENTRY 17. William Burton and his wife Martha asked the court to order an appraisement of the estate of Martha's deceased first husband, Thomas Folio, circa 11 March 1690 (1691). [Ruth and Sam Sparacio, eds., *Order Book Abstracts of Stafford County, Virginia, 1690-1692* (McLean, Virginia), 4-5. Copyright date unknown.]

The original document refers to this entry as "Burton's Petition," indicating that it was addressed "at a court held for the County of Stafford at the house of Thomas (Elsoy?)" on 11 March 1690. Those present included Coll. William Fitzhugh, Capt. George Mason, Mr. John Withers, Mr. Samuel (Haynard?) and Mr. Edward Thomason. The court ordered that Francis Hunt, Abram Bockington, John (Rousloy?), or any two of them appraise the estate of Thomas Folio on Wednesday the 18th.

The details indicate that Martha had been appointed the administrator of Folio's estate but had omitted to have the court order an appraisement. I am not sure if William Burton made the request alone or if he made it jointly with Martha (as the abstract, above, seems to suggest), but the details clearly indicate that William Burton had "intermarried" with Martha, the "widow and relict of Thomas Folio, late of this county." [*Court Records, 1664-1668, 1689-1693, Stafford County*, Records Office of the Clerk of the Circuit Court, Stafford County, Virginia, 123, 125.]

COMMENT: This was presumably the same William Burton, by the way, who witnessed the Will of Francis Hunt in 1701. (See 1701 entry.) - MB

ENTRY 18. William Burton served on either one jury investigating two different cases or on two different juries, circa 12 March 1690/1691. One case involved a dispute between Nicholas Goodridge and David Darnell. The other was a case involving Richard Gibson. [Ruth and Sam Sparacio, eds., *Order Book Abstracts of Stafford County, Virginia, 1690-1692* (McLean, Virginia), 9-11. Copyright date unknown.]

ENTRY 19. Will Burton was seen "going over Potomack Creek" in a boat with several other men, including John Waugh, according to the testimony of Richard Bryant. [Ruth and Sam Sparacio, eds., *Deed and Will Abstracts of Stafford County, Virginia, 1689-1693* (McLean, Virginia, 1989), 18.]

1691

ENTRY 20. William Burton served on a jury circa 20 May 1691 which ordered William Harris to free Benjamin Lewis, "a Negroe," on evidence that Lewis had been free in England and had only been a temporary indentured servant, not a slave. Harris appealed. [Ruth and Sam Sparacio, eds., *Order Book Abstracts of Stafford County, Virginia, 1690-1692* (McLean, Virginia), 20-21. Copyright date unknown.]

ENTRY 21. Martha Burton confirmed the inventory which had been taken of the estate of her deceased first husband, Thomas Folio. [Ruth and Sam Sparacio, eds., *Deed and Will Abstracts of Stafford County, Virginia, 1689-1693* (McLean, Virginia, 1989), 61.]

ENTRY 22. Thomas Burton, Sr. took an oath to be a grandjuryman on 6 October 1691. [Ruth and Sam Sparacio, eds., *Order Book Abstracts of Stafford County, Virginia, 1690-1692* (McLean, Virginia), 38. Copyright date unknown.]

COMMENT: I do not know if this is the same Thomas Burton mentioned in the 1666 or 1668 entries, but it seems a reasonable assumption. Also, I assume from the use of the suffix "Senior" that he was the father of Thomas Burton, Junior, although the use of such suffixes does always indicate a familial relationship. (See entry for 1700, below.)

It is possible, though, that this was Thomas Barton, Sr., who had a son named Thomas and whose surname was sometimes spelled Burton in other sources. (See 1728 entry.) - MB

ENTRY 23. A Mrs. Hewett was ordered, circa 7 October 1691, to pay William Burton for attending court regarding her suite (*sic*) against Captain George Mason. [Ruth and Sam Sparacio, eds., *Order Book Abstracts of Stafford County, Virginia, 1690-1692* (McLean, Virginia), 40. Copyright date unknown.]

ENTRY 24. William Burton was mentioned in a dispute with Joseph Newton circa 7 October 1691 regarding a debt of more than half a ton of tobacco. [Ruth and Sam Sparacio, eds., *Order Book Abstracts of Stafford County, 1690-1692* (McLean, Virginia), 40. Copyright date unknown.]

ENTRY 25. On 12 February of 1691 or 1692, William Burton was ordered to pay Joseph Sumner 2,000 pounds [literally one ton!] of tobacco for killing one of Sumner's hogs. [Ruth and Sam Sparacio, eds., *Order Book Abstracts of Stafford County, Virginia, 1690-1692* (McLean, Virginia), 92-93. Copyright date unknown.]

COMMENT: There was apparently a law at the time that imposed very stiff penalties on anyone found guilty of killing another's hog. I wonder if this law actually encouraged false accusations. See also the 1690 entry regarding the case between Bryant and Folio. - MB

1692

ENTRY 26. William Burton's cornfield was mentioned as being near "Maulles Swampe" in a 1 December 1692 deed between David Anderson and Thomas Harris. [Ruth and Sam Sparacio, eds., *Deed and Will Abstracts of Stafford County, Virginia, 1689-1693* (McLean, Virginia, 1989)]

ENTRY 27. William Burton received a "levy" for a wolf (apparently for shooting the wolf), circa 13 December 1692. [Ruth and Sam Sparacio, eds., *Deed and Will Abstracts of Stafford County, Virginia, 1689-1693* (McLean, Virginia, 1989), 136-137.]

1693

ENTRY 28. William Burton served on a jury circa 8 February 1692/1693. Joel Stribling had borrowed a horse from James Hall on or about 25 April 1692, and the horse died while in Stribling's care. The jury ordered that Stribling pay Hall 1500 pounds of tobacco plus costs. [Ruth and Sam Sparacio, eds., *Order Book Abstracts of Stafford County, Virginia, 1692-1693* (McLean, Virginia, 1988), 65.]

1698

ENTRY 29. According to an entry dated 12 February 1698, Thomas Burton apparently purchased 100 acres of land on Quanticutt Creek in Stafford County from the estate of William Mansbridge, who died in 1697. [Gertrude E. Gray, *Virginia Northern Neck Land Grants, 1694-1742* (Baltimore: Genealogical Publishing Co., Inc., 1987), 22.]

COMMENT: I did not find any documented evidence that this Thomas was the same one who was scheduled to be brought to the Colony by John Keech in 1666, but it might have been the same Thomas, or Thomas' son.

I suspect, though, that this was Thomas Barton, Sr. or Thomas Barton, Jr., who apparently owned land in the Quantico area. (See 1728 entry.) - MB

1699

ENTRY 30. William Burton was mentioned regarding debts and John Pike's estate, circa 1699 or 1700. [Ruth and Sam Sparacio, eds., *Deed and Will Abstracts of Stafford County, Virginia, 1699-1709* (McLean, Virginia, 1987), 6.]

1700

ENTRY 31. Thos. Burton was summoned to serve on a jury in 1700 regarding a dispute between Sml. Samford and Capt. John West. [Ruth and Sam Sparacio, eds., *Deed and Will Abstracts of Stafford County, Virginia, 1699-1709* (McLean, Virginia, 1987), 8.]

ENTRY 32. It was recorded on 8 May 1700 that William Burton and John Rowley had appraised goods of Henry Shalters. [Ruth and Sam Sparacio, eds., *Deed and Will Abstracts of Stafford County, Virginia, 1699-1709* (McLean, Virginia, 1987), 10.]

1701

ENTRY 33. William Burton, Richard Bryant, Sr., and Richard Bryant, Jr. witnessed the will of Francis Hunt. [Ruth and Sam Sparacio, eds., *Deed and Will Abstracts of Stafford County, Virginia, 1699-1709* (McLean, Virginia, 1987), 36.]

ENTRY 34. Samuel Burton received a levy for "post" circa 12 December 1701. [Ruth and Sam Sparacio, eds., *Deed and Will Abstracts of Stafford County, Virginia, 1699-1709* (McLean, Virginia, 1987), 41.]

1702

ENTRY 35. Samuel Burton received a levy for a journey to town circa 12 November 1702. [Ruth and Sam Sparacio, eds., *Deed and Will Abstracts of Stafford County, Virginia, 1699-1709* (McLean, Virginia, 1987), 51.]

1703

ENTRY 36. According to the Will of Richard Bryant, Sr., dated 5 April 1703, Samuel Burton had been living on a plantation apparently owned by Bryant, but Bryant had not required Burton to pay rent for the previous four years. Bryant left instructions in his Will, however, that Burton pay 450 pounds of tobacco in rent, plus the quitrents for 100 acres, if he continued to live on the plantation. Apparently, Bryant also wanted Burton to vacate the premises in the future, once Bryant's son turned 18, to allow the son the option of living there.

In addition, William Burton was one of two men listed as "security" for Richard's wife, Ann Bryant, who was to be the Executrix of Richard's estate. [Ruth and Sam Sparacio, eds., *Deed and Will Abstracts of Stafford County, Virginia, 1699-1709* (McLean, Virginia, 1987), 81-82.]

COMMENT: This is the only source I have that mentions both the "first" William Burton and Samuel Burton. Their mutual connection to the Bryants suggests that they were probably related to each other, if not to the Bryants as well.

Dr. Richard Bryant, Sr. was the grandfather of Richard Elkin/Ellkins. I don't know which spelling of Elkin is correct. (See the 1726 entry regarding the "second" William Burton on Richard Ellkin's plantation, indicating a continued relationship between the two families.)

By the way, Ann Bryant's maiden name might have been Meese. [William L. Deyo,
The Monteith Family and the Potomac Indians *(Colonial Beach, Virginia: DeJoux*
Publications, 2001.) From a chart near the back of the publication on an unnumbered
page.] - MB

1706

ENTRY 37. On 11 September 1706, William Burton, William Smith and Thos. Harris
presented their appraisal of the estate of William Wood. [Ruth and Sam Sparacio,
eds., *Deed and Will Abstracts of Stafford County, Virginia, 1699-1709* (McLean,
Virginia, 1987), 124.]]

1725

ENTRY 38. William Burton married Sarah Spicer on 14 December 1725. [George H.
S. King, ed., *St. Paul's Parish Register, 1715-1798* (Fredericksburg, Virginia, 1960), 20.]
[Therese A. Fisher, ed., *Marriage Records of the City of Fredericksburg and of Orange,*
Spotsylvania and Stafford Counties, Virginia, 1722-1850 (Bowie, MD: Heritage Books,
Inc., 1990), 28.]

   COMMENT: Is this William Burton the son of William and Martha? (See 1690
entries.) Or possibly the son of Samuel Burton? - MB

1726

ENTRY 39. Lettice Burton, daughter of William Burton and Sarah Spicer, was born
on 19 August 1726. [George H. S. King, ed., *St. Paul's Parish Register, 1715-1798*
(Fredericksburg, Virginia, 1960), 20.]

ENTRY 40. William Burton lived on a 75-acre plantation in St. Paul's parish in
Stafford County circa 13 April 1726, which Richard Ellkins (*sic*) sold to John
Fitzhugh. [Ruth and Sam Sparacio, eds., *Deed Abstracts of Stafford County, 1722-1728,*
1775-1765 (McLean, Virginia, 1987), 32.]

   COMMENT: This might have been the same plantation, or part of the same
plantation, mentioned in the Will of Elkin's/Ellkins' grandfather, Dr. Richard Bryant, Sr.,
where Samuel Burton lived in 1703. (See 1703 entry.)

I am not sure, however, because a source on the Internet indicates that, in 1690, Richard Elkin (sic) and Nathaniel Elkin had inherited 150-acre plantation that their father, Ralph Elkin, had purchased from a Major Ashton in 1681. The Internet source indicates, correctly or not, that a William Burton was living on the 150-acre plantation in 1681.

In any case, this suggests that the William Burton living on the 75-acre plantation in 1726 might have been a son, nephew or other relative of either Samuel Burton or the "first" William Burton. It's also possible, depending on the accuracy of the Internet source, that the "first" William Burton, Samuel Burton and the "second" William Burton all lived on the same plantation. - MB

1728

ENTRY 41. Deed J-507, made 4 April 1728, and deeds J-509 and J-510, made 5 April 1728, document transactions between Thomas T. Barton and Abram/Abraham (Farrow?). The details of J-507 appear to indicate that Barton's father, also named Thomas, had acquired 400 acres of land on Quanticoe Creek from Wm. (Bourne?) and Samll. and Mary (Masel?) at some point between 1665 and 1685. The younger Thomas sold these 400 acres to Farrow.

The land, by the way, had originally been granted by Governor Wm. Berkeley to Capt. John Lord, apparently on 27 September 1664. Lord conveyed it to Thos. (Bourne?) on 30 August 1665.

In some places in these deeds, however, Thomas Barton's surname is spelled Burton, even though it is also spelled Barton in other places of the very same deeds. [*Stafford Deeds, 1722-1728*, Records Office of the Clerk of the Circuit Court, Stafford County, Virginia, 507-510. ("Deed Book J" written on inside of front cover.)]

COMMENT: It seems clear from the signature blocks that this was Thomas Barton, not Burton. I mention these documents, though, because they raise the possibility that references in other documents from the same era to Thomas Burton might actually be references to Thomas Barton. (See 1666, 1668, 1691 and 1698 entries.)

By the way, according to another source, Abraham Farrow (circa 1670-1731) died with an estate of roughly 2,400 acres in what is now Prince William County. In 1709, he bought Richard Gibson's mill on Quantico Creek. [Jerrilynn Eby, Men of Mark: Officials of Stafford County, Virginia, 1664-1991 (Westminster, Maryland: Heritage Books, Inc., 2006), 45.]

I do not know, however, if this was the same Richard Gibson involved in the 1690 court case. (See 1690 entry.) - MB

1740

ENTRY 42. A reconstructed census for Virginia in 1740 indicates that a Mr. Burten (*sic*) lived in Stafford that year. [*Virginia in 1740: A Reconstructed Census* (Miami Beach, Florida: T. L. C. Genealogy, 1992), 49.]

COMMENT: Although I have doubts about the reliability of this source, "Burten" might have been a misspelled reference to the William Burton who married Sarah Spicer (see 1725 marriage entry), but I do not know for sure. The source indicates that the name Burten was found in Stafford County Will Book M, 1729-1748. *- MB*

1741

ENTRY 43. Lettice Burton married Alexander Jefferies on 30 September 1741. [Therese A. Fisher, ed., *Marriage Records of the City of Fredericksburg and of Orange, Spotsylvania and Stafford Counties, Virginia, 1722-1850* (Bowie, MD: Heritage Books, Inc., 1990), 90.]

COMMENT: Lettice was the daughter of William and Sarah Spicer and was 15 years old when she married. (See 1726 birth entry.) - MB

1746

ENTRY 44. Priscilla Burton, daughter of William Burton, was born on 17 January 1746. [The Register of Overwharton Parish, Stafford County, Virginia, 1723-1758.]

COMMENT: The mother's name was not given. I suspect that this William Burton was the husband of Sarah Spicer (see 1725 marriage entry), but I do not know for sure. - MB

1749

ENTRY 45. According to a March 1749 entry in a Stafford Court record, "William Bruton's will proved by (Isbell?) Davis (illegible) and is ordered to be certified." [*Order Book, 1749-1755*, Stafford County, Virginia, 15. (Digitized electronic copy, Library of Virginia Website. Viewed online by the author in 2012.)]

COMMENT: I do not know if this is a misspelled reference to a William Burton or not. Other sources also reference a William Bruton in Stafford at this time. - MB

ENTRY 46. William Burton was mentioned regarding a debt related to the estate of Chandler Fowke. [Ruth and Sam Sparacio, eds., *Will Abstracts of Stafford County, 1748-1767* (McLean, Virginia, 1987), 30.]

COMMENT: According to another source, Captain Chandler Fowke of Gunston Hall lived from 1692-1745. [Jerrilynn Eby, Men of Mark: Officials of Stafford County, Virginia, 1664-1991 (Westminster, Maryland: Heritage Books, Inc., 2006), 50-51.] - MB

1750

ENTRY 47. According to an April 1750 entry in a Stafford Court record, "administration with the will annexed of William Breuton decd. is granted John Smith—Bennett Beasly, Jeremiah Smith security; Howson Hooe, John Short, John Alexander & William Bumbury appraisers." [*Order Book, 1749-1755*, Records Office of the Clerk of the Circuit Court, Stafford County, Virginia, 30.]

COMMENT: I am not sure if the deceased was a Burton or not. - MB

ENTRY 48. According to an April 1750 entry in a Stafford Court record "in the action of trespafs (*sic*) upon the Case between Priscilla Bows (plt.?) & William Burton Deft., on the Deft.'s motion (anals capias?) (is?) ordered returnable to the next Court." [*Order Book, 1749-1755*, Records Office of the Clerk of the Circuit Court, Stafford County, Virginia, 38.]

COMMENT: This case was sent to a jury the following year. (See related 1751 entry, below.) - MB

ENTRY 49. According to a May 1750 entry in a Stafford Court record, "the Inventory and appraisment of the Estate of William Breuton decd. being returned is admitted to Record." [*Order Book, 1749-1755*, Records Office of the Clerk of the Circuit Court, Stafford County, Virginia, 44.]

COMMENT: I am not sure if the deceased was a Burton or not. - MB

ENTRY 50. According to a 10 July 1750 entry in a Stafford Court record "in the action of trespafs (*sic*) upon the Case between Priscilla Bows plt. & William Burton Deft., the Deft. not appearing Judgment is granted the plt. against him and Peter Maury his security for (illegible) of the sum sued for in the Declaration shall...." [*Order Book, 1749-1755*, Records Office of the Clerk of the Circuit Court, Stafford County, Virginia, 61.]

COMMENT: *This decision was appealed in court the following month and sent to a jury the following year. (See related entries, below, as well as 1751 entry.) The last sentence is incomplete in the original document. - MB*

ENTRY 51. According to a 16 August 1750 entry in a Stafford Court record, William Burton served on a jury in an "action of trespass upon the case between Martha (Horton?) plt. and William Ross & Mary his wife, defts." The other members of the jury were Calvert Porter, Joseph Combs, John Fitzpatrick, John (Paunall?), John Nelson, Thomas Nelson, Thomas (Wood?), Nathanel Gray, William (Holebrook?), George Randall and Robert (illegible).

According to another entry on the same page, William Breuton served on a jury for another case, with the same jury members that served with William Burton.

On the next page, a William Brunton served on a different jury in the case of *Edward Bush v. Thomas Porter*, and a William Burton served on a jury in the case of *Edward Bush v. John Fitzpatrick*. [*Order Book, 1749-1755*, Records Office of the Clerk of the Circuit Court, Stafford County, Virginia, 75,76.]

COMMENT: *Earlier records indicate that a William Bruton/Breuton had died in 1749. (See 1749 death entry.) So, was there a William Breuton, Jr. who served on the jury? Or did a clerk accidently transcribe Burton's name as Breuton?*

I suspect that the two juries mentioned on page 75 were the same jury being used for two different trials. If so, it would mean that the William Burton and the William Breuton mentioned were the same man.

The two juries mentioned on page 76 were not the same, but the problem is similar. I suspect that the William Brunton mentioned was actually William Burton or William Breuton.

Perhaps the same man served on all four juries. - MB

ENTRY 52. According to a 16 August 1750 entry in a Stafford Court record "in the action of trespafs (*sic*) upon the case between Priscilla (Bows?) Plt. and William Burton Deft. The Security for the Deft. having pleaded that the Deft. did not...(illegible)...till the next Court." [*Order Book, 1749-1755*, Records Office of the Clerk of the Circuit Court, Stafford County, Virginia, 77.]

COMMENT: This case was sent to a jury the following year. (See related 1751 entry, below.) - MB

ENTRY 53. According to an 11 September 1750 entry in a Stafford Court record, William Burton served on a jury regarding "an action of debt" between Robert (Million?) and Charles Harding. One of the other jurors, Charles Brent, was withdrawn and the case was dismissed, but the plaintiff was ordered to pay the defendant's costs. [*Order Book, 1749-1755*, Records Office of the Clerk of the Circuit Court, Stafford County, Virginia, 89.]

ENTRY 54. According to a 11 September 1750 entry in a Stafford Court record, "the action of trespass upon the case between Priscilla Bows Pltf. & William Burton Deft. is continued at the Pltf.'s costs." [*Order Book, 1749-1755*, Records Office of the Clerk of the Circuit Court, Stafford County, Virginia, 90.]

COMMENT: This case was sent to a jury the following year. (See related 1751 entry, below.) - MB

ENTRY 55. According to a 12 December 1750 entry in a Stafford Court record, "the action of Trespass upon the Case between Priscilla Bows Pltf. & William Burton Deft. is continued at the Deft.'s cost." [*Order Book, 1749-1755*, Records Office of the Clerk of the Circuit Court, Stafford County, Virginia, 104.]

COMMENT: This case was sent to a jury the following year. (See related 1751 entry, below.) - MB

1751

ENTRY 56. According to a 14 May 1751 entry in a Stafford Court record, "in the action of Trespass upon the Case between Prifcilla (*sic*) (Bows?) (Plt.?) & William Burton Deft. a Jury to wit: William Allen, John Ramay, Joseph (Bragg?), Elias Hore, William Matheny, Nathl. Gray, Innes Brent, Philip Peyton, Andrew Edward, John Kirk, William Mills & Thomas Matheny were fworn (*sic*) to try the (Ifsue joined?) who brought in their Verdict in these words We of the Jury find for the (Pltf.?) eight hundred & seventy five pounds of Tobacco Nathl. Gray foreman, which Verdict at the Pltf.'s motion is (admitted?) to record & its considered by the Court that the Pltf. recover of the sd. Deft. & Peter (Maury?) & Withrs. Conway his Security the sd. eight hundred seventy five pounds of Tobacco by the Jurors afsd. in their Verdict aforesd.

(apealed?), & his costs by him in this Behalf expended." [*Order Book, 1749-1755*, Records Office of the Clerk of the Circuit Court, Stafford County, Virginia, 116.]

COMMENT: *I don't know what this case was about, but I noticed that the same source document records numerous similar cases of unspecified "trespass" between other parties. - MB*

ENTRY 57. According to two 11 September 1751 entries in a Stafford Court record, "Will. Burton" served on two juries during that session of the Court. The first jury tried an "action of Trespass, Assault & Battery" between Chas. Regan Pltf. & Philip Payton & Winifred his wife, Defts. The jury found for the plaintiff one penny Sterling.

The second jury tried an "action of Trespass, Assault & Battery" between John Carpenter Pltf. & John Kirk & Sarah his wife, Defts. The jury found for the plaintiff forty shillings Sterling. [*Order Book, 1749-1755*, Records Office of the Clerk of the Circuit Court, Stafford County, Virginia, 130.]

ENTRY 58. According to a 12 September 1751 entry, the Stafford County Court "ordered that William Fuell pay Will. Burton two hundred pounds of Tobacco for eight days attendance as an Evidence for him at fuit (*sic*) of Smallwood." [*Order Book, 1749-1755*, Records Office of the Clerk of the Circuit Court, Stafford County, Virginia, 135.]

COMMENT: *Other entries in the same source indicate that defendant Fuell won a suit brought against him by plaintiff Bayn Smallwood, Gent. - MB*

1753

ENTRY 59. William Burton married Rachel Porch on 7 October 1753. [The Register of Overwharton Parish, Stafford County, Virginia, 1723-1758.]

COMMENT: *Is this William Burton the son of the "second" William Burton and Sarah Spicer? Or otherwise the grandson of the "first" William Burton? Or might this William be the widower of Sarah Spicer?*

Without additional evidence, I will assume that this is the "third" William Burton, son of the "second" William Burton and Sarah Spicer. - MB

1754

ENTRY 60. Mary Burton, daughter of William and Rachel Burton, was born on 30 May 1754. [George H. S. King, ed., *St. Paul's Parish Register, 1715-1798* (Fredericksburg, Virginia, 1960), 20.]

ENTRY 61. According to a 14 May 1754 entry in a Stafford Court record, "in the action of debt between William Black (Pltf.?) & William Burton & James Hansborough defts. the defts. came into Court & confefsed (*sic*) Judgment to the (Plt.?) for eleven pounds two shillings & eight pence & three hundred & fifty pounds of Tobacco (it's?) thereupon considered by the Court that the (Plt.?) recover the fame (*sic*) (of the sd.?) defts. & his Costs by him in this behalf expended. But this Judgment is to be discharged the Costs excepted on payment of five pounds eleven shillings & four pence & one hundred & seventy five pounds of Tobacco with Interest thereon from the (first?) day of June 1752 till the same is paid. (Mem^m?) This is to be paid in Crop Tobacco a (12/6?) (per?) hundred or transfer deducting six (per?) Cent." [*Order Book, 1749-1755*, Records Office of the Clerk of the Circuit Court, Stafford County, Virginia, 271.]

COMMENT: *A similar entry was made the following month. (See entry below.) - MB*

ENTRY 62. According to a 12 June 1754 entry in a Stafford Court record, "in the action of debt between William Black (Plt.?) & William Burton & James Hansbrough defents. the defts. came into Court and Confefsed (*sic*) Judgment to the (Plt.?) for eleven pounds & two shillings & two pence & three hundred & fifty pounds of Tobacco; It's thereupon considered by the Court that the Plt. recover fame (*sic*) of the sd. defts. & his Costs by him in this behalf expended. But this Judgment is to be discharged the Costs excepted on payment of five pounds eleven shillings and four pence & one hundred & seventy five pounds of Tobacco with interest thereon from the first day of June one thousand seven hundred & fifty two till the same is paid. Mem.^{m} To be paid in crop Tobacco as 12/6 (per?) Cent, or transfer deducting six (per?) Cent." [*Order Book, 1749-1755*, Records Office of the Clerk of the Circuit Court, Stafford County, Virginia, 300.]

COMMENT: *I do not know if this James Hansborough/Hansbrough was related to the Peter Hansbrough mentioned in the 1819 court case between William Burton's children. (See 1819 entry for* Burton vs. Burton.*) - MB*

ENTRY 63. According to an (11?) October 1754 entry in a Stafford Court record, "William Burton and (Derrick Mannon?) produced a certificate under the hand of Mott Doniphan Gent. for taking up a runaway Servant Man named John (Brown?) belonging to John (Brown?) of this County, who made Oath that the sd. Service was real & bonafide made done & performed & that they had not received any satisfaction for the same which is ordered to be certified to the General Assembly for allowance." [*Order Book, 1749-1755*, Records Office of the Clerk of the Circuit Court, Stafford County, Virginia, 333.]

ENTRY 64. According to a 13 November entry in a Stafford Court record, William Burton served on the jury for an "action of debt" between John Thornton Plt. and Andrew (Crawford?), Andrew Kenny & John Minor, defts. The other jury members were Thomas Suddon (*sic*), John Clark, John Kirk, George Randall, William Allen, Edward Pilcher, James Berry, Thomas Crawford, William King, George Bell and Charles Harding (foreman). The jury found for the Plt. 19 pounds, 13 shillings & 9 pence & 344 pounds of Tobacco. [*Order Book, 1749-1755*, Records Office of the Clerk of the Circuit Court, Stafford County, Virginia, 336.]

   COMMENT: *Thomas Suddon was probably Thomas Seddon. - MB*

1755

ENTRY 65. According to an April 1755 entry in a Stafford Court record, the Court "ordered that Thomas Hornbuckle pay William Burton one hundred and fifty pounds of Tobacco for six days attendance as an Evidence for him against Grigsby." [*Order Book, 1749-1755*, Records Office of the Clerk of the Circuit Court, Stafford County, Virginia, 360.]

ENTRY 66. According to a 9 April 1755 entry in a Stafford Court record, the Court "ordered that John Canaday pay William Burton three hundred pounds of Tobacco for twelve days attendance as an Evidence for him against Chambers." [*Order Book, 1749-1755*, Records Office of the Clerk of the Circuit Court, Stafford County, Virginia, 364.]

   COMMENT: *According to another entry on the same page of the same source, in an action of trespass, assault and battery made by Canady against Daniel Chambers, the jury found in favor of Chambers. - MB*

1756

ENTRY 67. Samuel Burton, son of William and Rachel Burton, was born on 20 April 1756 in Stafford. [The Register of Overwharton Parish, Stafford County, Virginia, 1723-1758.]

   COMMENT: Samuel moved to Culpeper County circa 1798 and died in October 1831. (See the entries for 1798 and 1831 for additional source citations.) Most sources indicate that his wife was named Mary. Some or all of their children were named in an 1840s court record. (See 1843 entry.) At least some of their children were born or lived in Stafford before they moved to Culpeper. - MB

ENTRY 68. William Burton lived in Overwharton parish in Stafford County circa 28 June 1756 and sold goods to Alexander Doniphan. [Ruth and Sam Sparacio, eds., *Deed Abstracts of Stafford County, 1722-1728, 1775-1765* (McLean, Virginia, 1987), 108.]

   Deed P-134, recorded 15 December 1756, lists William B. Burton as the grantor and Doniphan as the grantee. [*General Index to Deeds—Grantors*, Records Office of the Clerk of the Circuit Court, Stafford County, Virginia.]

   Another index refers to a deed of bargain and sale for "Burton to Doniphan" on page 134 of a court book covering 1754 to 1764. [*General Index, 1721-1845*, Records Office of the Clerk of the Circuit Court, Stafford County, Virginia.]

   COMMENT: I don't know if the "B" was Burton's middle initial or his "mark" (used in lieu of a signature by the illiterate). - MB

ENTRY 69. The 1850 census for Stafford indicates that James Burton was born circa 1756. [Source: 1850 United States Federal Census records on microfilm at the headquarters branch of the Central Rappahannock Regional Library and those obtained via AncestryLibrary.com and Heritage Quest (heritagequest online.com). Reviewed by the author in 2009.]

   COMMENT: My analysis of other sources, such as Nancy Burton's Will and codicil (see 1858 and 1860 entries), indicates that James was Nancy's cousin, James B. Burton, Sr. His father was probably the elder Nathaniel Burton. - MB

1764

ENTRY 70. Nathaniel ("Nathl.") Burton and Will Burton, along with Thos. Porch and George Hinson, took an inventory of the estate of William Berry, deceased, circa 28 September 1764. [Ruth and Sam Sparacio, eds., *Will Abstracts of Stafford County, Virginia, 1748-1767* (McLean, Virginia, 1987), 114.]

ENTRY 71. Nathaniel ("Nath.") Burton, Will Burton, Thomas Porch and George Hinson appraised the estate of John Hall (deceased), circa 8 October 1764. [Ruth and Sam Sparacio, eds., *Will Abstracts of Stafford County, 1748-1767* (McLean, Virginia, 1987), 114.]

   COMMENT: Nathaniel was the elder Nathaniel Burton of Stafford. I suspect that he and William Burton (the husband of Rachel Porch) were brothers. The Thomas Porch mentioned here might have been Rachel's brother. - MB

ENTRY 72. A Stafford deed summarized as "Burton from Waugh" is listed in the *General Index, 1721-1845.* The deed is supposed to be on page 396 of a 1764-1773 court book for Stafford County, but the exact year of the deed is not provided. [*General Index, 1721-1845*, Records Office of the Clerk of the Circuit Court, Stafford County, Virginia.]

   COMMENT: I do not know the date of the deed or the first names of the parties involved because the 1764-1773 deed book is apparently missing. To my knowledge, this deed is not mentioned in the computer index that purportedly covers 1699 to 1977, perhaps because the deed book was missing when they created the computer database. - MB

1767

ENTRY 73. Nathl. Burton of Stafford was listed as grantor and Hy Ellison of London, England was grantee regarding a mortgage of chattels in King George County Order Book 1721-1725, Page 674, recorded 2 July 1767. [*Embrey's General Index to Deeds and Wills, King George County, 1721-1924.*]

   An abstract indicates that the grantee was Henry Ellison, merchant of Whitehaven, and that Ellison's agent, Charles Yates, provided 21 pounds, 16 shillings and 9 pence to Burton, to be paid back within six months with interest. [Mary Marshall Brewer, ed., *Abstracts of Land Records of King George County, Virginia, 1752-1783* (Lewes, Delaware: Colonial Roots, 2006), 89.]

1769

ENTRY 74. During the 7 November 1769 session of the Virginia General Assembly, John Burton was among those appointed as commissioners by the President, Council and Burgesses, to investigate claims regarding damages at tobacco warehouses from floods and fires in Henrico, Chesterfield, Prince William, Northampton and King George counties. This included tobacco warehouses in Falmouth and Quantico.

The commissioners were, in order of the original listing: Richard Bland, Archibald Cary, Richard Adams, Patrick Henry, John Banister, William Macon, Roger Dixon, Walker Taliaferro, Henry Pendleton, William Fitzhugh, of Somerset, Joseph Jones, Fielding Lewis, Thomas Ludwell Lee, Thomas Blackburne, Mathew Whiting, Landon Carter, the younger, Bailey Washington, Severn Eyre, John Burton, Griffin Stith, John Bowdoin and Nathaniel Littleton Savage. [*The Statutes at Large*, William Waller Hening (Richmond, VA: J. & G. Cochran, Printers, 1821), from a 1969 facsimile reprint published by the University Press of Virginia for the Jamestown Foundation of the Commomwealth of Virginia.]

COMMENT: I do not know if the John Burton listed here came from the Stafford area or not. It is a common name and I can only speculate that this might have been the same John Burton who, ten years later, would sign a petition in favor of the relocation of the Stafford County courthouse. (See entry for 1779.)

Some of the commissioners, such as Patrick Henry, must have been living in the Richmond area at the time, given that they were expected to investigate the Henrico and Chesterfield warehouses. So this John Burton might also have been from that region.

Others, however, including the somewhat less famous Fielding Lewis and Landon Carter, had connections to the Fredericksburg area. They also included William Fitzhugh (1741-1809) of Somerset, in King George County, who was having his mansion, Chatham, built at the time, about a mile or so down River Road from the Falmouth warehouses. Construction on the famous house reportedly began in 1768 and ended in 1771. [Jerrilyn Eby, They Called Stafford Home (Bowie, Maryland: Heritage Books, Inc., 1997), 279.]

It is possible, then, that Burton was from the Falmouth area, or perhaps an area of Stafford near Quantico. - MB

ENTRY 75. The 1850 and 1860 census records for Stafford indicate that Ann "Nancy" Burton was born circa 1770. [Sources: 1850 and 1860 United States Federal Census records on microfilm at the headquarters branch of the Central Rappahannock

Regional Library and those obtained via AncestryLibrary.com and Heritage Quest (heritagequest-online.com). Reviewed by the author in 2009.]

COMMENT: *Ann was known as Nancy. Her parents were William Burton and Rachel Porch Burton. She apparently never married. - MB*

1771

ENTRY 76. According to a source of undetermined reliability, Isaac Burton was born in December 1771. [From unbound papers, titled *Family Record*, of unknown origin and unknown date in the author's family records.]

COMMENT: *I do not know the source of this information and I caution the reader that I have not been able to confirm it. I do not have any other source for Isaac's exact date of birth. Still, census records from 1830 and 1840 indicate that Isaac Burton was probably born between 1770 and 1780, assuming that Isaac was the oldest male member of his household. - MB*

1777

ENTRY 77. According to author Jerrilyn Eby, "Jarrett Burton was employed in Stafford County from 1777-1781 as an armorer and gunsmith. (Whisker, *Arms Makers of Virginia*, 25). According to Jarrett's pension application, he served in Stafford County under Capt. William Garrard (c. 1715-1786) and Maj. Henry Fitzhugh (1723-1783)." He was discharged after about three months but, in the fall of 1777, he went to work at the Fredericksburg Armory under Col. Fielding Lewis and Charles Dick. He worked there for about four years. By 1833, when he applied for his war pension, he was living in Mason County, Kentucky.

Eby comments that "the Burton family is still well represented in the southern end of Stafford County." [Jerrilynn Eby, *Laying the Hoe: A Century of Iron Manufacturing in Stafford County, Virginia* (Westminster, Maryland: Willow Bend Books, 2003), 197.]

Another source also includes Jarrett Burton among Stafford County Revolutionary War Veterans. [Homer J. Musselman, *Stafford County, Virginia, Veterans and Cemeteries* (Fredericksburg, Virginia: Bookcrafters, 1994), 10.]

COMMENT: *With all due respect to Eby, it appears that Jarrett was only employed in Stafford for a few months before going to work in Fredericksburg. For that reason, and because I do not know where he actually lived, I will only mention Jarrett as being in Stafford in 1777.*

Also, Eby's comment seems to imply, perhaps unintentionally, that some or all of the Burtons of southern Stafford were descendants of Jarrett Burton. Obviously, the Burtons were in Stafford long before he arrived. Furthermore, I have seen no evidence that Jarrett left any descendants in Stafford. - MB

1778

ENTRY 78. James Burton married Molly Brooks in Fauquier County circa 22 September 1778, with Samuel Brooks as bondsman. [*Fauquier County, Virginia, Marriage Bonds, 1759-1854, and Marriage Returns, 1785-1848*, John K. Gott (Bowie, Maryland: Heritage Books, Inc., 1991), 27.]

COMMENT: I am not sure if this James Burton was or would be a Stafford Burton. Given Fauquier's proximity to Stafford, the relatively few Burtons in Fauquier at the time and the presence of multiple James Burtons in Stafford in the late 18th and early 19th centuries, I thought I should mention him. (See also 1789 marriage entry.) - MB

ENTRY 79. According to one source, William Burton, possibly the husband of Rachel Porch, died circa 1778. [Fredericksburg *Court Record* extracts, Barry L. McGhee, www.historiccourtrecords.org, 2002-2009. Viewed by the author in 2009.]

COMMENT: This and other records (perhaps based on this one) suggest that William, the husband of Rachel Porch Burton, died in 1778 and that Rachel herself died in 1780. If this is correct, then the William Burton who died in 1778 was probably the man I have designated as "third" William, the son of the "second" William Burton and Sarah Spicer.

This "third" William was presumably born in the late 1720s or early 1730s, so he would have been no older than about 50 if he died in 1778. This makes me wonder if "third" William might have died fighting in the Revolutionary War, but I found no evidence to support or refute that possibility.

I'm not even sure who actually died in 1778 and 1780.

For example, perhaps it was Sarah Spicer Burton who died in 1780, not Rachel, given that each woman might have been a "widow of William Burton," as indicated in the original source. (See related 1780 entry.)

In addition, other records indicate that a Rachel Burton was the head of a large household in Stafford during the 1780s, so how could she have died in 1780? Was there another Rachel Burton, perhaps a daughter, who became head of the household? If so, why didn't one of the Burton sons become the head of the household instead? (See related 1782, 1785 and 1790 entries.)

It's also possible that the "second" and "third" Williams were one and the same. That is, perhaps the same William Burton married Spicer first and Porch second. I doubt it, though, in part because he would have been fathering children into his 60s and 70s. - MB

1779

ENTRY 80. According to a source of undetermined reliability, Mary Margress (*sic*) was born 12 May 1779. [From unbound papers, titled *Family Record*, of unknown origin and unknown date in the author's family records.]

COMMENT: This is probably a misspelling of Mary Marquess. She reportedly died 13 April 1843. (See 1843 death entry.) The Will of Anthony Marquess, presented in the court case of Marquess vs. Marquess, *reveals that Mary, one of Anthony's daughters, married Isaac Burton. (See 1826, 1827 and 1828 entries.) [George Harrison Sanford King, "Copies of Extant Wills from Counties Whose Records Have Been Destroyed: Will of Anthony Marquess of Stafford County," Mrs. Lyon G. Tyler, ed.,* Tyler's Quarterly Historical and Genealogical Magazine, *Volume 24 (1942-1943) (Richmond, Virginia: Richmond Press, Inc., Printers, 1943), 112.]*

I do not know the source of the alleged 12 May 1779 date of birth and I caution the reader that I have not been able to confirm it. I do not have any other source for Mary Marquess Burton's exact date of birth. - MB

ENTRY 81. James, John and Nathaniel Burton were among the signers of a 24 May 1779 petition to the Virginia House of Delegates to have the seat of Stafford County government moved to a more central location in the county. [*Stafford County, Virginia, Tithables: Quit Rents, Personal Property Taxes and Related Lists and Petitions, 1723-1790, in Two Volumes*, John Vogt and T. William Kethley, Jr. (Athens, GA: Iberian Publishing Company, 1990), 545.]

COMMENT: After Stafford and King George swapped large portions of territory in 1776—significantly reshaping the two counties—it would have made sense to have the seat of government relocated. - MB

ENTRY 82. William Burton was mentioned in a King George County deed, recorded 6 January 1779, regarding the sale (or lease?) of a 100-acre tract of land in Washington Parish from Anthony Price to John Price (both of King George). The land had previously been purchased by the father, Thomas Price, "of William Burton and Thomas Munday." [Mary Marshall Brewer, ed., *Abstracts of Land Records of King George County, Virginia, 1752-1783* (Lewes, Delaware: Colonial Roots, 2006), 167.]

COMMENT: *This might have been the "third" William Burton. I do not know if the transaction with Thomas Price occurred before or after the 1777 land swap. - MB*

1780

ENTRY 83. The widow of William Burton died circa 1780, according to Fredericksburg, Virginia court records. [Fredericksburg court record 36-7, *Burton vs. Burton*, recorded in 1820. Also see court record 567-1, recorded in 1804, regarding an inventory and appraisal of the estate of William Burton, deceased (1778 & 1781). Obtained via www.historic-courtrecords.org in 2009.]

An 1893 newspaper article indicates that Mrs. Rachel Burton died "one hundred and thirteen years ago;" i.e., in 1780. The article also noted that Rachel was an ancestor of Alexander Burton, who lived in Stafford with his wife near Berea Church in 1893. ["An Old Dress," The *Free Lance* newspaper, 14 February 1893, 3.]

COMMENT: *Other records indicate that Rachel Burton might not have died in 1780. (See 1790 census entry regarding Rachel Burton.) This is speculation, but perhaps it was Sarah Spicer Burton, the widow of the elder William Burton, who died in 1780. - MB*

ENTRY 84. George Thorn acquired land in Stafford County from "Tutt & Burton," on an unspecified date prior to 6 May 1780. This land was adjacent to that of James Bell, Jr., who owned 68 acres "on Barrel's Run Br. of Rappahannock R." in Stafford. Bell's land was also adjacent to land owned by James Hunter and Col. William Fitzhugh. [Gertrude E. Gray, *Virginia Northern Neck Land Grants, Vol. II, 1742-1775* (Baltimore: Genealogical Publishing Co., Inc., 1987), 111.]

COMMENT: *I do not know who this Burton might have been. - MB*

1782

See 1790 census entry regarding Rachel Burton.

1783

ENTRY 85. Stafford County personal property tax records for 1783 included entries for the following Burtons:

James Burton: one adult white male, one horse, five cattle and one "coty. levy" (probably a horse-drawn carriage or wagon of some kind). [*Stafford County, Virginia, Tithables: Quit Rents, Personal Property Taxes and Related Lists and Petitions, 1723-1790, in Two Volumes*, John Vogt and T. William Kethley, Jr. (Athens, GA: Iberian Publishing Company, 1990), 207.]

Gerrard Burton: one adult white male and one horse. [*Stafford County, Virginia, Personal Property Tax Lists, 1783-1806*, Virginia State Library microfilm, April 1955.]

COMMENT: I reviewed two sources for 18th and early 19th property tax records: The Vogt and Kethley, Jr. book, covering 1723 to 1790, and several rolls of microfilm of actual Stafford County tax books, covering 1783 to 1861. Despite the apparent overlap, I did not see the 1783 entry for James in the microfilm records, and I did not see the 1783 entry for Gerrard in the book.

In the original tax books, the column for horses often included mules, too, but I will just use "horse(s)" for convenience here and in subsequent entries. - MB

1784

ENTRY 86. Jesse Burton (a.k.a. Burden) was born circa 1784 in Stafford and died before 1840. [Carl P. Musselman and Mildred H. Musselman, eds., *Musselman-Powell & Bowling Families of Spotsylvania and Stafford Counties* (Fredericksburg, Va., 1993), 3.]

COMMENT: Census records for 1820 and 1830 are roughly consistent with this approximate year of birth. (See also the 1809 marriage entry and 1826 deed entry for more information on Jesse.) - MB

ENTRY 87. Stafford County personal property tax records for 1784 included entries for the following Burtons:

- Gerrard Burton: two separate entries; each listed one adult white male and one horse.
- James Barton (*sic*): one adult white male, one horse and four cattle.
- John Burton: one adult white male, four horses and three cattle.

[Source: *Stafford County, Virginia, Personal Property Tax Lists, 1783-1806*, Virginia State Library microfilm, April 1955.]

   COMMENT: James Barton was probably James Burton. In addition, I am not sure about the number of horses for John Burton because the original entry was hard to read. - MB

1785

ENTRY 88. Rachel Burton was the head of a household of nine whites, according to a 1785 listing of whites, dwellings and outhouses in Stafford County, compiled in accordance with an Act of the Virginia General Assembly passed in May 1784. [*Stafford County, Virginia, Tithables: Quit Rents, Personal Property Taxes and Related Lists and Petitions, 1723-1790, in Two Volumes*, John Vogt and T. William Kethley, Jr. (Athens, GA: Iberian Publishing Company, 1990), 194.]

   COMMENT: See 1790 census entry regarding Rachel Burton. - MB

ENTRY 89. A 1785 Stafford personal property tax entry for Richard Burton listed one adult white male, three horses and five cattle. [*Stafford County, Virginia, Tithables: Quit Rents, Personal Property Taxes and Related Lists and Petitions, 1723-1790, in Two Volumes*, John Vogt and T. William Kethley, Jr. (Athens, GA: Iberian Publishing Company, 1990), 245.]

   The original tax book entry, on microfilm, was similar, but listed him as Rich Burton. [*Stafford County, Virginia, Personal Property Tax Lists, 1783-1806*, Virginia State Library microfilm, April 1955.]

   · *COMMENT: These two sources are the only indication I have that there was a Richard Burton in Stafford at that time. - MB*

1786

ENTRY 90. Stafford County personal property tax records for 1786 included entries for the following Burtons:

G. Burton: one adult white male and two horses. [*Stafford County, Virginia, Tithables: Quit Rents, Personal Property Taxes and Related Lists and Petitions, 1723-1790, in Two Volumes*, John Vogt and T. William Kethley, Jr. (Athens, GA: Iberian Publishing Company, 1990), 279.]

John Burton: one adult white male and three horses. [*Stafford County, Virginia, Tithables: Quit Rents, Personal Property Taxes and Related Lists and Petitions, 1723-1790, in Two Volumes*, John Vogt and T. William Kethley, Jr. (Athens, GA: Iberian Publishing Company, 1990), 282.] [*Stafford County, Virginia, Personal Property Tax Lists, 1783-1806*, Virginia State Library microfilm, April 1955.]

Rachel Burton: one white male over 16, three horses and five cattle. [*Stafford County, Virginia, Tithables: Quit Rents, Personal Property Taxes and Related Lists and Petitions, 1723-1790, in Two Volumes*, John Vogt and T. William Kethley, Jr. (Athens, GA: Iberian Publishing Company, 1990), 268.] [*Stafford County, Virginia, Personal Property Tax Lists, 1783-1806*, Virginia State Library microfilm, April 1955.]

1787

ENTRY 91. William Burton was born in King George County circa 1787. He died of heart disease at the age of 73 in Culpeper County on 18 September 1859. His parents were Samuel and Mary. [*Culpeper County, Virginia, Deaths: 1854-1879*. (Provo, UT: Ancestry.com Operations, Inc., 2010.)]

COMMENT: Other records indicate that this was William S. Burton or William L. Burton. (It's one and the same man. There is a just discrepancy regarding his middle initial, probably because it is difficult to distinguish between a handwritten capital S and a handwritten capital L from that time period.)

King George author and genealogist Elizabeth Nuckols Lee, a descendant of Samuel Burton, told me in a 2010 email that she believes William was William Spicer Burton. This makes sense, given that one of Samuel's ancestors was Sarah Spicer Burton, and it was a convention at the time to use the maiden name of female ancestors as middle names.

Nevertheless, for other entries in this Chronology concerning this William, if the original source indicates William L. Burton, I use L, not S, as the middle initial.

Although he was apparently born in King George County, I include him as a Stafford Burton because tax records indicate that his parents lived in Stafford during the 1790s. His

father Samuel moved the family to Culpeper County circa 1798 and became the patriarch
of a long line of Culpeper Burtons.

An 1841 court record indicates that William married Margaret Pollard. (See 1841
entry.) She might have been Margaret A. Pollard. (See 1853 marriage entry for their
daughter, Virginia F. Burton, for the names of some of their children.) - MB

ENTRY 92. Stafford County personal property tax records for 1787 included entries
for the following Burtons:

Girard (*sic*) Burton: one adult white male and two horses. [*Stafford County,
Virginia, Tithables: Quit Rents, Personal Property Taxes and Related Lists and
Petitions, 1723-1790, in Two Volumes*, John Vogt and T. William Kethley, Jr.
(Athens, GA: Iberian Publishing Company, 1990), 307, 346.] [*Stafford County,
Virginia, Personal Property Tax Lists, 1783-1806*, Virginia State Library microfilm,
April 1955.]

James Burton: one adult white male, three horses and seven cattle. [*Stafford
County, Virginia, Tithables: Quit Rents, Personal Property Taxes and Related Lists
and Petitions, 1723-1790, in Two Volumes*, John Vogt and T. William Kethley, Jr.
(Athens, GA: Iberian Publishing Company, 1990), 307, 348.] [*Stafford County,
Virginia, Personal Property Tax Lists, 1783-1806*, Virginia State Library microfilm,
April 1955.]

John Burton: one adult white male and one horse. [*Stafford County, Virginia,
Tithables: Quit Rents, Personal Property Taxes and Related Lists and Petitions, 1723-
1790, in Two Volumes*, John Vogt and T. William Kethley, Jr. (Athens, GA:
Iberian Publishing Company, 1990), 307, 345.] The original tax book entry on
microfilm was similar, but also included one white male over 16, in addition to
the white male over 21. [*Stafford County, Virginia, Personal Property Tax Lists,
1783-1806*, Virginia State Library microfilm, April 1955.]

Rachel Burton: one white male 16-21 (apparently named Isaac Brimmer), three
horses and 10 cattle. [*Stafford County, Virginia, Tithables: Quit Rents, Personal
Property Taxes and Related Lists and Petitions, 1723-1790, in Two Volumes*, John
Vogt and T. William Kethley, Jr. (Athens, GA: Iberian Publishing Company,
1990), 307, 347.] The original tax book entry on microfilm is similar, but lists

Brimmer as over 21. [*Stafford County, Virginia, Personal Property Tax Lists, 1783-1806*, Virginia State Library microfilm, April 1955.]

William Burton: one adult white male with tax paid by William Reavley. [*Stafford County, Virginia, Tithables: Quit Rents, Personal Property Taxes and Related Lists and Petitions, 1723-1790, in Two Volumes*, John Vogt and T. William Kethley, Jr. (Athens, GA: Iberian Publishing Company, 1990), 315, 347.] The original tax book entry for Reavley lists William Burton as one of two adult white males. [*Stafford County, Virginia, Personal Property Tax Lists, 1783-1806*, Virginia State Library microfilm, April 1955.]

COMMENT: Despite Vogt and Kethley's spelling, I think Gerard's name was spelled with "e" in the original tax book entry, but I understand all too well how difficult it can be to read those old records.

Also, I wonder if William Burton was a servant of Reavley's, or possibly a tenant. Reavley must have been somewhat wealthy, because he paid tax that year on 5 slaves, four horses and 13 cattle.

In addition, a Samuel Burton was listed in the 1787 tax list for King George County. He paid tax on himself, one black above 16, one black under 16, three horses and five cattle. He was most likely the son of William Burton and Rachel Porch. A William "Burnot" was also listed in the same 1787 tax list for King George, paying tax on himself and two horses. I do not know, however, if he was actually a Burton. [Nettie Schreiner-Yantis and Florene Speakman Love, The 1787 Census of Virginia: King George County *(a.k.a.* The Personal Property Tax Lists for the Year 1787 for King George County, Virginia*) (Springfield, Virginia: Genealogical Books in Print, 1987), 364.] - MB*

1788

ENTRY 93. Elizabeth Musselman Brummett Burton Reed was born circa 1788 in Stafford. She was the daughter of Henry and Elizabeth Musselman. She died at some point after 1870. She married three times. [Carl P. Musselman and Mildred H. Musselman, eds., *Musselman-Powell & Bowling Families of Spotsylvania and Stafford Counties* (Fredericksburg, Va., 1993), 3.]

COMMENT: For most of her adult life, Elizabeth was known as a Burton, the surname of her second husband, Jesse. (Her first marriage only lasted a few years and she did not marry her third husband until she was 70.) For both her and for Jesse, the surname was sometimes spelled Burden instead of Burton.

Other sources indicate that Elizabeth's son was William Brummett and her sister was Alice Musselman (or Mussleman). (See 1843 entry for Deed NN-187.) For her marriages, see 1805, 1809 and 1858 entries. - MB

ENTRY 94. Stafford County personal property tax records for 1788 included entries for the following Burtons:

James Burton: two adult white males and three horses. [*Stafford County, Virginia, Tithables: Quit Rents, Personal Property Taxes and Related Lists and Petitions, 1723-1790, in Two Volumes*, John Vogt and T. William Kethley, Jr. (Athens, GA: Iberian Publishing Company, 1990), 372, 402.] [*Stafford County, Virginia, Personal Property Tax Lists, 1783-1806*, Virginia State Library microfilm, April 1955.]

Rachal (*sic*) Burton listed two whites over 16 and two horses. [*Stafford County, Virginia, Tithables: Quit Rents, Personal Property Taxes and Related Lists and Petitions, 1723-1790, in Two Volumes*, John Vogt and T. William Kethley, Jr. (Athens, GA: Iberian Publishing Company, 1990), 372, 403.] [*Stafford County, Virginia, Personal Property Tax Lists, 1783-1806*, Virginia State Library microfilm, April 1955.]

COMMENT: I think Rachel's name in the original tax book entry was spelled Rachel, not Rachal. - MB

1789

ENTRY 95. James Burton married Nancy Singer, the daughter of John Singer, circa 1 April 1789 in Fauquier County, Virginia. [*Fauquier County, Virginia, Marriage Bonds, 1759-1854, and Marriage Returns, 1785-1848*, John K. Gott (Bowie, Maryland: Heritage Books, Inc., 1991), 27.] [J. Estelle Stewart King, *Abstracts of Wills, Administrations and Marriages of Fauquier County, Virginia, 1759-1800, with Cemetery Inscriptions, Rent Rolls and Other Data* (Baltimore: Genealogical Publishing Co., Inc., 1978)]

COMMENT: I am not sure if this James Burton was, or would become, a Stafford Burton. Given Fauquier's proximity to Stafford, the relatively few Burtons in Fauquier at the time and the presence of multiple James Burtons in Stafford in the late 18th and early 19th centuries, I thought I should mention him. (See also 1789 bondsman entry, below.)

I do not know if this is the same James Burton who married Molly Brooks in 1778, also in Fauquier. (See 1778 marriage entry.) - MB

ENTRY 96. James Burton was listed as bondsman for the 11 February 1789 marriage of Leaner Murphy and Rose Duncan in Fauquier. [*Fauquier County, Virginia, Marriage Bonds, 1759-1854, and Marriage Returns, 1785-1848*, John K. Gott (Bowie, Maryland: Heritage Books, Inc., 1991), 145.]

COMMENT: I am not sure if this James Burton was, or would become, a Stafford Burton. Given Fauquier's proximity to Stafford, the relatively few Burtons in Fauquier at the time and the presence of multiple James Burtons in Stafford in the late 18th and early 19th centuries, I thought I should mention him. (See also 1789 marriage entry, above.)

ENTRY 97. Stafford County personal property tax records for 1789 included entries for the following Burtons:

Gerrard Burton: one white male over 16 and three horses. [*Stafford County, Virginia, Tithables: Quit Rents, Personal Property Taxes and Related Lists and Petitions, 1723-1790, in Two Volumes*, John Vogt and T. William Kethley, Jr. (Athens, GA: Iberian Publishing Company, 1990), 433, 467.] [*Stafford County, Virginia, Personal Property Tax Lists, 1783-1806*, Virginia State Library microfilm, April 1955.]

James Burton: one white male over 16 and four horses. [*Stafford County, Virginia, Tithables: Quit Rents, Personal Property Taxes and Related Lists and Petitions, 1723-1790, in Two Volumes*, John Vogt and T. William Kethley, Jr. (Athens, GA: Iberian Publishing Company, 1990), 433, 466.] [*Stafford County, Virginia, Personal Property Tax Lists, 1783-1806*, Virginia State Library microfilm, April 1955.]

Nathaniel Burton: one white male over 16, and either one or three horses. [*Stafford County, Virginia, Tithables: Quit Rents, Personal Property Taxes and Related Lists and Petitions, 1723-1790, in Two Volumes*, John Vogt and T. William

Kethley, Jr. (Athens, GA: Iberian Publishing Company, 1990), 433, 466.] The original tax book entry on microfilm lists one white male over 16 and three horses for "Nathal." Burton. [*Stafford County, Virginia, Personal Property Tax Lists, 1783-1806*, Virginia State Library microfilm, April 1955.]

Samuel Burton: two white males over 16, one black over 16 and one horse. [*Stafford County, Virginia, Tithables: Quit Rents, Personal Property Taxes and Related Lists and Petitions, 1723-1790, in Two Volumes*, John Vogt and T. William Kethley, Jr. (Athens, GA: Iberian Publishing Company, 1990), 433, 467.] [*Stafford County, Virginia, Personal Property Tax Lists, 1783-1806*, Virginia State Library microfilm, April 1955.]

William Burton: one white male over 16 and one horse. [*Stafford County, Virginia, Tithables: Quit Rents, Personal Property Taxes and Related Lists and Petitions, 1723-1790, in Two Volumes*, John Vogt and T. William Kethley, Jr. (Athens, GA: Iberian Publishing Company, 1990), 433, 467.] [*Stafford County, Virginia, Personal Property Tax Lists, 1783-1806*, Virginia State Library microfilm, April 1955.]

COMMENT: The entry for Nathaniel Burton on page 433 of Vogt and Kethley, Jr., lists one horse but the entry on page 466 lists three horses. It was clearly three in the original tax book. - MB

1790

ENTRY 98. Gerrard Burton and others were paid by Robert Wilford for being witnesses in court, circa 10 August 1790. [Ruth and Sam Sparacio, eds., *Deed and Will Abstracts of Stafford County, Virginia, 1780-1786* (McLean, Virginia, 1988), 114. (Includes Scheme Book Court Orders, 1790-1793.)]

The details are recorded on page 56 of the original Scheme Book. Robert's last name appears to be spelled Welford. He was ordered to pay Burton 25 pounds of tobacco for Burton's attending court for one day. [*Scheme Book, Court Orders, 1790-1793*, Records Office of the Clerk of the Circuit Court, Stafford County, Virginia, 56.]

ENTRY 99. According to one source, Cary Burton was born circa 1790 in Stafford. He died about 1860. His parents, Samuel and Mary Burton, moved their family to

Culpeper circa 1798. His brother was William L. Burton (possibly William Spicer Burton).

Cary's first wife was Susanna Walker (born 7 September 1799; died before 1832), daughter of Solomon Walker and Frances Taylor. Their children included Absolom (*sic*) Spicer Burton (born circa 1812) and Amanda Burton [born circa 1814 (*sic*); died 1894]. (See 1894 death entry for Amanda.)

His second wife was Nancy Burns (born circa 1794; died in 1870), whose mother was Lucy Burns. Their children were Thomas C. (*sic*) Burton (born circa 1833 in Culpeper); Lucy M. Burton (born circa 1835); and William Peter Burton (born circa 1841). (William Peter's death certificate, however, indicates that he was born 30 March 1839 and that his mother was Nancy Pollard. See 1914 death entry for William.)

Cary's son Absolom (Absalom?) married Sarah Francis Elizabeth Starkey, daughter of Samuel and Malinda Starkey. Their children included: James M. Samuel Burton (born 1841); Susan M. Burton (1843-1858) (*sic*); Amanda Burton (born 1845); Forsalia Burton (born circa 1849); Emmett H. Burton (1853-1926); Allenthia Burton (born circa 1857); Hezekiah Cooper Burton (24 May 1860-July 1899); William Washington Burton (24 May 1860-22 February 1900); Susan Mildred Burton (born 1863); and Alberta Burton (born circa 1865). (Most if not all of their children were born in Culpeper, though census records indicate that Absalom/Absolom and his family later moved to Orange and then to Spotsylvania.)

I do not know if Cary's daughter Amanda ever married or had children, but her probable death notice indicates that she never married. Amanda died at the age of 74 on Thursday, (19?) July 1894. (See 1894 death entry.)

Cary's son Thomas married Sarah Elley on 21 September 1854 in Culpeper. Their children included: Sarah Burton (born circa 1854); Benjamin Burton (born circa 1857); and Andrew J. Burton (born 23 May 1858). [Elizabeth Nuckols Lee, *Descendants of William Burton*, unpublished.]

According to another source, Thomas' middle initial was S, not C. It indicates that Thomas S. Burton of Culpeper married Sarah Elley, daughter of Edward Elley, on 18 September 1854.

According to the same source, their respective siblings apparently married each other, too. Lucy M. Burton married Edward Elley, Jr. on 17 December 1858. [*Culpeper Marriage Register*, Book 2, Page 17, Records Office of the Clerk of the Circuit Court, Culpeper, Virginia.] Another source (below) indicates that Elley might have been spelled Ely in later years.

Other sources indicate that Cary's other son, William Peter Burton, did not marry. He was a Confederate veteran of E Company, 13th Virginia Infantry, and died in March 1914. (See 1914 death enry.)

COMMENT: My own research into the Culpeper descendants of Stafford Burtons has been very limited and I cannot confirm all of the information about Cary's descendants. I emphasize that much of this information comes from an unpublished source, which was graciously provided to me by Mrs. Lee even though she had never finished it. Readers should therefore consider it "bonus material" and be more forgiving than usual if it contains any errors.

For example, Thomas C. Burton might have been Thomas S. Burton, but I do not for sure. (See my comments for the 1792 entry for Susannah Jett.)

Also, I have doubts about the date of death of the first of Absalom's daughters named Susan. Another source, however, of questionable reliability, indicates that the first Susan, died 18 March 1858 at the age of 15 from typhoid pneumonia. This source, however, misspells the surname as Burtin. [Culpeper County, Virginia, Deaths, 1854-1879. (Provo, UT: Ancestry.com Operations, Inc., 2010.)] - MB

ENTRY 100. Stafford County personal property tax records for 1790 included entries for the following Burtons:

Gerrard Burton: one white male over 16 and two horses. [*Stafford County, Virginia, Tithables: Quit Rents, Personal Property Taxes and Related Lists and Petitions, 1723-1790, in Two Volumes*, John Vogt and T. William Kethley, Jr. (Athens, GA: Iberian Publishing Company, 1990), 492, 523.] [*Stafford County, Virginia, Personal Property Tax Lists, 1783-1806*, Virginia State Library microfilm, April 1955.]

Nathaniel Burton: one white male over 16, one black over 16 and four horses. [*Stafford County, Virginia, Tithables: Quit Rents, Personal Property Taxes and Related Lists and Petitions, 1723-1790, in Two Volumes*, John Vogt and T. William Kethley, Jr. (Athens, GA: Iberian Publishing Company, 1990), 493, 531.] [*Stafford County, Virginia, Personal Property Tax Lists, 1783-1806*, Virginia State Library microfilm, April 1955.]

Samuel Burton: one or two white males over 16, one black over 16 and one horse. [*Stafford County, Virginia, Tithables: Quit Rents, Personal Property Taxes and*

Related Lists and Petitions, 1723-1790, in Two Volumes, John Vogt and T. William Kethley, Jr. (Athens, GA: Iberian Publishing Company, 1990), 493, 528, 532.] The original tax book on microfilm has two separate entries for Samuel Burton. One lists two white males over 16 and the other lists only one white male over 16.

William Burton: one white male over 16 and one horse. [*Stafford County, Virginia, Tithables: Quit Rents, Personal Property Taxes and Related Lists and Petitions, 1723-1790, in Two Volumes*, John Vogt and T. William Kethley, Jr. (Athens, GA: Iberian Publishing Company, 1990), 493, 530.] The original tax book entry on microfilm indicated that William Burton had 4 adult white males and four horses. [*Stafford County, Virginia, Personal Property Tax Lists, 1783-1806*, Virginia State Library microfilm, April 1955.]

COMMENT: It is possible that I misinterpreted ones for fours while taking notes from the microfilm record for William Burton. The Vogt and Kethley, Jr. figures are more consistent with the entries for William in preceding and subsequent years.

Also, the entries for Samuel Burton on pages 493 and 528 of Vogt and Kethley, Jr. list two white males over 16, but the entry on page 532 lists only 1 white male over 16. I doubt that there was more than one Samuel Burton in Stafford at the time, but I could be mistaken. Samuel might have been paying tax on behalf of another party that year, but usually the record would indicate the other party. In this case, no explanation was given for the second entry. - MB

ENTRY 101. According to 1790 Census records for Stafford County, Virginia:

Rachel Burton was listed as the head of a household consisting of nine "white souls." It is not clear, however, if she and her household were counted in 1790, or between 1782 and 1785, or at some point earlier. [*Heads of Families at the First Census of the United States Taken in the Year 1790: Records of the State Enumerations, 1782 - 1785* (Washington, D.C.: Government Printing Office, 1908), 108.]

COMMENT: The online census sources to which I had access via the library, AncestryLibrary and Heritage Quest, did not have 1790 census records for Virginia. I was able to find the above source, however, both on microfilm and in a book in the basement of the headquarters branch of the Central Rappahannock Regional Library in Fredericksburg, Virginia. Regrettably, this source did not list the names of the members of Rachel's household at that time. (For the names of some or all of Rachel and William Burton's children, see the entries for 1754, 1756 and 1810.)

But there's another problem: other records indicate that the Rachel Burton who married William in 1753 died circa 1780, apparently before the census. (See the related entry for 1780.) Perhaps the 1782 enumeration was merely published in 1782 from information collected prior to her death, but I doubt it because that would have been before the end of the Revolutionary War. Perhaps, then, the 1790 entry refers to another Rachel Burton.

It is possible, however, that Rachel did not die in 1780. In addition to the census, tax records indicate that a Rachel Burton was the head a household that included males "over 16" from the 1780s and into the early 1800s. Were Rachel merely a surviving daughter named after her mother, I suspect that her eldest brother would have been listed as head of household, not her. - MB

1791

ENTRY 102. William Burton was one of several people mentioned in the local newspaper as having letters at the Fredericksburg Post Office as of 5 January 1791. ["List of Letters," The *Virginia Herald* newspaper, 13 January 1791.]

COMMENT: It might seem odd today that a newspaper would print a notice informing people that they had mail waiting for them at the post office. I assume, however, that poor roads and other difficulties of travel at the time meant that people would not check the post office for mail very frequently, especially if they did not live in town. - MB

ENTRY 103. The elder Francis Jett signed his Will on 20 October 1791, designating William Alexander and William Burton as executors. [Geo. Harrison Sanford King, "Will of Francis Jett of Stafford County, Va."; ed. Mrs. Lyon G. Tyler, *Tyler's Quarterly Historical and Genealogical Magazine*, Vol. 20 (Richmond, Virginia: Richmond Press, Inc., Printers, 1939), 234-238.]

A secondary source, also citing Volume 20 of *Tyler*, includes an entry for Francis Jett's Will that mentions William Burton as one of Francis Jett's executors and Susannah Burton as one of Jett's daughters. This source, however, indicates that the Will was signed on 19 October 1791 (and recorded 8 December 1794). [William Lindsay Hopkins, *Some Wills From the Burned Counties of Virginia and Other Wills not listed in* <u>*Virginia Wills and Administrations, 1632-1800*</u>" (Richmond, Virginia, 1987), 129.]

   COMMENT: *The "fourth" William Burton married Susannah Jett, his first cousin, but I do not know if they were married at the time this Will was signed in 1791. - MB*

ENTRY 104. Stafford County personal property tax records for 1791 included entries for the following Burtons:

- George Burton: one white male over 16.
- Gerrard Burton: one white male over 16 and three horses.
- Rachel Burton: three white males over 16 and four horses.
- Samuel Burton: one white male over 16, one black over 16 and one horse.
- Wm. Burton: one white male over 16 and two horses.

[Source: *Stafford County, Virginia, Personal Property Tax Lists, 1783-1806*, Virginia State Library microfilm, April 1955.]

1792

ENTRY 105. Susannah Jett was mentioned in a court case circa 1792. [Ruth and Sam Sparacio, eds., *Deed and Will Abstracts of Stafford County, Virginia, 1780-1786 and Selected Entries from Scheme Book Court Orders, 1790-1793* (McLean, Virginia, 1988).]

   COMMENT: *According to Deyo's* Porch Family *(pp. 21, 30), Susannah "Sukey" Jett married her first cousin, William Burton. Their children included Barsheba Burton and Thomas S. Burton. Deyo cites neither dates nor sources for the marriage and births, but I suspect his source is an 1820 lawsuit regarding the Will of Susannah's father, Francis Jett, Sr. (See the 1820 entry regarding the heirs of Francis Jett. See also the 1836 entry regarding Thomas S. Burton and the 1807 entry regarding a court case mentioning the marriage of William and Susannah.)*

   Susannah's parents were Francis Jett, Sr. and Barsheba ("Barshba") Porch. Her brother Francis was born circa 1773, but I don't know when she was born. If Deyo is correct about Susannah and William being first cousins, it means that Barsheba Porch and Rachel Porch were sisters (along with Elizabeth Porch Curtis). William and Rachel Burton, by the way, did have a son named William. (See entry for 1810 for confirmation.)

Also, Barsheba Burton's brother should not be confused with the younger Thomas S. Burton of Culpeper, who was the son of Barsheba's cousin, Cary Burton (and, therefore, the grandson of Barsheba's uncle, Samuel Burton, who moved to Culpeper in 1798). - MB

ENTRY 106. Stafford County personal property tax records for 1792 included entries for the following Burtons:

-   Garrard (*sic*) Burton: one white male over 16 and two horses.
-   James Burton: two white males over 16 and three horses.
-   Rachel Burton: two white males over 16 and four horses.
-   Samuel Burton: one white male over 16, one black over 16 and two horses.
-   William Burton: one white male over 16 and two horses.

[Source: *Stafford County, Virginia, Personal Property Tax Lists, 1783-1806*, Virginia State Library microfilm, April 1955.]

1793

ENTRY 107. Stafford County personal property tax records for 1793 included entries for the following Burtons:

-   Garrard (*sic*) Burton: one white male over 16 and one horse.
-   James Burton: two white males over 16 and three horses.
-   Rachel Burton: two white males over 16 and four horses.
-   Samuel Burton: one white male over 16, one black over 16 and two horses.
-   William Burton: one white male over 16 and two horses.

[Source: *Stafford County, Virginia, Personal Property Tax Lists, 1783-1806*, Virginia State Library microfilm, April 1955.]

1794

ENTRY 108. Stafford County personal property tax records for 1794 included entries for the following Burtons:

- Garrard (*sic*) Burton: one white male over 16 and one horse. A second entry for Garrard listed one white male over 16 and either one or four horses.
- James Burton: one white male over 16 and three horses.
- Nathaniel Burton: one white male over 16.
- Rachel Burton: no white males over 16 and four horses.
- Samuel Burton: one white male over 16, one black over 16 and two horses.
- William Burton: one white male over 16 and two horses.

[Source: *Stafford County, Virginia, Personal Property Tax Lists, 1783-1806*, Virginia State Library microfilm, April 1955.]

COMMENT: *The number of horses in the second entry for Gerard Burton was difficult to read. I could not tell if it was a 1 or a 4. I don't know why a second entry was made, but it is possible that Gerard paid taxes once for himself and again on behalf of someone else. - MB*

1795

ENTRY 109. Stafford County personal property tax records for 1795 included entries for the following Burtons:

- Gerard Burton: one white male over 16 and one horse.
- Isaac Burton: one white male over 16.
- James Burton: one white male over 16 and three horses.
- Rachel Burton: one white male over 16 and four horses.
- Samuel Burton: one white male over 16, one black over 16 and one horse.
- William Burton: one white male over 16 and two horses.

[Source: *Stafford County, Virginia, Personal Property Tax Lists, 1783-1806*, Virginia State Library microfilm, April 1955.]

1796

ENTRY 110. Stafford County personal property tax records for 1796 included entries for the following Burtons:

- Gerard Burton: one white male over 16 and one horse.

- James Burton: one white male over 16 and three horses.
- Rachel Burton: no white males over 16 and four horses.
- Samuel Burton: one white male over 16, one black over 16 and one horse.
- William Burton: one white male over 16.

[Source: *Stafford County, Virginia, Personal Property Tax Lists, 1783-1806*, Virginia State Library microfilm, April 1955.]

1797

ENTRY 111. Stafford County personal property tax records for 1797 included entries for the following Burtons:

- Gerrard Burton: one white male over 16 and one horse. A second entry for Gerard Burton listed the same.
- James Burton: one white male over 16 and three horses.
- Rachel Burton: one white male over 16 and three horses.
- Samuel Burton: one white male over 16, one black over 16 and one horse.
- William Burton: one white male over 16. A second entry for William Burton listed one white male over 16 and two horses.

[Source: *Stafford County, Virginia, Personal Property Tax Lists, 1783-1806*, Virginia State Library microfilm, April 1955.]

COMMENT: I doubt that there were two Gerrard Burtons. As I commented above, I suspect that he was listed twice either because of an error or because was paying tax on behalf of someone else in addition to himself.

The two entries for William Burton, however, might refer to two separate people, as in later years. It is possible, though, that in 1797 William paid tax for himself and again on behalf of someone else. - MB

1798

ENTRY 112. According to a 1798 record of the 45th Regiment of the Virginia Militia, Isaac Burton was assigned to Captain John Fox's 2nd Battalion, under Lt. Col. James Primm. Burton was one of many men "fined for failure to appear at muster but had no property to fine." [Jerrilynn Eby, *45th Regiment of Virginia Militia, Stafford County, Virginia, 1781-1856* (Westminster, Maryland: Heritage Books, 2011), 18-19.]

ENTRY 113. Samuel Burton (see entry for birth in 1756, above) reportedly left Stafford County and moved to Culpeper County. [William L. Deyo, *Porch Family: The Forgotten Legacy of White Oak, Stafford County, Virginia* (Colonial Beach, Virginia: DeJoux Publications, 2001), 21.]

COMMENT: Other records confirm that Samuel moved to Culpeper with his wife and children, but this is the only source I could find regarding the date of the move. The year 1798 seems to be supported by Stafford County personal property tax records, in which Samuel appears every year beginning in 1789, but does not appear after 1797. - MB

ENTRY 114. Stafford County personal property tax records for 1798 included entries for the following Burtons:

- Gerrard Burton: one white tithe (presumably one white male over 16), four negroe (*sic*) tithes (presumably four blacks over 16) and three horses.
- James Burton: one white tithe and three horses.
- Nathaniel Burton: one white tithe and one horse.
- Rachel Burton: one white tithe and four horses.
- William Burton: one white tithe. A second entry for William Burton listed one white tithe and two horses.

[Source: *Stafford County, Virginia, Personal Property Tax Lists, 1783-1806*, Virginia State Library microfilm, April 1955.]

COMMENT: Gerrard appeared to be paying on behalf of someone else, because his name was followed by the word "for" and then something illegible, probably another name. Also, this year marks a change in the labeling of tax categories from previous years, such as "white tithes" rather than "white males" over 16.

In some years, there were many other categories, including multiple columns on the tally sheets for carriages, wagons and various types of furniture. These columns were rarely checked for Burtons, so I normally do not mention them. Also, the category for horses sometimes included mules as part of the same column, and sometimes a second column for "stud" horses. I only refer to "horses" because the original tally sheets do not indicate what type of animal in the "horses, mules, etc." column was being counted.

Once again, the two entries for William Burton might refer to two separate people. It is possible, though, that William paid tax for himself and again on behalf of someone else. - MB

1799

ENTRY 115. Stafford County personal property tax records for 1799 included entries for the following Burtons:

- James Burton: one white tithe and three horses.
- Nathaniel Burton: one white tithe and one horse.
- Rachel Burton and son: one white tithe and three horses.
- William Burton listed one white tithe and one horse.

[Source: *Stafford County, Virginia, Personal Property Tax Lists, 1783-1806*, Virginia State Library microfilm, April 1955.]

COMMENT: I point out that Rachel Burton is now listed as having a son, but I caution readers not to jump to conclusions. For example, if this Rachel was Rachel Porch Burton, then she would have been in her 60s and it would have been some other Burton widow who died in 1780.

If, however, this Rachel was Rachel Porch Burton's daughter, then she either had a son out of wedlock or she had married another Burton who, presumably, had died years earlier. It is also possible that this Rachel might have been a non-Burton who married a Burton. - MB

1800

ENTRY 116. According to surviving 1800 census records, George Burton was listed as the head of a household of one male and three females in Overwharton Parish in King George County. His household included one male, 26-45; one female, under 10; one female, 16-26; and one female, 26-45. [William Deyo, *King George County, Virginia, 1800 Census* (Colonial Beach, Virginia: DeJoux Publications, 1998), 16.]

COMMENT: I suspect that George was the son of William Burton and Rachel Porch of Stafford and, therefore, a Stafford Burton. Regrettably, I was unable to find 1800 census information for Stafford County, Virginia. - MB

ENTRY 117. According to a source of undetermined reliability, Harris W. Burton was born 17 March 1800. He died 21 September 1883. [From unbound papers, titled *Family Record*, of unknown origin and unknown date in the author's family records.]

COMMENT: Although I do not know the source of this information, multiple census records also indicate that Harris was born in 1800. Harris was one of the many sons of Isaac and Mary Burton. - MB

ENTRY 118. Stafford County personal property tax records for 1800 included entries for the following Burtons:

- Isaac Burton: one white tithe.
- James Burton: one white tithe and four horses.
- Rachel Burton and son: one white tithe and three horses.
- William Burton: one white tithe. A second entry listed one white tithe and two horses.

[Source: *Stafford County, Virginia, Personal Property Tax Lists, 1783-1806*, Virginia State Library microfilm, April 1955.]

COMMENT: The two entries for William Burton might refer to two separate people. It is possible, though, that William paid tax for himself and again on behalf of someone else. - MB

Continued in Volume II